"'A Handful of Hard Men' has me shaking with fury at our double standards where whites are concerned, and at the gauzy mythology of 'political correctness' that has painted white Rhodesians as oppressors."
'Taki' Theodoracopulos. *The Spectator* UK.

"What we saw on the BBC TV news while all this was going on was the various meetings between Harold Wilson, his ministers and Ian Smith, who had declared independence for Rhodesia. We were unaware of what was actually taking place in the country... Hannes Wessels redresses the balance with an amazing tale of daring and courage."
Books Monthly UK

"Wessels has a talent for bringing the lengthy list of battles and skirmishes to life. However, his account regularly connects the events in southern Africa to the larger context. Deprived of the opportunity to assassinate Robert Mugabe before he could assume control of the nation and transform it into the horrific slaughterhouse called Zimbabwe, the brave men of the SAS stood down. They did their duty; the loss of Rhodesia was a tragedy willed by forces beyond their control. Wessels' book is a worthy tribute to their sacrifice, and will be of benefit to all readers who desire a better comprehension of this aspect of the worldwide war against the forces of Marxism-Leninism."
New American Magazine

"'A Handful of Hard Men' ... is an absolutely stunning record of the Rhodesian Special Air Service ... a soldier's story told through the weapons' sights of Rhodesian SAS veterans as they carved through the massed ranks of their enemies - employing ruthless aggression and initiative instead of soft 'hearts and minds' COIN policies in a heroic but ultimately doomed bid to stay free from Robert Mugabe's dictatorship. .... a true story about the death of a brave little nation that went down fighting like demons before impossible odds. Buy it."
J.H. Farrell. *Australian & NZ Defender*

"'A Handful of Hard Men' must rank as one of the most riveting books on contemporary African military history that I have read. Hannes Wessels has captured the essence of true combat by this handful of very hard men... I was left breathless and it was as though I could smell the cordite and taste the blood in my mouth. I would highly recommend this magnificent book to any serious student of contemporary African warfare and history."
Lt. Colonel Eeben Barlow. (SADF; 32 Battalion Reconnaissance Wing. Executive Outcomes and STTEP International)

"The story of a virtuoso fighter and the brave men who stood with him against impossible odds. Hannes Wessels has achieved a literary grand slam with 'A Handful of Hard Men', published in the United States and Britain late 2015. A classic expose of the role of Rhodesia's Special Air Service during a twelve-year conflict that involved half-a-dozen African states. Public acclaim for the book among military buffs was so enthusiastic that within months it went into a second edition. Readers' comments on websites (both UK and US) have echoed these sentiments: it achieved more 5-star reviews than any other recent work of Southern African military history."
Author Al. J. Venter.

"Wessels has produced an intimate study of rugged war that surpasses other publications of this era in its detail of the well-trodden path from Rhodesian schoolboy to soldier.

Simon Reader. *BizNews*

"… a highly entertaining, detailed and thorough account of the Bush War and the role played by the Rhodesian SAS. Considering the small size of the unit its accomplishments are outstanding."

Morgan Haselau. *Man Magnum*

"This is the most unbelievable story about an incredible soldier and his other comrades in arms. If you had not recorded this, this story would have never been told."

Former SAS sergeant.

"One of the best SAS stories I have ever read".

W.D. Tennant

"The real deal. The pure, special-forces soldiering of Darrell Watt and his men, is to this very day, jaw dropping. I got scared all over again reading about it. Nothing around the world beats it. These guys would be international legends if they had done this in the service of England or America. The author does a brilliant job of weaving the political threads in time to the years of soldiering. Simple and revealing and awful to read about. The best account you will ever read."

Former Rhodesian SAS officer.

"This is the first time in my life that I have read a 350 page book in a weekend, and I didn't skip a single line. What an unbelievable story of toughness, courage, professionalism and sheer grit. For better or for worse, what an era that was, and the nostalgia one gets from reading it is immense."

Paul Connolly

"The book was just magnificent. One of the best reads about incredible men (and friends) I have ever read."

Brian Hayes.

"I am in absolute awe of the courage and bravery shown by the men of the RLI and SAS. I just did not realise, until reading the book, how close we came to defeating the bastards. I have read quite a few of the books written about the bush war and this one is clearly the best."

Barrie Hocking

"The greatest hero I have ever heard of in Darrell Watt. What an incredible man! I know of some of the actions of our great soldiers, but, never to the extent, consistency of purpose, courage and valour beyond any reasonable expectation of a human being. I sincerely congratulate the author on an excellent book. It captivates one from the beginning to the end and the depth of that time rises up again. Many are saying, as I am, this is possibly the very best book to come out in all the books on the Rhodesian War."

Trevor Knoetzen

"Your recent book, 'A Handful of Hard Men' is an important contribution to understanding the Rhodesian Bush War. We receive requests for it from Special Operations Command at MacDill Air Force Base, Combined Arms Research Library at Fort Leavenworth and the Marine Corps senior command courses and special operations courses. They use your book as part of their teaching lessons learned in fighting terrorism and in counterinsurgency techniques and practices."
Editor

The Best book ever! This is probably one of the best books I have ever read. The author provides an accurate account of the war, the politics behind the war and the key players, however, above all, the author keeps you interested and in suspense all the time. The horror of this war is portrayed better than anything I've ever read.
Anton van Reenen

This is one of the best books on Rhodesia and the Bush War I have read. It tells of the exploits of the Rhodesian SAS and in particular those of Darrell Watt, who seemed positively superhuman at times.
Daniel J. Fortune

One of the best books ever written on Rhodesia. Read it if you want to find out the truth behind their war for the right to live in a country without the world sticking their bloody noses in where it didn't belong.
D.O.L

This is an incredibly well written account on what most of us there did NOT know We were hoodwinked, misinformed or simply NOT informed.
Brian Graham

This book is great story of the men who gave their all for their country and who should be held in high esteem for all time as some of the bravest to ever fight the scourge of communism.
Robert Mullin

Great story of the accomplishments of the Rhodesian SAS. By far the best account that I've ever seen of the disgusting betrayal of that country, to the murdering Marxists, by Britain and the Western world.
John McKluckie

A Handful of Hard Men is easily one the finest books I've read on the counterinsurgency in Rhodesia.
David

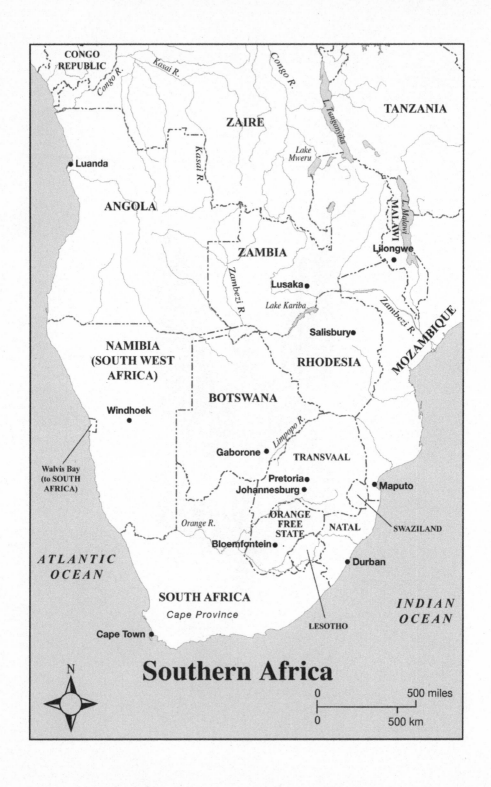

Southern Africa

A HANDFUL OF HARD MEN

The SAS and the Battle for Rhodesia

Hannes Wessels

EX MONTIBUS MEDIA
DARLING

Published in the Republic of South Africa in 2016 by
EX MONTIBUS MEDIA
PO Box 73, Darling, 7345

First Published in the United States of America and Great Britain in 2015 by
CASEMATE PUBLISHERS
1950 Lawrence Road, Havertown, PA 19083
and
10 Hythe Bridge Street, Oxford, OX1 2EW

Copyright 2015 © Hannes Wessels

Second edition 2017

ISBN 978-0-620-74204-7
Digital Edition: ISBN 978-0-620-68644-0

Cataloguing-in-publication data is available from the South African National
Library, Library of Congress and the British Library.

10 9 8 7 6 5 4 3 1

Printed and bound in the Republic of South Africa.

For a complete list of Ex-Montibus Media titles please contact:

EX MONTIBUS MEDIA
Web: www.exmontibusmedia.co.za
E-mail: admin@ExmontibusMedia.co.za

CONTENTS

DEDICATION

TO THAT SPECIAL BREED OF PEOPLE WHO
BUILT A SPECIAL COUNTRY.

ACKNOWLEDGEMENTS

To all the former members of the Rhodesian SAS and other members of the armed forces who helped and encouraged me with this book but with special thanks to Darrell, André and Richard without whom I could not have written it at all.

Thanks to Mark Jackson, Steve Kluzniak, Frans Botha, Bas Jolliffe, Rob Johnstone and Willem for use of photographs and reference material. I know there are others who I should thank in this regard but in the mists of time I have not been able to identify or find all those whose photos have been used. Johan Bezhuidenhout for allowing me to use his stories. Peter Stanton for his help with information on the early history of the war. Special thanks to Chas Lotter for allowing me to use his poems which so poignantly capture the mood of those times.

Dave and Jill Stone, Robin and Jill Hammond, Jerry Engelbrecht, Dick Oldridge and my sister Helga for reading, proofing and advising. To Jerry Buirski for quick editing when I needed it and for his encouragement. To Alan Mezzetti for the technical and moral support that has been gratefully received.

To my long-suffering wife Mandy for her patience, resilience and unwavering support as we have rolled with the punches that have challenged us in writing and publishing.

AUTHOR'S NOTE

So much has been written about the Special Air Service, one may well ask if it has not been overdone. I asked myself that question.

The answer might be a qualified yes, particularly if one holds the view that in recent years, fact has repeatedly been mixed with fiction, leaving an element of confusion in the minds of readers as to what is true and what is not. Everyone loves a hero and sometimes they are hard to find in real life, so enter the novelists to manufacture the characters they need under the legend of the 'Winged Dagger.'

I am happy to say that in writing this book, I faced no such dilemma; the material is true and speaks for itself. But this is more than a war story; it is also the story of a people and a country.

To the best of my knowledge, history offers no record of a nation more isolated, ostracised and bereft of allies and no soldiers who fought against greater odds with fewer men or resources as paltry, than those of what was known as Rhodesia. Nor does history tell us of any polity that developed as fast: from tribal primitivism to First World civility and sophistication in sixty years, only to be destroyed with even greater rapidity in little more than two decades.

While the country once known as Rhodesia survived only ninety years, it existed in the tumult that surrounded two world wars, the collapse of the European empires and the unfolding of the Cold War. Victims of the vicissitudes of history, the Rhodesians suddenly found themselves international outlaws facing down Western opprobrium and Communist aggression. The proxy war for the world was on and southern Africa, particularly South Africa, possessing enormous mineral and strategic value, was firmly in Sino-Soviet sights. But a primary obstacle was Rhodesia, so it should come as no surprise that Moscow and Beijing supported the 'liberation' movements energetically and generously. It was into this vortex that the Rhodesian soldier was thrown and so it begs the question: what if they had chosen not to fight and capitulated in the mid-1960s as the world demanded they do? Stalinist-type rule would almost certainly have followed and powerful direct economic, political and military pressure would have immediately been applied to South Africa. Just how this would have affected world history is impossible to deduce but the ramifications would have been enormous. Simply put, this did not happen because the Rhodesians chose to fight and this is the story of some of the stalwarts of that struggle.

It is also an honest, and I sincerely hope, readable attempt to tell some of the story of the country through the eyes and deeds of exemplary soldiers battling unbelievable odds, against a backdrop of relentless treachery and sometimes deadly political intrigue. Out of this emerges a testament to what the few are capable of achieving when they possess skill, stamina, courage and, above all, a belief in the righteousness of their cause. But this is not about supermen; it is about uncomplicated people imbued with simple but powerful values which drove them to extraordinary performances. It is about the same breed of fighting men from the same country who battled so valiantly in two world wars to keep the free world free.

Much of this tale is about a self-effacing, quietly spoken man by the name of Darrell Watt and some of those with whom he served. It tells how they, in the face of sometimes impossible adversity, came within an ace of thwarting history by destroying the forces ranged against their country by killing many and demolishing the platforms that launched them. Sadly, one is left in little doubt that if his peers in the political and military hierarchy had displayed a semblance of the same devotion to duty, the outcome of the conflict would have been radically different.

Just where Watt's feats place him in the pantheon of Special Forces soldiers may be grist for the discussion mill but what is unquestionable is that he demonstrated extraordinary professionalism in the course of a thirteen-year war during which he was seldom far from the cauldron. Astonishingly, despite his almost routine heroics, he received precious little recognition and many of his exploits appear to have gone unrecorded. The reasons for this remain unclear but the Rhodesian army was certainly not immune to the blight brought by professional jealousy. What is abundantly clear is his achievements are the stuff of legend and the grandeur of the regiment he so gallantly served is massively enhanced by his contribution.

I have used the word 'terrorist' in the book with some reservation when referring to the armed members of 'ZANLA' {Zimbabwe African National Liberation Army, ZANU's military wing} and 'ZIPRA'. {Zimbabwe People's Revolutionary Army, ZAPU's military wing} Some would argue a terrorist is simply someone who uses violence in order to achieve a political end. That is to oversimplify. Few wars are fought without a political objective and we invariably accept that the combatants are soldiers, not terrorists. I use the word because their methodology for waging war was, in the main, not synonymous with what one expects from soldiers. I say 'in the main' because all who fought in this war will readily acknowledge that there were men and women within the ranks of the enemy who fought bravely and honourably for a cause they believed in and are deserving of respect, but alas they were the minority.

The facts show very clearly that the overwhelming majority of targets attacked by the armed forces deployed by the anti-Rhodesian movements were of a civilian nature and only in relatively rare cases were military facilities or personnel the focus of their attention. This conduct has no symmetry with soldiering and so I feel at liberty to generalise at times and refer to the men who served Robert Mugabe and Joshua Nkomo as 'terrorists.'

Efforts by the wartime Rhodesian government to draw the world's attention to the conduct of the men who served Mugabe and Nkomo fell on resolutely deaf ears. The ire of the international community was reserved almost exclusively for those who sought to stem their terrible tide. This was partly because this conflict was erroneously viewed as 'black' versus 'white' and in Africa, as in much of the world, when such a comparison is made there can only possibly be one 'victim' and one 'villain.' This dreadful misjudgement resulted in power passing to new rulers in the name of 'freedom' and a country brim-full of promise has been ruined, reducing millions to poverty and misery.

Regrettably this perception continues to this day where people of European descent, following fundamental Christian values, are relentlessly vilified for their historic association with capitalism, colonialism and slavery, making them the villains of the modern world. This perversion of the truth has proved highly effective and some of the most successful civilisations in history are drowning under waves of self-induced guilt and giving way to the demands of fast growing minorities that appear determined to destroy rather than nurture and improve.

It is my fervent hope that those legions of supposedly liberal politicians, pressmen and men and women of the cloth who did so much to assist in the 'liberation process' will read this book and reflect on their actions. For those genuinely misinformed, one must have some sympathy, but they are in the minority. Most knew the truth but lacked the moral courage to stand up and be counted. I can only hope they feel a deep sense of shame. They disgraced the democracies they were elected to represent and in doing so, shamed their countries.

For those who fought so hard to prevent this tragedy, all is lost but their pride and their place in history. When that is written undistorted by the prism that reflects the colonial sense of guilt that has corrupted policy towards Africa for six decades, they will have found their rightful place: on the roll of honourable heroes who fought with enormous courage and skill to save their country from destruction.

What is written here is as accurate an account of the events described as possible. It is quite possible that dates and some details may not be quite correct. The war finished 35 years ago and I have had to rely to a large extent on the memories of the men involved, and there is always the possibility for some error. In the event that has transpired I apologise, but all reasonable efforts were taken to be true to history.

Hannes Wessels
Western Cape, South Africa

A BRIEF HISTORY OF RHODESIA

Never complete. Never whole.
White skin and an African soul.
—ANON

The seeds of future conflict were sown when Kimberley mining magnate Cecil John Rhodes turned his attentions to spreading the imperial gospel north into the wild and uncharted African hinterland. He was frustrated by the timidity of a British government that refused to share his expansionist zeal and decided to do it himself, with his own money and his own men, and he resolved that they would be good men.

Over lunch at the Kimberley Club in the diamond capital of South Africa, he explained his thoughts to Frank Johnson, the man who would lead his force. They agreed most recruits would be from a military background, but Rhodes wanted more. Tough and resolute he insisted they must be, but they also had to be gentlemen in the classical sense of the time and possessed of the eclectic array of skills required to build a country. It has been suggested that the same qualities he would later mandate for those applying for his scholarships were applied to selection of the chosen few who would be deployed in this extension of Empire. As a result, top Cape families were invited to contribute their sons, and doctors, lawyers, pharmacists and farmers filled the ranks of this elite body of men who rode north and colonised the country that came to bear its founder's name.

In a harbinger of what was to come, on the day the column camped on the Shashi River, the first activity engaged in had nothing to do with conquest: it was a game of rugby. Then they crossed into the territory that would become Rhodesia and into a dangerous new land. Lives would later be lost in battle, to disease, wild animals and other natural calamities, but the tide of history was swiftly turning and for better or worse, the white man had arrived. On 13 September 1890, some 200 men stood at attention as the Union Flag was raised at a place they called Fort Salisbury. The claim had been staked.

While the initial occupation had been surprisingly peaceful, it was not long before hostilities broke out and the pioneers were called on to show their mettle. On the battlefield Lobengula's Matabeles fought with courage and fortitude. Mostly dissolute Zulus on the run from Shaka's tyranny in the south, they were also recent arrivals north of the Limpopo, but they had got there first and the white man was shaping up to become a nuisance. As warriors, they earned the respect of their white adversaries, but the same could not be said of the motley collection of tribes that came to be known as the Mashona, who were found in the main to be cowering in caves and crevices on the rocky hills of the central Highveld, where they resided in perpetual fear of marauding Matabele *impis.*

Ultimately, the native rebellions were suppressed with a mixture of force and diplomacy, but with conquest, the white interlopers put an end to the endemic tribal genocide and quickly insisted upon changing the mind-set that killing another human being was a right of might. This was anathema to the blacks but they were forced to live with it on pain of punishment. The irony following from this is the *Zezuru* people {one of the six or seven tribes making up the Mashona} who would probably have been wiped out by the Matabele in the course of time, were saved by white intervention. Had this not happened, a *Zezuru* child by the name of Robert Gabriel Mugabe might never have been. His journey into the living world was made safe by the white man he would grow to revile.

Frontiersmen in the classic sense, the pioneers were essentially magnanimous in victory and, unlike their counterparts in North America and Australia, they refrained from further attacks on the natives who now fell under their authority. Once in control of their domain they in fact nurtured the indigenous populace rather than annihilate it, and in a feat of nation building unmatched anywhere, they took a barbarous land by the scruff of the neck and by 1923 when self-rule was granted they had transformed it into an orderly polity with a diverse and dynamic economy capable of generating real wealth and lifting the living standards of all its inhabitants. Relishing a period of unusual peace, population growth among the black people was spectacular: from an estimated 300,000 at the point of occupation to six million by the middle of the century.

But it was never a settled and easy existence for the Rhodesians. Right from the start there was tension between them and the Afrikaners of the republics of Transvaal and Orange Free State, who had also been studying the northern reaches with acquisitive eyes. To the east, the Portuguese were wary of their cocky new neighbours who were limbering up to block the expansionist plan being plotted in

Lisbon that would have absorbed the vast hinterland between the colonies of Angola and Mozambique, thereby establishing a Lusitanian empire of massive proportion in Africa.

Unsurprisingly, it was not long before the Portuguese problem escalated into fighting, and following several skirmishes on the eastern frontier, a bold young captain by the name of Patrick Forbes decided to take matters into his own hands. With pluck, daring and less than a dozen troopers, he invaded Mozambique and attacked the Portuguese garrison at Vila de Manica. Determined to seize the port of Beira for the Crown, his plan was thwarted by British Prime Minister Salisbury who wasted no time in ordering Forbes to desist and return to British territory immediately. Unbeknown to Forbes, the attack was a breach of a non-aggression pact between Portugal and Britain that had not been violated in several hundred years. But the world had seen an early indicator of the fighting talents of the Rhodesians.

As the new century entered its teens however, events in distant places were spinning out of control. No sooner had the pioneers established order and basic government in the colony than the First World War broke out. Nation-building had to be put on hold while most of the able-bodied men left Rhodesia to battle the Germans in Tanganyika and the bogs of Belgium and eastern France {Over 5,000 whites, some 25% of the population volunteered for the war}. Many did not return, but in the years between that war and the next, great progress was made, albeit again in the face of much adversity. Rinderpest and foot and mouth disease took a heavy toll on livestock, added to which a series of crippling droughts devastated farmers, throwing the nascent agricultural economy into turmoil. Malaria killed hundreds of settlers and the global depression of the 1930s ended the hopes of many aspiring businessmen. The added challenge of distance to the sea made it costly to get export goods to the ports. But in spite of all the obstacles, a spirit of enterprise and endurance prevailed and most of the problems were tackled and eventually overcome. Against this backdrop, a parsimonious British government merely looked on, offering little more than moral support. With the advent of self-rule in 1923 the settlers were largely masters of their own destiny. For better or for worse they were pretty much on their own, but that was how they liked it.

The 'Spirit of Rhodesia' was summed up by an anonymous writer when the country was divided over whether or not to forsake self-rule and become part of the

Union of South Africa: "We have experienced a Native War, a Native Rebellion, the Boer War, The Great War, the Rinderpest, East Coast Fever, drought and floods, adversity and prosperity. From these the Spirit of Rhodesia has been compounded; and everyone who has been touched by the magic wand of the spirit of Rhodesia is a 'Rhodesian.' Our people have come from the four corners of the earth, mostly British, but no matter what nationality they were; if they were of the fit the country took them unto herself and gave herself unto them and they became Rhodesians. That is what we mean when we say 'Rhodesia for the Rhodesians.'[1]

When the Second World War erupted Rhodesia had an infrastructure and governmental organisation that could compare favourably with any nation in the world. Across the country schools and hospitals had been built, roads and bridges constructed and a modern telecommunications system installed. An extremely professional police force, the majority of its members black, brought peace and security.[2] Courts presided over by highly qualified judges and magistrates dispensed justice fairly and firmly without any hint of political interference and 'native administrators' worked in tandem with chiefs and other traditional leaders in administering the 'Native Reserves' {later known as Tribal Trust Lands} set aside for exclusively black habitation. Not even the Rhodesians' most virulent critics could see their way clear to accusing the civil administration of being corrupt, incompetent or inefficient.

With war looming, such was the enthusiasm of the men to enlist that steps were taken to compel a proportion to remain at home for fear that the colony would collapse due to lack of manpower. Nevertheless, pro rata as a percentage of the white population, Rhodesia contributed more manpower to the Second World War and suffered greater casualties than any other country in the Empire, including Great Britain herself. Because so many volunteered there was a real fear at official level that big Rhodesian losses would decimate their numbers to such an extent the future of the colony would be in jeopardy. As a result, the Rhodesian volunteers were deliberately distributed throughout the various services to spread the risk as widely as possible.

Being men who had weathered a variety of challenges in the wilds of an untamed continent, they adapted easily to the rough realities of war and took the responsibilities of leadership in their stride. A large number were quickly assessed as officer material and found their way to playing distinguished roles in a variety of services, ranging from flying in the Battle of Britain to becoming specialised operatives in the Long Range Desert Group which provided the platform for the formation of the SAS.

With Hitler vanquished, the post-war period saw the colony enter a golden era. The soldiers, sailors and airmen returned and brought with them a considerable number of ex-servicemen who had decided to leave Britain and build a new future in a new country. But true to Rhodes's ethos, the Rhodesian immigration authorities were selective and high standards had to be met to gain entry. The new arrivals were deemed to be people of stature and means, who were prepared to take a chance and work hard.

With an inflow of capital and expertise the country grew and prospered at a rate matched only in South Africa. By 1960 Rhodesia was, after South Africa, the second most-developed country in Africa and was completely self-supporting. A vibrant economy grew without incurring any debt.

The future looked bright but then came decolonisation and the imperial powers rushed to abandon their African territories. On 24 October 1964 Northern Rhodesia became the independent Republic of Zambia under Kenneth Kaunda. The pressure mounted on Southern Rhodesia to follow suit but the Southern Rhodesians were defiant and Prime Minister Ian Smith led a rebellion against the British Crown. The gauntlet had been thrown.

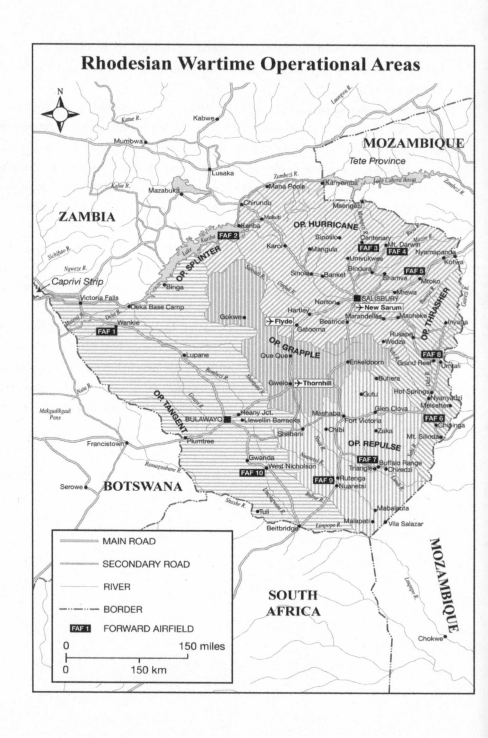

CHAPTER 1

This is my land my home,
I yearn not
For that strange unfamiliar place called Europe
I am an African
A white African.
—CHAS LOTTER

REBELLION

"**I**n *the lives of most nations there comes a moment when a stand has to be made for principles, whatever the consequences. This moment has come to Rhodesia.*

I call upon all of you in this historic hour to support me and my government in the struggle in which we are engaged. I believe that we are a courageous people and history has cast us in a heroic role. To us has been given the privilege of being the first Western nation in the last two decades to have the determination and fortitude to say: 'So far and no further.'

We may be a small country but we are a determined people who have been called upon to play a role of worldwide significance. We Rhodesians have rejected . . . appeasement and surrender.

We have struck a blow for the preservation of justice, civilisation and Christianity—and in the spirit of this we have thus assumed our sovereign independence.

God bless you all."
—RHODESIAN PRIME MINISTER
IAN DOUGLAS SMITH UNILATERALLY
DECLARING INDEPENDENCE FROM
BRITAIN

With the British government led by Harold Wilson insisting on 'No Independence before Majority Rule' {NIBMAR}. Rhodesian Prime Minister Ian Smith decided the black rule that would then follow spelled doom for his country and decided it was time to go it alone. On 11 November 1965, surrounded by his cabinet, he reached for his pen and signed a document that signalled open rebellion against the Crown. Not since the American Declaration of Independence was promulgated in 1776 has such an event taken place. It was a unilateral declaration of independence {UDI} and the die was cast; the country would soon be at war with the world. At midday Rhodesians sat riveted to their radios as Smith told them of his momentous decision.

DARRELL WATT

One young man listening to that fateful broadcast was Darrell Watt. "I was at school when we heard the news. There was uncertainty about what it all meant. I was quite frightened. I spoke to my Dad who was pro-Smith so I took my cue from him. I was reminded that many of my forebears were soldiers so if there was going to be a fight I was up for it.

"My dad was born in Bulawayo in 1921 and went to Milton Boys' High where he was head boy. At eighteen he was called up for service in the Second World War and after training in Salisbury he was railed to Cape Town where he, along with his Rhodesian contingent, was shipped to Liverpool and on to Catterick in Yorkshire. In 1941 he was deployed to Algiers as part of the 78th British Infantry Division. He did not like it there because of the lack of hygiene. From there he went to Tunisia and took part in the battles against Rommel's Afrika Korps. From there he was evacuated to Italy and trekked to Rogio and Taranto via Sicily. The advance north through Italy was a tough one and he told me of his high regard for the German soldiers. The weapon they appear to have most feared was the German 88mm with its high velocity and low trajectory.

"The Battle at Monte Cassino left the biggest impression on him and he never quite got over the terrible loss of life he witnessed there. Wounded by shrapnel and sick with yellow fever, he was hospitalised in Bari on the coast before continuing the march into Austria. His final battles were in the Po Valley west of Naples. He also spoke highly of the civilised way in which the Germans soldiers conducted themselves. His lasting impression at the end of the war was Britain's ingratitude.

He was told to find his own way home. My grandmother nursed in both world wars and gave me her medals before she died.

"I was born in Fort Victoria in April 1949 but we moved to Gwelo and I went to school at Thornhill Boys' High. Eventually my family ended up in Salisbury. All I can remember about life in Fort Victoria was sitting on the bonnet of my Dad's old Citroën and having a hornet sting me on the arse. It was bloody painful, and I've been careful where I sit ever since.

"I loved the bush from an early age. I had access to surrounding farms and ranches, most of which were situated in open country teeming with game. I learned about the natural world from my black friends. It was the first part of a long learning curve that would help me in ways I never dreamed of then.

"My father, being in the Rhodesian Department of Water Development, used to spend a lot of time in the Tribal Trust Lands₃ providing water to the black people and when not in school I used to travel with him. He was typical of so many of the Rhodesian civil servants; he was out in the field working hard to help the Africans improve the quality of their lives. This is something the world never wanted to know about. With my father on his government bush trips I met men from the Game Department like Paul and Clem Coetzee.

"School mirrored life in Rhodesia—very tough but very fair. People often wonder why young Rhodesians were so quick to make the transition from schoolboy to soldier. I think the toughness of the country's education system and the emphasis on team sports had a lot to do with this. While I did not shine in the classroom, I did play rugby for the 1st XV.

"When they told me I had to repeat Form IV I informed my parents I'd had enough, talked my Dad into buying me an old Land Rover and rifle, and headed to Gwaai Forest Area in Matabeleland to work for Allan Savory."

Savory, a brilliant but controversial wildlife expert, was about to make his mark in the Rhodesian political and military arenas. A former game ranger in Northern Rhodesia, he was an opinionated forward-thinker who would win a seat in parliament as a member of Ian Smith's Rhodesian Front Party, only to later defect and align himself with the African Nationalists.

"Initially we camped at Amandundumela up on the hill in Gwaai and there we 'culled' eland and sable which were there in numbers surplus to the carrying capacity of the area. Today I gather there is almost nothing left but then the numbers needed to be controlled. Later I moved to Liebigs Ranch in the south-east Lowveld. Then Allan and his associates formed a company called the Rhodesia Meat Company.

"We were paid according to the number of animals we shot and I was getting quite good at this. I ended up being the top earner and this irritated the senior guys who had more experience than me. Mike Bunce, who was a veteran, got so pissed off he wanted to beat me up a couple of times. I was only seventeen and I think they saw me as a bit of an upstart earning more than they were. £1 was a lot of money then and in one month I made £400 which was enough to buy a vehicle. This shocked everyone. I reached a point where I became highly effective with my 30.06. My trackers were Shangaans; one was Jacob and the other Philemon. We would hunt on foot and run the animals down. The problem was what we shot had to be loaded and processed and that was a lot of work. One day Jacob said he had enough and we must stop shooting. I said no, we must continue but he bolted with my bag of bullets, shouting at me as he ran away, 'You have shot sixteen zebras out of one herd and we have to load them; we have had enough; you must stop now!' Then he went and hid in the bush till dark. It sounds excessive but the game numbers were so high that there had to be a managed reduction to protect the habitat.

"Jacob and Philemon helped me learn the lessons of the bush which would later keep me alive. They were tremendous trackers. We would practise back-tracking human and animal spoor back to the vehicle. I learned how to age spoor and identify an animal that was tiring. Vegetation was a good way to age tracks and 'aerial' spoor helped identify numbers. Termite activity and the rate at which blood dried were important to timings. They also taught me how to anticipate the direction an animal was going, a difficult lesson to learn.

"While my black friends taught me the vital basics, Savory had a big impact. With his help I learned the additional skills that enable one to survive in the bush. Probably most importantly I learned how to anti-track. I never forgot those lessons and am convinced this is the reason that I and most of the men I commanded, survived.

"Lessons well learnt were the value of the extended line rather than a single file where walking on top of tracks makes the trail easier to follow; choosing your footfalls to avoid soft ground; flat soles without treads; walking in rivers wherever possible; using hessian sacks to traverse sandy soil."

It was while perfecting the skills of the hunter that Watt received his compulsory military service call-up papers to join intake 89 in June 1967. He travelled to Llewellin Barracks in Bulawayo by train, with no real idea of what to expect.

"On our arrival in Bulawayo there were the 'Red Caps' {Military Police} and 'RP's' {Regimental Police} shouting out orders. We were herded onto waiting trucks—a bit like cattle, really—and taken to Llewellin Barracks. I did not realise it then but a big story was about to unfold."

THE WIND OF CHANGE

In a sense an important chapter in that 'story' began in 1957 when Ghana {formerly the Gold Coast} became independent of Britain and Kwame Nkrumah assumed power. Europe then began 'freeing' its colonies with extravagant haste as African Nationalism took root across the continent. Rhodesians looked on in horror as mostly chaos, carnage and bloodshed followed.

Southern Rhodesia's African Nationalists began seeking external schooling, believing it was denied them at home. Many also sought sanctuary from government watch-lists, banning orders and proscriptions. They headed to communist-bloc institutions where they rubbed shoulders with like-minded anti-colonial activists, all of whom regarded Nkrumah as a hero. It was at this time that Robert Mugabe took up a teaching post in Ghana and married his first wife, Sally.

Within the Rhodesian dynamic an early tribal split saw Joshua Nkomo head up the 'Zimbabwe African People's Union' {ZAPU} with Soviet patronage and Ndabaningi Sithole the 'Zimbabwe African National Union' {ZANU} with Chinese help.

In 1963 ZANU sent five candidates on a military course to China. Among them was future Zimbabwean government minister Emmerson Mnangagwa. Ghana and Tanzania also offered Chinese-run military institutions. In 1964 the first Ghanaian-trained group was flown to China to be trained as instructors. In 1965 a group of twenty-eight candidates underwent training in Cuba. In the same year the infamous 'Crocodile Gang' which included Mnangagwa became the first graduates of the Itumbi Reefs academy near Chunya in south-west Tanzania. They would return to the country and murder Petrus Oberholzer in the Eastern Districts of Rhodesia and set a precedent for the many farm murders to follow.4 Josiah Tongogara, who would go on to become ZANU's military leader, was in the second intake.₅ By the fourth intake the number of recruits had risen to a hundred and twenty. In 1966 ZANU sent eleven recruits including Tongogara to the Nanking Military Academy in China.

Scandinavian countries were especially sympathetic to African Nationalism and offered educational and professional assistance to young Rhodesians. This facility was often exploited to dupe recruits into attending military camps.

Contrary to the popular view that white oppression was driving thousands of recruits into the arms of Communist-bloc instructors, Bhebhe and Ranger, both sympathetic to the Nationalist cause, concede this in their book 'Soldiers in Zimbabwe's Liberation War': "As a result of the dearth of volunteers, both ZAPU and ZANU engaged in a policy of forced conscription in Zambia . . . ZAPU and ZANU . . . decided to employ . . . press-ganging. Many young men originally from Rhodesia and living in the Mumbwa rural area and in Lusaka were press-ganged into going for training."

Deception, they write, was also used. "Both ZAPU and ZANU made it their custom to welcome such students at the airports but instead of finding themselves in colleges and universities as they had intended, they found themselves whisked off to military training camps."

Josiah Tungamirai who would later command the Zimbabwe Air Force and Ernest Kadungure who would be a minister in Zimbabwe's first cabinet were both products of the forced recruitment programme that laid the foundation for armed resistance.

CHAPTER 2

The regiment has been,
is, will always be his life
and his reason for life.
—CHAS LOTTER

FORMATION OF THE SAS

The Special Air Service {SAS} originated in the desert war of North Africa. With Erwin Rommel rampaging and the Allied forces reeling, British commanders sought a means to destroy the Luftwaffe on the ground and to disrupt the enemy's lines of communication. A young British subaltern named David Stirling sent parachutists behind German lines to destroy an airfield.[6] Stirling was convinced that small groups maximising the element of surprise could inflict losses disproportionate to their numbers.

Although that first operation was a disaster, requiring the Long Range Desert Group to rescue the men, the seeds were sown. Made up from LRDG troops containing Rhodesian volunteers, the unit had destroyed more than 400 enemy aircraft, also airfields, fuel, munitions dumps and lines of communication by the end of the war. Hitler paid them the supreme compliment when he noted, "These men are dangerous . . ." and exhorted Rommel to do all that was necessary to eliminate the threat.

In June 1950 volunteers were sought for a Rhodesian task force to Korea. There was an overwhelming response but only a hundred men were selected. When a new emergency developed in Malaya where Communist insurgents were gaining ground in a campaign against British colonial rule, the men were shipped there instead. Highly trained troops who could sustain themselves in the jungle were needed and the Rhodesians helped fill the need.

The legendary World War II veteran Major 'Mad Mike' Calvert was given the task of planning the British-led counter-insurgency. He decided to spearhead his effort with a Special Forces unit that became known as 22 SAS (Malayan) Scouts. The Rhodesian contingent, under the command of Lieutenant Peter Walls, would be known as C Squadron SAS (Malayan) Scouts. Among the Rhodesian ranks was ex-postal technician Ron Reid-Daly who had left his employment on the toss of a coin. C Squadron arrived in the Far East late in 1951. The Rhodesian SAS was born.

Three years later the Rhodesians returned home having performed with distinction under arduous circumstances. Peter Walls, who had rapidly been promoted to major, was awarded an MBE.

The unit was briefly disbanded but then resurrected when paratroopers were added to the 'Federal Army' {Federation of Northern Rhodesia, Southern Rhodesia and Nyasaland}. A core group was sent to the UK for training at Hereford. On their return, the first selection course was run in the Matopos Hills in May 1961. By the end of the year the squadron strength was 184 and the Rhodesian SAS was looking for a home.

For financial reasons the SAS was initially based in Ndola where it was bankrolled by Northern Rhodesia's Federal copper revenues. This was not a popular choice because of the need to continually rotate troops between Northern and Southern Rhodesia for training. During this period some elements were seconded to 22 SAS and deployed in Aden. In the middle of 1962 Rhodesian SAS troops were sent to Northern Rhodesia's border with the Congo to assist Belgian refugees fleeing independence atrocities. This spectacle would have a profound effect on soldiers and civilians alike when, three years later, Southern Rhodesia was told to submit to a timetable for black majority rule.

At the breakup of the Federation in December 1963 the Federal Army was disbanded. Numbering only thirty men, C Squadron was re-formed in Salisbury and recruitment begun under the command of Major Dudley Coventry. One of the SAS 'originals,' Coventry was already a legend. On one occasion he was reputed to have killed a German soldier with a single punch.[7] But despite a charismatic and colourful commander, morale was low, as were resources.

In 1965, C Squadron was offered an opportunity for an officer to be attached to the parent regiment in Hereford and Lieutenant Brian Robinson was given the slot. When he reported for duty the British SAS was heavily involved in operations in Borneo. He was fascinated to learn that they had a squadron permanently deployed on deep-penetration operations in Indonesia where, at times, they engaged in cross-border raids against Indonesian regulars supporting the insurgents.

He remembers, "The British were initially highly circumspect about passing on any operational information to me, but gradually the atmosphere improved and the stiff upper lip relaxed." After a great deal of persuasion, Robinson was able to convince the commanding officer of 22 SAS to send him on a training operation to Borneo, but political fate was about to intervene.

"After UDI I instantly became a 'Rebel Rhodesian' and had to decide on my loyalties." Offered a choice, he declined to stay with 22 SAS. "I was desperate to get into a punch-up back in Rhodesia," he acknowledged.

HAROLD WILSON AND THE SOVIETS

Following the unilateral declaration in Salisbury, British Prime Minister Harold Wilson took his problem to the United Nations to have the 'Rebel Regime' declared 'a threat to world peace' and on 19 December probably the harshest and most comprehensive economic sanctions in history were introduced while outraged OAU {Organisation of African Unity – replaced with the AU African Union in 2002} members threatened to sever diplomatic relations with London if the rebellion was not crushed immediately. Wilson met with his commanders to weigh up the military options. The Rhodesian government was denied that most fundamental of human rights and refused an opportunity to defend itself in any international forum, including the United Nations. Relations with virtually the entire world were suspended and Rhodesian passports were declared invalid.

At this time senior figures within the Rhodesian political establishment, noting the synergy between Whitehall and the Kremlin, insisted that Harold Wilson and some of his senior lieutenants were in league with the Soviets. Predictably they were roundly condemned as members of the lunatic fringe of the 'racist regime' but recent revelations now tend to support their view.

The Soviet contact man in the West at this time was Alexander Chernyaev and his recently revealed diaries disclose the existence of a 'special relationship' between the British Labour Party and Moscow and a 'reverential approach' of the party leaders to their Russian 'comrades.' It is also now known that Jack Jones, who became the leader of the Transport and General Workers' Union which helped Wilson win and maintain power, was a paid-up agent of the KGB.[8]

What is also now known is that the British Security Service had a file on Wilson and had been monitoring his frequent visits to Moscow since his election as an MP in 1945. MI5 and MI6 intercepted his communications and on one occasion burgled his house in a search for evidence. The intelligence services also knew that Wilson was in regular contact with KGB London operative Ivan Skripov and that the British Council for the Promotion of International Trade which Wilson headed was, according to them, "Communist controlled."[9]

Just what happened then is revealed by Carl Watts[10] where he details how advanced and detailed the British invasion plans were. Logistical support was sought from the air forces of the United States and Canada to supplement the air transport capabilities of the Royal Air Force. Fighters and bombers were to be dispatched to Zambia and Tanzania with the bombers tasked to destroy the Rhodesian air bases at Thornhill and New Sarum while the SAS was to be used to secure the civilian airports in Salisbury and Bulawayo. Infantry and parachute battalions were to be deployed in Botswana and Zambia and a carrier task force was to be sent to the Mozambique Channel. One regiment that made it clear there would be extreme unhappiness if ordered into action against the Rhodesians was the British Special Air Service. They had only recently been fighting alongside their Rhodesian counterparts against communist terrorists in Malaya and it was hard for them to contemplate so radical a change in circumstance.

Ken Connor, a serving member of the British SAS at the time, later wrote: "Black African leaders immediately began pressing [Prime Minister] Wilson for armed intervention to bring the settlers to heel. His first reaction was to use the SAS and 39 Brigade, based in Aden, to put down the illegal regime. What stopped him was a near mutiny in the regiment."[11]

It is also now known that by February 1966 Ken Flower, who would soon become the Rhodesian intelligence chief, secretly briefed Harold Wilson on the country's military capabilities. This information was doubtless of significant assistance to those planning to invade the country and proof that Flower's loyalties were at best, split.[12]

Adding to the pressure it became clear that Britain's Labour government was replete with men and women who disliked their tropical cousins on a highly personalised and partly class-based basis. The Rhodesians were seen as an embarrassing imperial hangover, but also rambunctious elitists who were too cocky for their own good and reeked of the old establishment that the Labourites wished to destroy. The scene was not well-set for Smith and his people; there was bad chemistry before the political dimension was even examined.

"On more than one occasion," Ian Smith recalled, "Harold Wilson implored me to appreciate the wonders of being English. It was simply beyond his comprehension that we did not want to be English and fully integrated into their establishment. The fact that we actually preferred to be Rhodesians was seen as an outrageous affront."

With pressure mounting, the Rhodesians felt their options were limited in terms of places to go: this was their home, most planned to stay and they were prepared to fight for it. Unfortunately for them, that brashness of spirit was what irritated a Western world riddled with the perceived shame of an imperial association. In much of the West the 'nanny state' had arrived, elitism of any form was scorned and mediocrity against a backdrop of rampant egalitarianism had become the norm. The majority of white Rhodesians were the very antithesis of this and they refused to be constrained by a fashionable liberalism that frowned upon free enterprise and self-reliance.

As post-UDI Rhodesia fell out of favour with the rest of the world, the press painted a picture of whites living a life of undeserved luxury at the expense of the impoverished blacks and antipathy towards them escalated sharply.

"Rhodesia was divided along racial lines and the black standard of living was lower than ours," says Watt, "but still much of an improvement over their traditional lifestyle and where they had been when the white man arrived. The relationship between white and black was relaxed and friendly which is why I always questioned the need for war. Although the whites were politically dominant, there was a great deal of mutual respect between the races. That was very much a part of our way of life. I don't think many whites took anything for granted; they were mostly honest and hardworking and just wanted to be left alone to get on with the job of building the country."

But that was not to be.

THE FIRST FARM ATTACK

On 16 May 1966, just over five months after UDI was declared, Johannes Viljoen and his wife were attacked in their homestead and murdered by terrorists on their farm near the town of Hartley {now Chegutu} north of Salisbury. It was a grim warning of what was to come.

With the threat of a British-sponsored invasion looming, a decision was taken in October 1966 to have the SAS destroy the rail bridge spanning the Kafue River in Zambia in order to sever the line that would bring troops and matériel to the frontier. But the operation ended in tragedy when the device being readied for the task exploded, killing four men. SAS Commander Major Coventry was a lucky survivor, but the unit had lost three of its most experienced non-commissioned officers {NCOs}.

RECRUIT WATT

"I did my basic training at Llewellin Barracks. I recall an infantry major there and a lieutenant giving me hell for the way I was shooting at targets on the range. Rather than kneel, I was on my haunches and they didn't like that but I pointed out I had hit all the targets and with a very tight grouping. An angry argument followed between them with the lieutenant coming to my side, telling the major that he too was a hunter and had used the same shooting position. The major then quietened down and both of them wanted to know more about my days as a hunter.

"It was after that that Ken Phillipson and Stan Hornby arrived to recruit for SAS Salisbury. They took us on a cross-country run from the gate of Llewellin Barracks across the Bulawayo road towards Gwelo over two hills with rifle, full battle-dress and webbing. It was Stan Hornby, dressed in his running shoes, shorts and vest who challenged us to keep up his pace but then suggested I slow down! Stan then ran out of gas and another instructor took over but he also fell away. I was in peak physical fitness then from running about twenty kilometres a day hunting animals.

"In those days we did selection first at Inyanga, then the training course and at the end of the training we did what was known as 'All in' which was a very physically demanding, non-stop exercise designed to weed out those who were still deemed 'suspect.'"

Candidates commenced the selection ordeal with the punishing 'pre-rev' exercise during which men were subjected to non-stop physical and mental abuse. Dispensing with sleep, food, self-respect and modesty, they boxed, wrestled in mud, ran, swam, went over assault courses and participated in any other activity on hand that would wear them down. Most exercises were done carrying a rifle and a steel ball. One favourite was 'chariot races' which saw recruits hauling screaming instructors around the bush in vehicle trailers. It was an exercise designed to humiliate and exhaust before the real demands even began. No talking was allowed.

An easy escape from the pain was to accept a hot meal and a cold beverage. Those who prevailed and refused to accept assurances from the instructors that they were certain failures, were then transported to the cold, forbidding landscape of the Inyanga highlands in the east of the country, where the mountains are massive, their slopes sheer and the undergrowth thick and thorny.

Here, the selection began at night. Cold and hungry recruits were dumped in the wilderness, told to meet at a given 'locstat,' {a map grid reference}, within twenty-four hours, and thrown a jumble of maps along with a steel trunk full of metal balls. Apart from the steel trunk, which was shared, each man carried a loaded weapon, heavy pack and steel balls. Misdemeanours such as presenting at any stage with a dirty rifle would see the load of balls increased. Disoriented, unseeing, they were left to stumble and fall while battling to reach an uncertain destination. Those who made it to the rendezvous found no more than a map and another 'locstat' and so the grind went on. When instructors appeared it was invariably for no other reason than to heap invective on those who would share their colours and encourage them to give in.

Five days later, those who had not fallen were taken aside for interviews. Instructors questioned them closely to ascertain from the observations of the recruits themselves who in their respective teams had performed and in what way. This information was considered vital in making the final assessments.

With the team phase completed, the emphasis shifted to individual endurance and initiative. Apart from water, the only other liquid generously supplied was blister medication. On the final day, with the survivors literally on their last legs, they were given their ultimate instructions: march more than nine kilometres back into the mountains with full loads. But this time, they had a five-hour time limit. For many who had already suffered so severely for so long it was a bridge too far and they went down trying at the final, heart-breaking hurdle.

ROBINSON ON SAS SELECTION

"The world is bored to tears reading about the various selection courses run by Special Forces units worldwide. Each unit tries to outdo the next, introducing new methods of torture designed to break the incumbent but I think we worked out a very effective process.

"Compatibility is probably the most important aspect of all. Operating in enemy territory for protracted periods calls for a special kind of tolerance. Perpetual sniffing or unacceptable eating habits of an operator could easily lead to dissension in the ranks, a breakdown in morale and, eventually, tragedy.

"Mental strength: operating in enemy territory for protracted periods is dangerous. It is essential to have the mental strength to cope with this unnatural way of life.

"Physical strength: re-supply is the most vulnerable phase of any operation. It is therefore imperative to try and reduce the frequency of re-supply. This means that an operator must be capable of carrying a heavy rucksack for long periods over difficult terrain and be able to survive with as little as possible.

"Initiative: we looked for chaps who could think fast on their feet, no matter how exhausted. A junior leader might have to make instant decisions under severe pressure which in some cases might lead to the fall of a government should things go wrong.

"Skills: the SAS soldier must have the necessary military skills to allow him to operate in a clandestine manner against an enemy."

Robinson continues: "In the course of his training the SAS recruit would learn a variety of skills including tracking, bush craft, survival, demolition, attack-diving, watermanship, mines, mortars, foreign weapons, signals, parachuting, navigation and marksmanship. All this was premised on parade-square drill and punishing physical training. In the critically important area of shooting the SAS instructors were well aware that the majority of exchanges were taking place at close range with the enemy invariably hugging the ground. We therefore deviated from conventional shooting drills which encouraged a 'shoot-high' tendency, with targets consistently just above ground level on the ranges."

Dave Westerhout, Rhodesia's World Practical Pistol Champion, provided expert instruction on the use of side-arms and extremely high standards were expected. Rob Johnstone, former SAS training officer, recalled: "Shooting was always competitive and a prize was presented to the worst shot in the form of a cowbell, suspended around the neck and quaintly named the 'Shit-Shot Bell.' This prize was open to all ranks and was to be worn at all times except in bed. Amazingly, no one ever won it twice." On his course Watt impressed immediately. Out of a hundred volunteers he emerged as the top marksman and won all the runs and route marches. It was clear that a man of substance with all the requisite skills had found his way to the SAS. Training officer Ken Phillipson told the young recruit: "We need naturals, Watt, and you are a natural."

"Ten of us made it into the unit under the command then of Major Dudley Coventry," remembers Watt. "If I had known then what I was heading for, I think I would still have signed up, but I might have thought about it a little longer."

CHAPTER 3

Into the cauldron
Walk the fields of war with me,
With a people blown in the winds of change.
—CHAS LOTTER

FIRST BLOOD

The first time the Squadron would draw enemy blood was in May 1967 when word was received of a pantechnicon suspiciously parked on the side of the road thirty-five kilometres north of the town of Karoi. Then Squadron Commander Dudley Coventry took a team to investigate and heard movement inside. Called on to present themselves, the occupants opened fire through the sides of the vehicle. Launching himself at the man directing the fire, Corporal Jo Conway dragged him from the vehicle while his team opened fire, killing four.

Throughout the late 1960s, incursions from Zambia took place along the length of Rhodesia's northern border, from the Victoria Falls in the west to Kanyemba on the eastern border with Mozambique.

In late 1967 a significant incursion took place at the Batoka Gorge near Victoria Falls when a combined ZAPU and South African ANC {SAANC} force of close to a hundred crossed into Rhodesia, comprising the biggest incursion to date. Planned and launched by Oliver Tambo of the SAANC, and James Chikerema acting for the anti-Rhodesian fighters, the precipitous crossing using ropes and pulleys was organised by Soviet advisers. The prime objectives were to support the SAANC insurgents through western Rhodesia to the Limpopo River so they could infiltrate South Africa and to establish friendly supply routes in Matabeleland for future incursions. They believed the size of the group was large enough to take on the Rhodesian security forces if required. Included in the ANC force were future stalwarts Chris Hani and Joe Modise who would later become the first Defence Minister under Nelson Mandela.

Word of the incursion reached the ears of Rhodesian intelligence operatives but the whereabouts of the enemy remained unclear until a railway repair team on the Victoria Falls line heard of a suspicious presence and reported it. Troops of the Rhodesian African Rifles were deployed and a series of rolling contacts took place over a period of weeks with much of the action taking place in the Wankie {now Hwange} National Park. At the end of the operation Rhodesian forces suffered eight deaths, the enemy forty dead and thirty-four captured. The ANC element, known as the Luthuli Detachment, by all accounts gave a good account of themselves, earning the respect of their Rhodesian adversaries while awakening the South African authorities to the need to bolster their military presence in Rhodesia.

Looking at the lie of the land, the vast expanses that had to be covered and low troop levels making conventional border control difficult, a decision was taken to send two-man SAS teams into Zambia to identify infiltration routes being used by ZAPU insurgents.

"Unfortunately, remaining covert was vital," said Robinson, "and much to the chagrin of lurking operators, some wonderful killing opportunities had to be passed up in favour of remaining clandestine and carrying out the true SAS role."

Forbidden to wear Rhodesian uniforms, the men carried no weapons or equipment that could be identified as Rhodesian, and if captured their orders were to insist that they were dissidents operating at their own behest. While operational successes were minimal, the SAS men were learning valuable lessons all the time that would stand them in good stead in the years ahead.

To combat the growing threat 'tracker-combat teams' were formed consisting largely of white game rangers and their scouts from the Department of National Parks who worked closely with soldiers of the Rhodesian Light Infantry, but this arrangement had its limitations. The National Parks trackers were skilful, but when their casualties mounted their enthusiasm to close with the enemy and kill, waned. A pressing need arose for soldiers who could track and kill and this was a role that Watt fitted into perfectly.

"Soon we began to hear about incidents regarding so-called 'terrorists,'" remembers Watt. "These contacts with the enemy involved mainly National Parks rangers trained by Savory. The unit was known as the TCU {Tracker Combat

Unit}. The first contact I recall hearing of took place near Bulawayo and was a successful demonstration of our ability to track to combat. The idea was then brought to the SAS to run our own tracking courses under Savory's supervision and this was done close to Pandamatenga on the Botswanan border.

"I was really pleased when they made me an instructor as a 'troopie' as all the instructors were NCOs and officers. Also there were 'Stretch' Franklin, Hennie Pretorius and 'Jop' Oosthuizen. After doing this course we were deployed to the Zambezi Valley in an operational role."

THE TWO-TOED TRIBE

"It was during this time I first made contact with the Vadoma[13] people near the Redcliffs on the Zambezi and it was an incredible experience that I will never forget. These people were hiding from the *Zezuru* people who hunted them down and killed them. We managed to catch two tame ones and asked them to show us the main group somewhere in the hills near Kanyemba. We found them; they were like wild animals, dressed only in animal skins; they had no homes, pots or blankets. They ate only what they found: berries, birds and the occasional small animal. We knew a waterhole in those hills where they would drink from and there were large stones there and we put down tobacco, salt and sugar and lay for days waiting to see them while watching with binoculars. We eventually were feeding them daily like wild animals.

"Only when we moved well away to the top of a mountain did they approach our offerings. We sat on an 'OP' {Observation Post} and watched them through the binoculars rushing in to get the food when they were happy we'd disappeared. I became fascinated and did not want to leave. We watched them make their traps and copied them—they worked very well. They smoked a lot through a short stick in which they mixed *dagga* {cannabis} with the tobacco.

"One old man was living on his own in the bush. We approached him very quietly and he was ever so angry with us when we greeted him from very close. He admonished us and asked angrily why we had not warned him to say we were coming. He wore impala-skin pants with nothing else on. He had used two fires on either side of his chest area to keep him warm at night and he had the most terrible burn marks on his back and chest. He had been ousted by his family and was surviving alone. We discovered the old people were simply thrown out of the group to die alone in the bush where they were eaten by the hyenas that seemed to trail them. They were completely wild.

"On one occasion we managed to sneak up on a small group and give them a fright. They were very angry and disappeared for a while. Later I found remnants of this same tribe in the hills of Mozambique near Cabora Bassa dam wall. They were also completely wild. They were living as they had done for hundreds of years, avoiding the other tribes that were killing them. Thanks to them I learned an awful lot about how to survive in the bush with very little.

"This was all part of a learning curve along with Savory's lessons which were very valuable. He pioneered the original tracking and bush craft courses. He was a very good tracker, a captain in the Territorial Army and was very much a forward-thinker. A lot of people didn't like him but he was a smart guy and he knew a great deal about the bush. Looking back, I still think we were remiss in not being more committed to his tactic of finding tracks and following them till you found the enemy and killed him. The army ended up taking a few shortcuts and we shouldn't have. There is no substitute for the hard work of tracking through whatever terrain and for whatever distance until you find the people you need to destroy. For a lot of guys, I think the strain of an extended follow-up was too much. For the guy on spoor it is a demanding task: keeping an eye on the signs on the ground, knowing where your troops are and watching out for an ambush. The thicker the bush the harder it got but if you could stay on the tracks you got them eventually."

WATT'S FIRST ACTION

Watt's first engagement with the enemy followed when SAS headquarters reported that an alert game scout had found 'unusual' tracks of two people near the National Parks camp known as Marongora on the brink of the Zambezi escarpment. Watt along with Sergeant Jo Conway and Troopers T.C. Woods and Stretch Franklin reacted.

"We were based at Makuti at the time," recalls Watt. "There were a few incursions but not a lot of activity. We picked up the tracks at Marongora Dam and followed them into the escarpment. I was on spoor with Sergeant Conway behind me and two flankers. The bush was so thick the flankers had to file behind me at times. It was bloody hot but we kept going through the morning and by midday I could tell from the tracks they were tiring. I told the guys we were close when I found a place they had rested and then run so they must have heard us. Then we picked up equipment they had dropped and followed them into very thick thorn-bush split by narrow gorges. I said to Jo he and the other guys were best getting to high ground to cover me while I followed and flushed them. On my own I moved quietly and stopping to listen I heard a rifle scraping on rock. I moved closer and there I was looking down his barrel only feet away. I fired and missed but they came out with their hands up. We took them to a point where a chopper came and collected them. Back at Makuti I was told I had done the Squadron proud and we drank plenty of beer. It was my first contact with the enemy and it did my confidence a lot of good."

OPERATION CAULDRON

"After the Marongora incident we found ourselves engaged in a number of contacts after follow-ups and I felt we were getting better and better when we received word that Dave Scammell, a National Parks Ranger, had cut tracks coming in from Zambia and Jo, Stretch, Hennie Pretorius and I were choppered in from Salisbury. This was March 1968, the time of 'Operation Cauldron' and the biggest battles of the war to date were about to begin.[14] We picked up tracks of over thirty and followed them for three days into Mana Pools, along the Angwa River and towards the Zambezi Escarpment. It was a long follow-up through deep gullies in thick bush.

"As we closed on the Angwa Tsetse Camp, I was in front and knew we were close to contact so I reminded Jo there were only four of us and over thirty of them and suggested we get reinforcements. I was only a 'troopie' and Jo was a sergeant. Luckily the RLI {Rhodesian Light Infantry} were close and Lieutenant Bert Sachse soon arrived with his troop who came in behind us. I went ahead with Jo and told him to tell the RLI guys to wait while we went in to reconnoitre. Soon as we had the enemy position visual I suggested we get the RLI in to shoot them. We crept up and without them seeing us we saw they were lying in ambush for us. We watched them for a while and eventually they must have got hungry or thirsty because they started to move around. We carried on watching and soon they started to relax while some started eating. I told Jo it was time to bring the RLI in the same way we had approached and they could get on with killing them. They came in and got busy. When the firing stopped thirty were dead and five wounded, if I remember correctly.

A few limped away. I remember getting into trouble because I was shouting at the 'terrs' {terrorists} in Shona during the fighting. Running contacts followed and the RLI took casualties. This was one of the first examples of us being used in this role: leading the infantry to contact. Al Tourle[15] the RLI RSM {Regimental Sergeant-Major} put me up for a gong but it was turned down."

One of those killed was Eric Ridge who had recently left Plumtree School.[16] His death is recalled by Lieutenant-Colonel Jeremy Strong:[17] "As we approached the contact area, I saw Bert Sachse standing on a small island in the riverbed with a body lying next to him. We landed and I went and helped pick up the dead soldier and put him on the chopper. I immediately recognised him as Trooper Ridge. He had been one of our 'fags' {whereby younger pupils were required to act as personal servants to the most senior boys} at school. I couldn't believe it. My blood boiled."[18]

In the rolling contacts that followed, Group Captain Peter Petter-Bowyer of the Rhodesian Air Force Recalls 'Operation Cauldron': "In the Zambezi Valley, the RLI continued to have contacts of short duration, killing and capturing many terrorists which caused further disintegration of an already scattered force. Many of the guerrillas tried to make their way back to Zambia, unaware that the line of camps they had set up had become death traps. Many were killed in RLI ambushes at these camps and along the Zambezi River. One ZAPU terrorist decided not to follow the Chewore River route but set off for Zambia in a north-easterly direction. After more than a week without food, this emaciated man stumbled into an SAS patrol somewhere near Kanyemba. Given normal army field rations, he gulped them down and promptly dropped dead. When Captain Brian Robinson had recovered from the surprise of the incident, he sent a signal to the Quartermaster General offering SAS congratulations for his unit's first confirmed kill. The QMG was not amused."

HADEBE

Petter-Bowyer continues: "Everything was going the RLI's way until, on 18 March 1968, contact was made at the Mwaura River with a large group led by Hadebe, a ZAPU leader. Under Lieutenant 'Dumpy' Pearce, troops of 3 Commando RLI were pinned down on the north bank by intensive fire coming from heavy bush on the higher south bank. John Barnes and a senior technician, 'Monty' Maughan, arrived in their helicopter and put down 600 rounds of MAG {Rhodesian Army standard belt-fed light machine gun} fire into the unseen enemy's position. Their intention was to draw fire and give the ground commander a chance to move his troops to a safer position. Since this had no effect whatsoever, and the troops remained pinned down, Barnes called for a heavy air strike.

"Meanwhile, Mark McLean and Corporal Brian Warren came in at lower level to draw terrorist gunfire, which was returned in short measured bursts. Though the helicopter expended only 150 rounds of 7.62mm MAG ammunition, McLean's actions gave Pearce the break he needed to move his men to safer ground. Then, under McLean's directions, a pair of Vampires put in accurate strikes with 60lb squash-head rockets and 20mm cannon fire, before a Canberra checked in preparatory to making an attack with ninety-six 28lb fragmentation bombs.

"Much to the annoyance of his experienced Canberra crews, the newly appointed officer commanding 5 Squadron, Squadron Leader John Rogers, had elected to make the airstrike. When he called one minute out, McLean passed low over the target to put down a phosphorus grenade as a visual marker. It was on target but wind carried the white cloud away and the bombs, aimed at this cloud of smoke, were released off target, some exploding close to ground troops waiting on 'safe' ground. Fortunately, no one was seriously hurt.

"When the somewhat annoyed troops moved forward, the terrorists had gone. By the time they had swept through the abandoned area and established the direction of flight, it was too dark to pursue the fleeing enemy, but at first light the next day, the tracker-combat 'call sign' {Every section or 'stick' of four in the Rhodesian Army carried a radio and that radio had a call sign or radio identification designation, e.g. 'Two Five Alpha'} was moving on a trail heading straight for the escarpment.

"At the same time, a smaller 'call sign' was following frothy pink blood spatter from a single terrorist who obviously had a serious lung wound. By late afternoon the trackers reported that the spoor of two hyenas overlaid that of the wounded terrorist. Believing their quarry would not survive the night, the follow-up troops were uplifted for redeployment to a more important task.

"It was probably five years later when I was asked by Special Branch if I remembered the 'Operation Cauldron' terrorist we had given up for dead because hyenas were following him. I certainly did. 'Would you like to meet the man?' I was asked. It seemed unbelievable, but I did indeed meet the recently captured terrorist whose beaming face showed he was pleased to be alive following his second brush with our security forces. His story was amazing. No white man would have survived the ordeal he described.

"He had been wounded in the attack by the Vampires. He panicked and ran off even before the main group under Hadebe left the contact site. All night and the next day he struggled for breath as he made his way to the foot of the escarpment. In the late afternoon, his attention was drawn to a helicopter coming from behind him. Only then did he see, for the first time, the two hyenas as the helicopter frightened them off. When the aircraft landed it was so close that he could see the rotor blades whirling above low scrub. He tried to get back to it for help but moved too slowly. As the helicopter rose into full view he waved madly trying to attract attention, but he was not seen before the helicopter turned and disappeared.

"The two hyenas then reappeared and stayed about thirty metres behind him as he commenced his breathless ascent of the steep escarpment. By then it was almost dark and he was too tired and breathless to continue. So he sat down and faced the hyenas as they moved left and right in short runs, each time coming closer. When they were no more than ten metres away he shot one but missed the other, and chased it with a long burst from his AK-47 rifle. Overwhelmed by tiredness, he lay down to sleep, surely to die.

"He was amazed when he woke at dawn, wheezing and frothing, with his clothing covered in freezing-cold, caked blood. But he was still alive. All day he struggled slowly up the steep escarpment until evening when he lay down, exhausted and wanting to die. Again he was amazed at the dawning of the third day. Still wheezing and frothing he struggled to his feet and wobbled on ever higher. By nightfall he had reached the high ground and was about to lie down when he noticed a light shining some way off. He noted its position by reference to a tree and went to sleep, again not expecting to survive the night. But, yet again, he awoke on the fourth day.

"Taking a line on the tree and noting the relative position of the sun, he plodded off. At around 10h00 he came to a farm store that sold goods to the local black people. He was recognised for what he was but told the superstitious storekeeper how he had been unharmed by hyenas—an omen the keeper should know was deadly to anyone reporting his presence.

"Using his Rhodesian money he bought a large bottle of Dettol for his wound as well as something to eat and drink. He repeated his warnings of doom to anyone reporting him and returned to the bush. Under shade in good cover, he cut a long thin stick and stripped the bark away. He then inserted the stick into the wound in his chest and manoeuvred it until it came through the exit hole on his left shoulder blade. Then, moving the stick in and out slowly in long strokes, he poured the undiluted Dettol into the entry point and down his shoulder into the large exit hole of his terrible wound. Having emptied the bottle and removed the stick, he knew in his mind that he would heal. He settled down to eat and drink before falling into a deep sleep that lasted for at least two days.

"The Special Branch man asked the terrorist to remove his shirt so that I could see his scars. The shiny black puckered skin and the dent caused by the loss of a section of shoulder blade showed how large the chunk of shrapnel from a Vampire rocket must have been. I asked the man, 'Was it not very painful when you pushed the stick through your body? Didn't the Dettol burn like crazy?' He said that this was not a problem. 'I was choking on neat Dettol blowing out of both holes and into my throat. It was the choking that nearly killed me.'"[19]

EARLY MOZAMBIQUE OPERATIONS

"I enjoyed working with the RLI," recalls Watt. "On another occasion I directed them to an ambush position and told them to expect some action. Sure enough the 'gooks' came in and they got hammered. The RLI boys were very pleased.

"I was sitting with my 'call sign' watching this happen from a hill and noticed three 'gooks' were coming up on our tracks. I got into position and waited then dropped the three of them with three shots."

By the end of 'Operation Cauldron', the enemy had been dealt a punishing blow. Of the 126 insurgents that had crossed fifty-eight were killed, fifty-one captured and seventeen unaccounted for. Of these, nine were known to have made it back to Zambia, probably to die of their wounds. In continuing operations, a further seven were accounted for, one of whom was eaten by a crocodile while trying to swim back to Zambia and another was eaten by a lion.[20]

But while the Rhodesian security forces had every reason to be cheery, a new threat was emerging. The armed wing of FRELIMO, {Frente de Libertação de Moçambique} the Black Nationalist movement battling the Portuguese colonial administration, opened a new front centred around Tete which stretched to the north-eastern border of Rhodesia. And by 1968 the Communist bloc, led by the

Soviet Union and China, had joined the Rhodesian fray with alacrity. The Western retreat from Africa had not gone unnoticed and the Communist bloc quickly seized the opportunity to foment strife and further their respective neo-imperial aims in the void that followed. When the African Nationalists went looking for military support they did not have to go far. In some shape or form, the Rhodesians had found themselves at war with virtually the entire world. With the notable exceptions of Portugal and South Africa, there was not a single country they could call a friend.

In a measured response to the growing threat from the east Darrell Watt and his tracking team were dispatched to assist the Portuguese army in 1969.

"We went all over Mozambique," he recalls, "but in the main we were on the Zambezi trying to keep the enemy north of the river. "We deployed with their infantry and spent some of the time with their paratroopers—the *paraquedistas*—who were pretty good but generally the Portuguese troops were not as committed to the fight as were the Rhodesians. We did not succeed in getting them to do what we wanted them to do but still we did have some successes. Understandable I suppose, because for most of them their homeland was Portugal not Mozambique."

Also in the theatre with Watt at the time was Ron Reid-Daly, then a captain in the RLI, who would later command the Selous Scouts. "I really liked the Portuguese," he remembers. "Much maligned by us, some of them were bloody good soldiers and they had some very fine officers. They were also very hospitable and appreciative of what we did for them.

"On one occasion I followed tracks. Norman Walsh {Later Air Marshal Norman Walsh} was in the chopper and we did some leap-frogging and I found a huge camp. It was quite a revelation to me. We did an attack with Portuguese troops and killed some of them but when I returned to Salisbury I told the hierarchy that we in Rhodesia had a bigger problem than we thought and we needed to get ourselves organised. Unfortunately, most of what I said fell on deaf ears."

"After some time in Mozambique," recalls Watt, "I went with Brian Robinson and Charlie Crouch to Angola to train elements of the Portuguese army with particular emphasis on tracking and bush skills. Based in Luanda, we were then deployed east of the capital and spent some time working with the *Flechas*, {A multiracial special forces unit specialising in tracking and reconnaissance} mainly blacks, who were pretty good soldiers."

In 1970, with the help of both Savory and Watt, Robinson set about establishing a bush warfare school called Tracking Wing, based at Kariba and under command of the School of Infantry in Gwelo. Many of the graduates went on to play a decisive role in the developing conflict.

"These were fun days," remembers Watt. "The war had gone quiet and off duty we had time to dive, spearfish and mess around on the lake. Carribea Bay was our favourite drinking hole. Crocs were a problem but we learned to deal with them or thought we had until one of the guys was bitten. We managed to pull him out the water before he got eaten."

"The Squadron was fortunate to have several young soldiers who hunted for a living before joining the military," says Robinson. "Darrell Watt, Hennie Pretorius and André Rabie were typical of the bush men of the early days. Darrell was one of the first soldier-trackers to track to contact. He was to become involved in countless enemy contacts throughout his career."

CAMP ATTACK

"In early 1971 I was sent with Bert Sachse on a camp reconnaissance," remembers Watt. "A spy working for Rhodesian intelligence had come across the river on an inflatable mattress to report details of an enemy camp. Bert and I were sent in to have a good look. Bert wanted to go in by day which I didn't like but he was in charge. It was pretty nerve-wracking; there were 'gooks' and tracks all over the place and we did a lot of ducking and diving. Fortunately, we weren't compromised but we ended up near a pool where they were doing all their washing so there was plenty of movement and lots of noise: singing, shouting, radios blaring. We were stuck behind some rocks for hours unable to move. Eventually it went quiet but Bert seemed settled. I said, 'Bert let's get the fuck out of here. We know what we need to know. How much more do you need to see?' Eventually we made our way out of there in broad daylight and I considered ourselves lucky not to have been seen. We went back home and Bert filed his report.

"Next we were told to take the camp out. Barney Bentley was in command. When I heard the plan I was quite surprised. Each one of us was given a specific individual to target. I would have been happier to simply get into extended line and sweep through killing them all but I was a corporal and my views were irrelevant. Once we were all at our designated positions in the camp we were to await Barney's order which would be two words: 'Wake up!' We were then to shoot the 'gook' we had been allocated. On the sound of Barney's whistle, we were to evacuate the position and return to our initial position.

"Bert and I were instructed to lead the group in once we were near the target. Everything went well and soon we were close outside the camp. We could hear them snoring as we went inside and fanned out to our designated targets but one of the 'gooks' must have seen or heard something. They were sleeping under small canvas shelters and I think this guy must have seen army boots right next to his nose, and he was busy trying to come to his feet taking the shelter with him when Danny Smith had no option but to nail him and that was the end of the element of surprise, but I heard no whistle as the 'gooks' rushed to a defensive position. When the commotion was over I realised everyone had gone and I was on my own. I could hear a heavy machine gun being cocked when all went quiet. A short time later I decided to make my return slowly to where I thought my guys were. Luckily I blew my dog-whistle because Rob Warraker had me in his sights and he told me later he was just about to pull the trigger.

"I asked Barney why everyone had gapped it without the whistle being blown but never received an answer. There seemed to be lack of clarity as to what to do next. I said I know where they are lying and offered to lead the attack back in which I did and when we got close we all opened up. Then when all went quiet we withdrew.

"Later radio interceptors reported hearing the enemy signallers talking about twelve casualties."

Despite the demands of being a frontline soldier, Watt was enjoying 1971. Together with getting married to Gwen Rowles, playing rugby and enjoying Salisbury's social distractions, life was good. "At this stage, things were still quite relaxed and we still had time to play rugby," says Watt. "The RLI/SAS rugby team was damn strong and we could compete with any club in the country. Later Brian Robinson stopped us playing because too many blokes were getting injured and it started to affect operations. I snuck into town and continued playing for another club for a while. Then things got too hot and I stopped. Weekends were mostly spent at Lake McIlwaine outside Salisbury. We used to spearfish there, drink beer and barbeque. We had a lot of fun there.

"I was enjoying the army but I was still not convinced that the war had to be fought. We had had an incident back at the Squadron where one of the men, a good chap, who had passed selection and done everything expected of him, suddenly changed his mind. He had found God and he appeared on the parade square with a bible under his arm and announced he was refusing to fight. He was promptly arrested, charged and sentenced to 200 days in Detention Barracks which was a very severe punishment. I disagreed with his position but admired his courage of conviction. Savory had made me think and I asked Brian Robinson if I and my pal Archie Moore could go to a political meeting he was going to address. Brian said fine but to keep your mouths shut. I was very taken by Savory's ideas on finding a political solution that would prevent war. We'll never know if that was really possible but I often wonder about it."

In November 1971 the enemy was busy. Two senior ZANLA officers collected forty-five newly trained ZANLA personnel from Tanzania. Some twenty-three of them conveyed war matériel to the Zambezi whilst the rest continued to the Mozambican–Rhodesian border area. From this time onwards ZANLA, following Mao's stratagem, recruited large numbers of young men and women from the north-east of the country prior to training in Mozambique. Steady progress was being made.

SMITH SETTLES

On the political front Ian Smith had made some unexpected headway in his discussions with Britain's new foreign secretary, Sir Alec Douglas-Home. Unlike the Labourites with their socialist agenda, Smith liked Home, a Tory, and found him refreshingly sincere in his approach to the problem of Rhodesian independence. To the surprise of many and with the help of Sir Max Aitken and Lord Goodman, a solution was worked out that became a reality with the signing of an agreement between the governments of Rhodesia and the United Kingdom on 21 November 1971.

It seemed lasting peace was at hand and that Watt and the other young soldiers scouring the frontiers for an elusive enemy might be asked to stand down. But Smith, ever wary of the machinations of the wily mandarins who lurked in the shadows of Whitehall, was on his guard. There remained one hurdle: the agreement had to be adjudged 'acceptable' to the majority of the citizenry. Here the prime minister, now wise to wily British politicians and bureaucrats, could see ample room for chicanery by the faceless men in the ministries who were not happy to see the Rhodesians let off the hook so easily. For many in the British political and bureaucratic establishment, the Rhodesians had not yet been punished severely enough for the insult they had visited upon the Crown with the act of rebellion in 1965.

Smith agreed that the Rhodesian government would not actively campaign for acceptance of the proposals by the people; the administration would remain neutral on the side lines, but he expressed concern that any unnecessary delay in canvassing opinion would play into the hands of political agitators. Given time, they would have free rein to poison the minds of an unsophisticated populace, the majority of whom appeared to be keen to accept the agreement. Home agreed to expedite the process and the commission was expected to start gathering opinion in December 1971 but, no surprise to Smith, nothing happened. Requests for clarity on the situation went unanswered, while radical political cells were activated and a counter-propaganda campaign was waged in black townships with little opposition.

Eventually the commissioners, led by Lord Pearce, arrived well into the New Year, having allowed plenty of time for seeds of discord to be sown unchallenged. In a bid to placate Smith, Pearce made it clear that he was confident all was on track and then, out of the blue, one of the commissioners, Lord Harlech, suddenly returned to London. Smith wrote in his memoirs that it was ". . . most unusual in the middle of such an important exercise. We wondered why but were told it was for personal, family reasons."[21]

This, as it turned out, was a lie. The real reason was that British Prime Minister Edward Heath, dealing with fractiousness in his own ranks, was having problems getting Liberal Party support for UK entry into the European Common Market. He needed a sweetener and Rhodesia looked like a plump, ripe strawberry. The Liberal Party leader Jeremy Thorpe was open to some political horse-trading. Having earned himself the sobriquet 'Bomber' for his passionate calls in parliament for the Royal Air Force to bomb the errant colony into submission, he was in no mood to compromise. Thorpe was known to harbour an intense dislike of white Rhodesians who he considered homophobic and an embarrassing relic of a shameful imperial past.[22]

Heath agreed to pull the plug on the Rhodesian agreement in return for Liberal support on Europe. Thorpe agreed to the deal. Pearce was told to find in favour of the 'nays' and he duly did, thus summarily dashing hopes of peace.

This was a tragic event. The country, it seemed, would remain a rogue nation and on course for conflict. During this period, Rhodesian troops were deployed across the country, providing military support to the civil power tasked with keeping the peace. Apart from isolated incidents of civil unrest, the country seemed quiet. But there was mischief afoot.

MBUYA NEHANDA

Early 1972 the spirit medium, or 'witchdoctor,' Mbuya Nehanda,[23] an old crone living in the Dande Tribal Trust Lands close to the Mozambican border, was approached by ZANLA and carried in a blanket to Chifombo in Mozambique close to the Zambian border. The ZANLA leadership was acutely aware of the value of the spirit mediums or witchdoctors and her connection with the Chimurenga War of 1896 considerably elevated her status in the eyes of the peasantry. She was a critically important conversion to the cause and her association with ZANLA boosted recruitment within the border areas of Rhodesia. While at Chifombo she was tasked with 'blessing' groups heading for the front as well as the matériel being carried to ensure that when cached within Rhodesia it would escape detection by the security forces. When she died at Chifombo in 1973 her body was placed in a shallow grave with her head facing south and all groups heading for the front had to walk past her grave.

CHAPTER 4

A dead soldier's boots
Draped out of a chopper
With the toes turned out
Is the saddest sight of them all.
—CHAS LOTTER

THE END OF THE BEGINNING

On 21 December 1972, a ZANLA group, recently 'blessed' at Chifombo, stalked a remote farmhouse among the lush fields in the Centenary farming district of the north-east. In the dead of night, a group under the command of Rex Nhongo[24] attacked. Their target was the De Borchgrave homestead on Altena Farm, 240 kilometres north of Salisbury, which was raked with rocket and machine-gun fire, wounding one of the children and wrecking the house. The farmer, Marc de Borchgrave reached for the phone to summon help, only to find the line had been cut. Keeping his wits about him but fearing a vehicle ambush, he crept out of the house with his rifle and ran two miles to a neighbouring farm to raise the alarm.

Security forces responded while the besieged family sought sanctuary with their neighbours at Whistlefield Farm. But the reprieve was to be brief. Two nights later, the terrorists struck again, wounding de Borchgrave and another of his children. An RLI reaction team going to their aid hit a mine, resulting in the death of a trooper. The war for Rhodesia had been re-joined in earnest.

As an SAS troop commander, Captain Brian Robinson led the first 'call signs' into the area. "By this time I was flying high as a corporal," remembers Watt, "and was in charge of the tracking team. We moved all over the Centenary– Mount Darwin area looking for the enemy in what had become part of 'Operation Hurricane'."

Working from the 'JOC' {Joint Operations Centre} at Centenary, Robinson deployed Watt and his tracking team who were soon hot on the spoor of the terrorists. In a bid to buy time Robinson decided to leapfrog them and deployed 'call signs' ahead by helicopter. One group, led by Corporal Danny Smith, was barely in position close to the Musengezi River when they saw the culprits hurrying towards them. Moving quickly to improve the tactical position of his men, Smith opened fire at very close range on ten terrorists. Advancing with two men under heavy fire, he attacked with grenades, accounting for most of the group. The shots fired were to be the first of many in the north-east and, according to Robinson, this contact marked the beginning of the real war for Rhodesia.

Fate then took a hand and an incident occurred that Robinson would rue for the rest of his life: "My spell attached to 22 SAS in the UK left me indoctrinated by the term, 'hearts and minds,' which I must confess I had never heard of before. I therefore gave my troops strict instructions during which I explained that shooting civilians would not please me. If you take a shot, I insisted, make damn sure the target is a terrorist.

"Noel Robey was part of a 'call sign' that had one of 'Operation Hurricane's' early contacts.25 It was a fleeting engagement that sent the enemy fleeing in all directions. Robey took aim on an unarmed 'gook' running like hell for the trees then, and, with his finger tight on the trigger, remembered my stern admonishment," Robinson recalled. "Unable to see a weapon, he followed orders and declined to fire. It turned out later it was Rex Nhongo!"

"Later on we got back on tracks," remembers Robey, "and caught sight of the 'gooks' going over a hill rise at speed and we could not run them down. We lost sight of them and came by a store so I went in to ask the bloke behind the counter if he'd seen these guys. He said yes and pointed out where they'd gone, so off we went. The bloke I had just spoken to turned out to be the same guy I had just decided not to shoot: Rex Nhongo."

'Torty' King remembers an incident soon after the farm attacks. "Willem Ratte and I were with Darrell when we were summoned to the Special Branch HQ in Mount Darwin for a briefing. We were tasked with finding a group of 'gooks' who were causing untold shit in the farming area. Jim Lafferty, who would later serve with the Selous Scouts, took us in with some of his informers but we found nothing.

We then sat on a hill for a few nights with light intensifiers looking for movement until Darrell decided that we were wasting time."

Willem Ratte remembers: "Darrell lost interest in the clandestine approach and suddenly barked an order: 'This is all a waste of time, pack up, we're going!' My half-boiled tea went into the bush, a biscuit was quickly crammed into my mouth, and then we packed up, soon crawling down the hill, trying to stay behind the little cover there was. It was sometime in the afternoon, everywhere herdsmen were driving cattle in the lands, mamas were chattering on the footpaths, and old men were sitting in the shade looking out over the fields. And in between it all, four whiteys were ducking and diving and dashing around this hut and running behind that one to try and keep out of sight and follow our mad sergeant in his insane rush to get to where we had no idea! The other 'call sign' had been sitting on one hill all these days and nights, carefully chosen to give maximum coverage of the area, watching, observing like you were taught in training how to observe, with skill at concealment and patience, especially patience.

"How the hell did this idiot expect us to pick up anything if he just charges from one hill to the other, and in broad daylight! Bent double while hurrying after the others, trying to keep my rucksack as far down as possible to prevent it sticking out, I was muttering unprintable obscenities aimed at the back of the short figure of our team-leader as he was rushing across the sunlit lands. I was sure that our tracks and we ourselves would be picked up; there was no way anyone could anti-track in this mad rush to nowhere, never mind stay clandestine, the way this so-and-so was carrying on.

"Soon we were back by the river, and there a herd boy was standing right in the middle of where we were heading. All I heard was 'Fuck it, let's go!' and down we ran, through the water and up the other side into the bush lining the bank. Then this idiot turned left, winding his way through the trees, with us struggling to keep up as close to any semblance of an extended line as we could manage. Suddenly, he held up his hand and went down. We followed suit.

"In front of us there was one of these typical Rhodesian rocky outcrops covered by bush and trees. And from it, a radio blared. To my amazement, our sergeant, whom I had been quietly cursing for aimlessly running around the countryside, gave us the thumbs-down sign, the signal for 'enemy.' I still couldn't believe it. But he was sure; that I could see when he signalled 'Torty' and Trevor Kershaw over and whispered instructions.

"They were to go to our right, uphill, and then come down onto the suspect outcrop in a classical right-hook move, opening up with their RPD machine gun as soon as they could make out and confirm the 'terrs.' Sergeant Watt and I would stay where we were, kneeling next to each other, ready to fire our 'FNs' {Standard issue in the Rhodesian Army, a 7.62mm automatic rifle made in Belgium by Fabrique Nationale.} into the enemy position as soon as the shooting started. The other two left, and we waited. The radio was still playing and snatches of Shona conversation were reaching our straining ears. My heart going ninety miles a minute and I felt totally exposed and vulnerable in the clearing. Then a shout and our RPD opened up from the right in front of us, and at the same time we pumped our rounds into the bushes where we had heard the voices coming from. Changing magazines, we carried on firing as fast as possible."

"When we ran through the position there was already one dead 'gook' lying on the ground and one was trying to climb the bank on the opposite side of the river," remembers 'Torty'. "I shot him in the back and emptied half my magazine into him. A shot from Darrell hit the rifle of one of the 'terrs' and wounded him."

Willem Ratte: "The next moment a figure jumped out of the outcrop, literally flying through the air and landing to our left and then legged it past us. It was actually quite funny, the way he high-stepped with super long strides as he ran through our rounds kicking up dust in between and left and right and behind, his legs pumping like pistons as he disappeared down the bank. Gone. When the firing ceased and we had wrapped up the contact scene, it appeared there had been six of them: three dead and the rest had got away. It was the gang SB lad been looking for, no mistake about that, and only Darrell Watt's dogged determination, ability to read a situation correctly and refusal to waste time sitting in one place doing nothing, had achieved success. He had, after having a look around the open TTL, realised that the gang's best place to hide would be in the dense bush along the riverbank on the farmland side.

"When we got back to Mount Darwin, his reputation went up another notch, while I humbly apologised for all my swearing and cursing—in private. And later they told us about the one who had run past us. Apparently, he was one lucky bastard . . . for a short while. It appeared he was wounded but fled all the way down the escarpment to the border in record time, where he ran smack-bang into an ambush by the fenced minefield which was at that stage being laid. Picking up another wound but getting away again, he ran back to a place called Chiswiti, where he stumbled into yet another ambush, part of a major operation taking place at that time. According to the soldiers involved, he was hit once more and again survived, but then just sat down in the middle of the killing ground and started crying."

"Brian Robinson flew into Mount Darwin to congratulate us and we were given the day off to have a beer in the SB pub," remembers King.

HAWKESWORTH

Less than three weeks after the attack on Altena Farm three white land inspectors along with their black staff were ambushed on a lonely road in the Mount Darwin area. Dennis Sanderson and Bob Bland were killed, while Gerald Hawkesworth and his black staff were abducted and marched into Mozambique. Watt boarded a helicopter with his team and was soon on the tracks which were clearly headed into Mozambique. Permission to follow across the frontier was sought and the Portuguese authorities granted it.

"The black abductees either escaped or were released but not Hawkesworth. We followed his group all the way to the Zambezi where they crossed in a canoe but we were unable to catch up with them before they crossed the river and continued north. It was very frustrating—we were very close to recovering him."

Using the abduction partly as a pretext for a larger deployment into Mozambique, two teams of pathfinders, one under the command of SAS Captain Garth Barrett, the other led by Lieutenant Chris Schulenburg, prepared to freefall into the salient. It was the first 'external' {'external': a euphemism for a military operation outside the country} airborne operation of the war. Directed to take up positions either side of the Musengezi–Zambezi confluence, the two four-man groups would then await the arrival of reinforcements in the form of static-line paratroopers, whereupon they would set about interdicting and killing the enemy. In the course of this it was hoped the group holding Hawkesworth would be engaged, but tragedy was immediate when Sergeant Frank Wilmot's parachute failed to open: Chris Schulenburg's group were off to a deadly start.

Despite the setback Garth Barrett initiated an ambush which resulted in the death of one terrorist. On him was a note requesting permission from the

FRELIMO area commander for ZANLA to transit the area with Gerald Hawkesworth. It was the closest anyone would come to rescuing him.[26]

Also involved in the search for Hawkesworth was then Corporal Phil Cripps. "This exercise was supposed to be of short duration; we were told we only needed small packs and four days' rations. It lasted six weeks and I had taken the bare minimum for four days. During that time, we would see nobody else other than the people we killed. Resupply was every ten days by air and on one occasion we were starving when our patrol leader botched the arrangements and nothing came. Bush craft survival skills were no help there because there was nothing to eat. We hankered for the leaves on the baobabs but could not shin up the trunks. I ended up eating used teabags after they had been brewed several times."

But more civilians were soon caught in the line of fire. In May 1973, a tragedy that would attract world attention occurred at the popular tourist attraction of Victoria Falls when Zambian soldiers, by all accounts drunk, opened fire in broad daylight on an unsuspecting group of visitors, killing two Canadian girls and wounding an American. Sustained gunfire after the attack made it impossible for rescuers to reach the party immediately, forcing the survivors to hunker down till nightfall when they were finally rescued. Kurt Waldheim, the UN secretary-general, was soon on the scene to exonerate the Zambian authorities and blame the Rhodesians. It was one of many early indications that in the battle ahead world judgement was going to be very one-sided.

MACOMBE

At the same time, in the north-east of the country it had become clear to the Rhodesian commanders that a change of strategy was needed. The decision to access Rhodesia from Mozambique was working for the enemy. Once into Rhodesia ZANLA commanders and political commissars, along with local witchdoctors, most of who paid obeisance to Mbuya Nehanda, had been working quietly and effectively at convincing the local people of the merits of their cause. The war to win the hearts and minds of the populace had been joined and the enemy were out in front.

The SAS had a fight on their hands. "The first 'external' Squadron operation to counter the renewed threat coming out of Mozambique came about as a request from me to the 2 Brigade commander, Brigadier John Hickman," remembers Robinson. "I presented the plan and indicated the proposed deployments on a

1:50,000 map of the area. Permission was only granted for us to take up a position in Mozambique on the specific order from the Brigade Commander that this was strictly a reconnaissance operation and not an offensive task. The Portuguese high command would only accept this deployment under the conditions described."

As a result, a remote, abandoned Portuguese *aldeamento* {Fortified or protected village} known as Macombe, on the Zambezi, was chosen as a base and became operational in September 1973. The landscape was flat, sandy underfoot and wooded, broken by low hills and rivers. The summer heat was oppressive, making day operations tough on the troops.

While Robinson insisted the emphasis be on surveillance and remaining covert, this had a caveat: where tracks were found and there were no other troops in the vicinity capable of reacting, then the men on spoor would do the job. Aircraft were positioned at the base during daylight hours, returning to a rear HQ in Rhodesia at night.

Brian Jackson remembers his first operation out of Macombe. "Late 1973 I was with a group tasked to locate and do the reconnaissance on a camp called Mpapaya. We had a tame terrorist to assist us. Six of us canoed over the Zambezi after dark, covered our tracks and walked for three days. Early on the morning of the fourth day our guide said, 'Stop, we are here.' We set up a temporary base then realised we were in the middle of a large village complex and we were thirsty. With one of the other guys I took all the water bottles and went barefoot to a hole that had been dug into the dry riverbed and filled the bottles. It was a testing time because the enemy camp was very close by and we were told there were over a hundred FRELIMO there too.

"Come first light the whole area was alive but we were well concealed in the patch of bush overlooking the river. Some women came to collect water and there was much shouting and gesturing before they took off.

"About an hour later our lookout spotted about ten terrorists in extended line moving towards the waterhole. We did not want to engage them and compromise our position but if they came too close we were ready.

"After looking around the waterhole they appeared to be moving off but then suddenly turned towards us. It was their bad call. From close range we killed the lot and, as we expected, triggered a heavy reaction from the camp. We packed with much speed and hightailed out of there. We heard later that the enemy immediately abandoned their camp, expecting an airstrike.

"Two days later we were back on our beach on the Zambezi where our clearance patrol bumped into a group of FRELIMO and there was a heavy exchange of fire, then silence. We decided that they were unaware of our crossing point so just after last light we were all picked up."

Watt remembers: "On another occasion we picked up tracks heading south from the Macombe area and started following them. I always told my fellow soldiers that if I was shown fresh tracks there were no excuse for not finding the enemy. The terrorists were moving fast but not fast enough. They must have sensed the pursuit because their pace never slackened but we moved at a very fast walk. We followed them all the way into Rhodesia. It was a follow-up that covered more than a hundred kilometres and took us four days of hard walking. I think it may have been the longest follow-up of the Rhodesian war. There were twelve of us and unfortunately some of the blokes could not maintain the pace and slowed us up. I was not happy; these were SAS troops and I expected more of them. I had to leave some of the blokes that couldn't keep going behind which obviously reduced our numbers. There were about fifty of the enemy all heading in the same direction but periodically splitting up. By that time operational headquarters and a lot of other people had heard what was going on and were listening closely to their radios to see how it would all pan out. For them it was a little like listening to running commentary on a sports match. There were great excitement as other troops were told to clear out of our way while we closed in for the kill.

"We were getting very close when an RAR {Rhodesian African Rifles} platoon cut the spoor and went ahead of us. They made contact first, killing some of the enemy and throwing the rest into disarray as they fled in different directions. We were able to ascertain their lines of flight and figured— correctly—that they would try and escape on their entry route. We split into two four-man teams and laid ambushes and in they walked. We hit them and then ran to new positions and we hit them again. We captured a few. They told us they were headed for Sipolilo to set up a permanent presence from where they planned to escalate the war. If there were any survivors that made it back to their bases, they would have had a tale of woe to tell. They did not enjoy their tour of Rhodesia."

ANDY CHAIT

Also operating from Macombe with Watt was Phil Cripps along with a new arrival by the name of Andy Chait. Cripps was pioneer stock from the Vumba Mountains in the Eastern Highlands but Chait was a South African. Educated at Jeppe Boys' High in Johannesburg he arrived in the SAS with a reputation as a brawler with a hot temper but would quickly make his mark as a soldier.

"We had just come off the operation looking for Hawkesworth," remembers Cripps. "Andy then joined us and we were deployed to Macombe and ordered to infiltrate north of the Zambezi in two five-man patrols: one would head east and the other west. We were some of the first sent north of the river where we knew Chris Schulenburg had already discovered enemy camps.

"On crossing the river in 'Klepper' canoes we moved—anti-tracking as best we could—to high ground and settled on a plateau looking down on the Zambezi floodplain. At first light we made contact with HQ then Andy and I went on a bit of a recce along the river to get a better look at the lay of the land. We were entering an area of long grass along a small game trail when Andy behind me shouted a warning, and as I dropped he opened up over my head with a couple of aimed shots. I saw nothing of the 'terr' but all hell broke loose as his comrades opened up on us. About 200 metres away was a large group of FRELIMO in their green uniforms preparing an assault, so we broke away and made for our position on the plateau where our mates welcomed us with some apprehension.

"Having been told no air support would be forthcoming, we quickly abandoned our position while doing the best to anti-track as we withdrew. We trekked west over the next few days until we crossed a large path with plenty of fresh tracks and followed it north. I was nervous as I knew we were going deeper and deeper into enemy territory. Then concern turned to alarm when we discovered another even larger track going east and heavily used. The tracks were only hours old.

"Andy decided to cross it and continue north until we reached a dry riverbed with high banks where we took shelter from the heat under a large tree and went into all-round defence. Soon we heard voices below and Andy had two 'terrs' in his sights. He signalled to them to come to us. He motioned them closer but to no avail and as they made a break for it Andy opened up but they disappeared. An eerie silence returned.

"Andy knew we had just poked a hornets' nest so we prepared to move while he took a quick piss, but without completing his discharge he suddenly ducked to the ground having seen a green cap bouncing along in the reeds below. Then there was the crunch of many feet in the river and a large group of FRELIMO marching three-abreast advanced towards us.

"I rushed to my pack to cover an incoming path and as I did so, I spied another group of FRELIMO approaching. A little fellow in front was moving fitfully and he was brushed aside by a big guy who strode boldly towards me. His move would cost him his life because I downed him with a volley to the chest and then fired into the rest of the group. By this time there was incoming fire from points all around us and amidst this I caught sight of Andy standing calmly atop the river bank revving the enemy below.

"Wings Wilson was ordered to get on the radio and request an airstrike immediately. I remember watching him trying to get the aerial over a branch while being showered with leaves and splinters as bullets shredded the tree. An intense barrage of fire continued for what seemed like hours and then suddenly it stopped and the only sound was the ringing in our ears. Then we heard a distant drone and an old 'Provost' aircraft closed on us but as he neared the enemy guns roared into life again and all fire was directed at the aircraft. The pilot reacted calmly and held his orbit while we tried to locate the enemy and give him a target but then we saw fuel spewing from his wing-tanks. Sadly, this meant he had to abort but we received the welcome news that reinforcements were on their way.

"While waiting for help, Andy and I went down to the riverbed but saw only blood and skid-marks. The bodies had been dragged off. When we went back to look for the body of the big guy I had shot he too was gone. Only his AK and a pool of blood remained.

"Two choppers each with five men aboard flew through intense fire to get to us but made it safely and once we had regrouped, Andy gave us orders to move out and we headed back to the Zambezi.

"On crossing the large track again, he led us up to high ground but as we approached the rise we heard incoming mortars from above us. Andy ordered us forward and then to ground. Huddled together we listened to the pops as the bombs left the tubes and buried our heads in the earth. Then I heard a deadly thump as a bomb hit the ground nearby but incredibly it did not explode and so we lived. While we lay low Andy charged right up the hill and at the mortar teams. They, in their wisdom, fled and the firing stopped.

"Still shaken, we were dismayed when Andy told us to prepare to ambush the big track. I am not lying when I concede I was relieved nobody came. My nerves were in tatters. Any hopes of going home were dashed when we were ordered west in the morning to cross-grain looking for new tracks. Later in the day we stopped for a smoke break and just as I was relaxing there was a bang and I looked up. There was Andy looking down on a dead 'Fred' {FRELIMO soldier} who had been following our spoor.

"The next day I was leading when we walked straight into a group of ZANLA coming towards us barely thirty metres away. I shouted and dropped the bloke in front then Andy raced past me trying to get at the rest but they 'gapped it' {fled} at the speed of light.

"Intelligence later confirmed that the camp we had virtually been in the middle of days earlier was a large FRELIMO camp called Kadzimafala. It was also confirmed that we had killed twelve 'terrs' there. The large gentleman I had shot was confirmed as the camp commander, Moses.

"Still no uplift; we were then tasked to move east along the Zambezi and pick up a large track going north which had been spotted by air reconnaissance a few days earlier. The first day we followed it through some hilly country with large trees scattered about and as we came out of the hills late that afternoon we found a small 'terr' transit camp just off the main track. Here we stopped for a break and Andy decided, much to my horror, to bed down in the camp in the hope the enemy would return to their base and we would then deal with them. I think Andy could see the look of sheer terror on my face because he then made a remark I shall never ever forget: 'You Rhodesians are too interested in self-preservation,' he said with a smile. We had to agree but I kept thinking I was too young to die and I found his approach to death bewildering.

"The night was uneventful but the next day we were mobile again. Mid-afternoon we halted at the base of a hill overlooking a *vlei* {swamp} area. Two men were left to watch the track while the rest of us went to the top of the hill to brew up and establish communications for the last radio schedule of the day. My water was close to boiling and I was savouring a smoke in the shade when there was a fusillade below and the guys on the path signalled they had downed one of two 'terrs' who had been tracking us. The other had vanished into the riverine bush. Scanning below we saw his head bobbing up and down in the reeds and immediately tried to pick him off but the target was too distant and elusive. This irritated Andy and he told me to guide him in before sprinting down the slope and into the thicket where he knew his quarry was hiding. We shouted instructions to him and then heard two quick shots. Andy then strolled nonchalantly up the hill with a satisfied smile.

"The next day we were back at work following tracks when we stopped for lunch in flat country where the path swung east. Andy, canny as ever, had us move off the path and into cover behind a low rocky ridge while early-warning sentries were posted on either side about thirty metres away.

"Just before tea was served there was an urgent whisper from the sentry to the east signalling the approach of 'lots of terrs.' Hardly had the message been passed than the enemy were right in front of us moving quickly on their way to reinforce their comrades.

"Andy opened up instantly but needed to get closer so he ran right into their ranks, gun blazing. I followed and in no time there were four bodies on the road with blood spoor all over the place. For all of us who fought alongside him we marvelled at Andy's courage and coolness. We all knew we had been blessed with the company of an exceptional soldier."

"But looking back," says Watt, "the Macombe days were pretty pointless for me: probably the most boring period of my time in the SAS. We spent too much time watching the enemy rather than killing them. Rather than being in four-man sticks I would rather have been in bigger groups and in a position to go after the enemy as and when we sighted them. I think there were political considerations in play at this time but for us soldiers it was very frustrating.

"It was interesting being in that area from a historic point of view because it had once constituted the ancient kingdom of Monomotapa. Within it, some believed King Solomon's mines were situated, so it was a part of the country that attracted much attention from Portuguese explorers in the sixteenth century and quite a few fights had taken place there."

RHODESIANS ON TOP

With Rhodesian special forces changing the dynamic FRELIMO's growing paranoia about the interlopers was understandable. The more the SAS meddled in

Mozambique the harder their task of infiltrating southward became. FRELIMO leader Samora Machel pleaded with all who would listen in the international community to compel the rebel Rhodesians to mind their own business and go home. The British government was sympathetic to his pleas, but at a loss about how to meet his bellicose demands.

After the initial setbacks, starting with the farm attacks of late 1972, the tide had turned and by 1974 the enemy, while far from beaten, was having a very torrid time. The SAS had effectively neutralised the problematic Tete area and slowed the flow of infiltrators from Mozambique into Rhodesia. Embryonic RLI 'Fire Forces' {A rapid reaction assault force consisting of airborne troops with air support} operating out of Mount Darwin, in concert with newly formed Selous Scouts pseudo-operators,[27] were proving devastatingly effective and the enemy was in disarray. From a military point of view, the Rhodesians had seized the upper hand when, yet again, politics trumped soldiering. For the little SAS teams sitting atop the remote Mozambican hills, watching and waiting, matters beyond their control in faraway places were about to deal them a harsh blow against which they had no defence.

COUP IN PORTUGAL

In Portugal the populace was tiring of war in Africa. It had all seemed a fine idea initially but the financial strains were telling, the economy was struggling, their sons were dying on distant shores and international criticism was mounting. To turn up the heat the missionaries added their voices with reports (most of which subsequently proved false) of atrocities being committed by colonial troops. The disinformation had the desired effect and there were international outcries. The debit side of the colonial ledger was mounting.

Into the breach stepped the aloof, monocled figure of General Antonio de Spinola who, having written a seminal book on a proposed route out of the colonial quagmire, led a bloodless coup, ousted the autocratic Caetano regime and cast the die in Lisbon. It was no longer a question of whether Portugal was leaving Africa, but when. As providence would have it, Samora Machel's star was soaring along with his dream of a Marxist dictatorship in East Africa and as his star rose, so did Robert Mugabe's. Machel would soon receive Mozambique on a silver platter to the sound of deafening applause from across the globe, and Africa would never be the same again.

For the Rhodesians the implications were devastating. In one turn of a distant political wheel in a small European country, they had lost their shortest route to the sea, their one semblance of a friend and their entire eastern flank was now dangerously exposed. The war was certain to intensify and the odds against them increased dramatically.

DÉTENTE

Despite Rhodesia winning the war thus far, its future looked precarious. Smith found himself increasingly hostage to South African political chicanery. In a bid to deflect world opprobrium from its apartheid policies premier John Vorster initiated 'African Détente.' Smith was arm-locked into de facto unilateral ceasefire and the releasing of political detainees. Heavily reliant on South African military support, he was reminded of his position when South African arms shipments were halted. The Portuguese withdrawal from Mozambique opened a long hostile eastern flank.

All Smith's fears of the initiative's folly soon proved well-founded. Barely a fortnight after the announcement four South African policemen deployed in Rhodesia were murdered by a group of ZANLA posing as being peaceful, but this did not change Pretoria's approach and its contingent of policemen and helicopters were ordered back to South Africa.

"I'm often asked why we, the politicians were not more aggressive," remembers Ian Smith. "Why we did not give freer rein to our chaps to go and hit the enemy where it hurt most. The answer is the South Africans had a gun at our heads. Without them we were finished and they were still determined to ingratiate themselves with the black leaders to the north. They looked at all our military actions in that light and if we pushed our luck we ran the risk of having them pull the plug. We had to be very mindful of that because I knew they were quite capable of doing it."

"I think there were less than twenty terrorists left in the country at the time of the Détente initiative," recalls General John Hickman. "This process ruined us militarily. Pik Botha[28] played a large part in organising our demise. He saw Rhodesia as a liability and wanted to be rid of us at almost any cost. It should also not be forgotten, that an ardent supporter of this initiative was the CIO {Central Intelligence Organisation} head Ken Flower.[29] He was very strenuous in arguing for us to adopt a policy of maximum restraint which suited the enemy."

Watt recalled: "There's no doubt that when Vorster came up with Détente the enemy was in retreat. There was huge resentment within the SAS when we were told to back off. This was a time when we wanted to really hammer the enemy and put them down for good. If not for the politics, I think we would have done so.

"We were based on the Angwa River on the Mozambique border during the ceasefire. We were forbidden to do anything really. We sat there watching the enemy walk past us and were not allowed to react; it was very distressing and morale took a big knock.

"With the war on hold there was not much happening so I was looking for something else to do. One of our guys, a chap by the name of Hornby, had tried to row single-handed from Japan to the United States and this idea had caught my attention. Hornby failed and was rescued but he was planning another rowing trip from Walvis Bay in South West Africa {now Namibia} to South America and I was keen to do something similar but it did not work out for me. Hornby tried but was never seen again. I decided to do something closer to home and wanted to put my effort into raising money for the 'Terrorist Victims' Relief Fund' and St Giles Rehabilitation Centre which was doing so much for those wounded in the war. With a boat provided by a sponsor I then rowed the length of Kariba [300 kilometres] and then walked from Kariba to Salisbury which was a fourteen-day walk. I did it with my fox terrier who was a great companion and we raised quite a lot of money for a good cause."

HERBERT CHITEPO

On 19 March 1975, ZAPU nationalist leader Herbert Chitepo was killed in Lusaka by an explosive device fitted to his car. No fan of Robert Mugabe's, Chitepo's star was rising. Two suspects were Alan Brice and Hugh Hind, both ex-British SAS and then in the employ of the Rhodesian CIO who would have been acting on Ken Flower's orders, but this remains a matter of debate. In an interview with the Financial Times the day after the murder, James Chikerema, then a senior figure in the ZAPU hierarchy, reported that Chitepo had been killed by what he called 'the Karanga Mafia' {the ZANLA high command}.

In a later interview in Harare in June 1995 Chikerema told the same reporter that on the morning of Chitepo's death he saw Josiah Tongogara[30] at the East Wing of State House in Lusaka. Chikerema, who was in a highly emotional state at the time, tried to draw his pistol as he warned Josiah Tongogara, "You will never get away with this!" State House guards intervened and calmed Chikerema down. Until the day he died Chikerema insisted the 'Karanga Mafia' was responsible for Chitepo's murder.

However, Brian Robinson is emphatic. "Chuck Hind did the deed on instructions from Jack Berry of the CIO. I know this for a fact because Jack ran his operations from our pub, the Winged Stagger. The faction fighting that erupted subsequently delighted and amazed Jack. It was entirely a CIO operation so must have been cleared by Flower. Chuck simply put a mine down behind the wheel, to great effect. I think the Brits must have decided it was fine to take out Chitepo and clear the way for Mugabe."

With the assailants unknown a row erupted within enemy ranks which threatened to turn violent, prompting the Zambian government to imprison then expel the ZANLA hierarchy. One of those jailed was Josiah Tongogara who had emerged as a powerful figure within the ZANU military ranks while Ndabaningi Sithole remained the pre-eminent political leader of the movement.

However, Sithole was soon neutralised following his arrest by 'Mac' McGuinness of police Special Branch on charges of plotting to kill Ian Smith. He was subsequently jailed on the strength of evidence supplied by a female friend of Sithole's who became an informer for McGuinness.

With Chitepo, Sithole and Tongogara out the way, the road was clear for Mugabe. He soon arrived at the home of Jesuit Father John Gough to seek assistance. Gough was soon in touch with his friend and fellow Catholic, Assistant Police Commissioner Peter Allum. Allum immediately undertook to assist. Also summoned to help was Dan Stannard of the 'British South Africa Police' {BSAP} who was then serving in the town of Rusape on the road to the eastern border. Stannard recalls: "I was made aware of the fact that Mugabe and Tekere would be exiting Rhodesia via Inyanga . . . I was told that no attempts were to be made to stop this exfiltration."[31]

This was a defining moment in the fugitive nationalist's rise to power and changed the course of history. It seems safe to assume Allum, Flower and McGuinness were acting on behalf of British Intelligence services and one is therefore left wondering, bearing in mind British operatives being possibly involved in the killing of Chitepo, if Mugabe's ascent to power was not already being orchestrated by Whitehall.

CHAPTER 5

These stark men
Who have not yet celebrated?
Their coming of age
Whose carefree years have been pickpocketed
Out of their lives
By the war.
Who have lost the carelessness of youth,
Gained the callousness of Death's companions.
—CHAS LOTTER

THE VICTORIA FALLS DÉBÂCLE

In June 1975, Samora Machel became president of the avowedly Marxist and newly independent republic of Mozambique. In a sweeping, often brutal nationalisation programme the concept of private ownership was abolished and citizens of Portuguese descent were dispossessed of virtually all they owned, turned into the streets and forced to flee to sanctuary in South Africa and Rhodesia in their thousands. Many of those whites who remained in the former colony were banished to Machel's 're-education camps.' Those whites not imprisoned were then forced to join work gangs in the spirit of true communism and their homes became communal dormitories. Life in Mozambique, only recently so pleasant, rapidly became a living hell for many. Political opposition was banned with severe penalties for dissenters.

As the threat grew, frustrated Rhodesian soldiers followed orders to conduct themselves with restraint. Their fate now lay largely in the fumbling hands of an Afrocentric South African prime minister, John Vorster, who remained convinced that he could use Rhodesia as the sacrificial lamb that would see his country accepted into the community of African nations and the end of South Africa's pariah status.

His efforts finally culminated in talks commencing on 29 August 1975 which he chaired on a train strategically parked on a bridge at the Victoria Falls. The carriage containing the delegates was bisected by the international boundary, with the African nationalist leaders technically seated in Zambia and the Smith delegation in Rhodesia. Smith's defence minister P.K. van der Byl, mindful of what was to come, went armed with a pistol in a shoulder holster. Taking his seat next to Smith he nudged the prime minister and allowed his jacket to flare, giving Smith a sneak view of what was hidden. "Just in case these terrorists get out of hand, sir," he explained, nudging the firearm, "I'll be able to give us some covering fire."

Politically it was a non-event, but the nationalist leaders and their coterie took full advantage of the generous supply of wine and whisky supplied by their South African hosts and some were reported falling off the train at the end of the day. His hospitality abused, his grand plan in tatters, Vorster left the venue in disgust. On his return to Pretoria he ordered all South African assets back to South Africa.

EXODUS FROM THE SAS

In early September 1975 a large group of FRELIMO attacked a four-man SAS 'call-sign', killing Corporal Kelvin Storie instantly and wounding 'Ginger' Thompson. With only Troopers Mike Smith$_{32}$ and Gary Stack left to fight, the FRELIMO commander assumed victory and was standing proudly astride the body of the SAS corporal when the two troopers counter-attacked, killing him and putting a bewildered enemy to flight. It was Stack's first deployment and a bloody baptism of fire.

This death came at a time when SAS morale was low for other reasons. Many of the unit's best operators were leaving to join the Selous Scouts and serve under the charismatic Reid-Daly who was wasting no time in creating an enviable esprit de corps. With SAS numbers diminishing rapidly alarm bells started to ring.

"I have to be quite honest," remembers Robinson. "Ron Reid-Daly proved a powerful magnet for some of our best chaps and we watched our numbers steadily decline. I think if Darrell Watt had gone with the rest he would have taken a lot of blokes with him and it might well have been the end of the unit. I asked him to stay and to his great credit he did so."

"I very nearly left the SAS at this time," says Watt. "Most of my friends had decided to leave and I liked what I heard about the Scouts but Brian asked me to stay and I felt a certain loyalty to him and the Squadron. In later years the rivalry between the Scouts and us reached an unhealthy level. I was one of the few SAS men allowed into their cantonment at Mtoko. On one occasion I arrived there in uniform to be confronted by a Scouts major. He looked me up and down as if I'd just crawled out from behind a bush. 'What the fuck do you want here?' he asked. I was pissed off but kept my cool. I told him I had been invited over by Colonel Reid-Daly. Then he went quiet and changed his attitude but the relationship between us was hardly a happy one. Looking back, I'm not so sure there should have been two special forces units competing against one another rather than having everyone under one roof. In my view Ron Reid-Daly was an excellent special forces commander."

MACHIPANDA

"After Mozambique received independence I spent time based at Umtali doing short operations into Mozambique, mainly on the railway, blowing it up a few times. Some nights I visited the railway marshalling yards at Machipanda near the Rhodesian border armed with explosives fitted with timing devices set to detonate en route to Beira. Terrorist camps were mushrooming in the vicinity and the trains were providing the necessary logistical support.

"They never knew what the hell was going on," said Watt. "I watched and waited in the dark near the station. Then when it was noisy and everyone started looking busy I approached the train. The lighting was poor so I was able to sneak onto the tracks, crawl up under the carriages, approach the locomotive unseen and plant my bomb with surprising ease. On one occasion I managed to dig deep into the coal and bury it underneath. I heard later this set off a hell of a blast, followed by a good fire. But the place I used to try for was the axle so when it went off the whole train went into the bush taking some of the track with it.

"The Mozambicans had little salvage equipment that was serviceable so these derailments presented a major problem for them and I believe South African engineers had to come in to help.33 The less movement on that line, the less arms and equipment the enemy could bring to our doorstep."

Politically, it had dawned on everyone by this time that the whole détente exercise had been a resounding flop and the political hierarchy finally gave in to pleas from Brian Robinson to be allowed to send reconnaissance teams back into Tete province, but with the rider that they were to do so 'quietly' and avoid confronting

FRELIMO at all costs. Central Intelligence Organisation boss Ken Flower persisted with his call to refrain from attacking targets in Mozambique, preferring an ultra-defensive posture to an aggressive one, but the military men had had just about enough.

Meanwhile, a problem of a different magnitude and type presented itself in the operational area. Marymount Mission, near where the SAS were based, had a swimming pool which the soldiers eyed longingly, but the Catholic priest, Father Carl Stephens, was pro-ZANLA and would not allow the Rhodesian soldiers to use it. But that all changed when Defence Minister P.K. van der Byl arrived.

"On hearing we were denied use of the pool," recalls Watt, "he was very annoyed and went to confront the priest. Reading him the riot act, he told him to let the SAS use the pool or he'd have him deported back to Ireland. The priest got quite a fright and so the soldiers got access to the pool, albeit grudgingly. PK also brought some whisky which went down very well with the troops."

LIFE ON THE 'FRONT'

"In late 1975 I became more involved in specialised operations and began long periods in Gaza in southern Mozambique in what would become known as the 'Russian Front,'" remembers Watt. "It was called this because in the context of the Rhodesian war it was probably the toughest deployment of them all. It was now clear the entire eastern border of the country was exposed and we had a big fight on our hands.

"It was very frustrating, we were being followed virtually constantly and it was very difficult to anti-track in the sandy soils that covered most of the area. Villagers in the area were primed to be vigilant and report any suspicious activity promptly to the authorities or suffer the consequences, so we found ourselves in extremely tough territory among a populace that was overwhelmingly hostile to us. We spent an awful lot of time running. I constantly needed to look for somewhere to hide and in parts of that area it was very open, making it difficult.

"Metallic shine was a big factor. We learnt to dull absolutely everything; a lesson lost on the enemy. So often the glint of sunlight on the magazines of the AKs gave them away. If I sensed there was a presence close by I would sit and watch the area for hours and let the sun move. Sooner or later, I'd pick up a glint of metal and then I would know their position. It was a deadly giveaway that paid off many times.

"Snoring could also be a problem. Generally, we all slept lightly enough," said Watt, "and were sensitive enough to pick up the first sign of danger. Cigarette smoke was another giveaway. I could smell it a long way off and discouraged my blokes from smoking for that reason.

"Listening to the birds was a great help. Honey guides and go-away birds were particularly useful. Their calls changed when they were surprised. That almost always meant someone was coming and gave us time to get ready.

"In Gaza I wanted to hit the enemy to trigger a response, then lure them into well-planned ambushes and teach them a lesson that would encourage them to stop following us, but that didn't happen. Hundreds of well-armed and competent troops were deployed to find and kill us. This was the most intense area of the war for me and the FRELIMO units there were the most aggressive troops I encountered throughout the war.

"Added to that there was always a problem with water—or the lack of it," remembers Watt. "You can go a long time without food but not water; it was a constant problem and we had to be very disciplined about our intake. When blokes ran out it was a big test of friendship: to share or not to share. The days were bloody hot and we generally laid up until nightfall when we normally walked throughout the night but often we were being chased so we had to keep going. Sometimes we had to run, and bearing in mind we were always carrying in the region of forty-five kilograms in kit, ammunition and weaponry, we were pushed right to the limit."

Johan Bezuidenhout remembers an unusual event during a Mozambique deployment. "We were deployed in central Mozambique with Darrell. The summer rains had fallen, the countryside was beautiful and game was plentiful. We had been there almost a month so the boys were smelly. We were in a typical ambush position on a road close to a rocky hill feature. At night we withdrew to higher ground to rest. Gerry de Lange slept alone a long way away so as not to be pelted with rocks for snoring.

"On this particular night the moon was full, visibility excellent and the hyenas cackled in the distance. In the early hours I heard a different sound, a mournful wailing, as if someone was being throttled. I immediately assumed we were under attack and Gerry was in trouble. We all sprang into action and approached the screams in a line with weapons cocked. As we closed in on Gerry we could see no 'gook' had him by the throat. He must have stunk so much that he had attracted one of the hyenas which had locked its teeth into Gerry's sleeping bag and was shaking it ferociously. Gerry was screaming, 'Ooooh, pleeease, will somebody help me, for fuck's sakes!'

"The hyena saw us, took fright and tried to bolt with Gerry and the sleeping bag and off he went over branches and boulders with the five of us in hot pursuit. Every rock hit brought a scream of 'Oooh fuck' from Gerry still stuck in the sleeping bag. Luckily for him the bag and Gerry got wedged between rocks and the hyena tore off a piece, leaving the body and bag behind. Realising he had lost his meal, the hyena stopped to look at us in disgust before trotting away, cackling madly as if he found it all very funny.

"In the process Gerry had been turned completely around in the bag and his head was where his feet had been and he was kicking and wildly punching the bag like a mad boxer and still screaming, 'For fuck's sake, pleeease help me.' It took us a while to convince him it was safe and he could come out the bag. Gerry refused to sleep on the perimeter again so he got pummelled by us instead for snoring."

A 'KIWI' ENTRY

"We, the 'troopies' on those operations were really little more than mules," recalls Terry. "On one occasion we ran and ran. In addition to all the normal stuff, I was also carrying a landmine and mortar bombs so I was heavy. I don't know for how long we walked but it seemed like forever. Eventually Darrell brought us to a halt in a tree line. I was so exhausted I think I was asleep before my bum hit the ground and I slumped against a tree. But no sooner had my eyes closed than I awoke to firing and I looked up to see Darrell rushing past me with his RPK blazing away. FRELIMO had followed us and fortunately Darrell had been watching our rear and seen them. He killed two of them a stone's-throw away from where I sat and almost certainly saved my life.

"I sat there thinking fate sure as hell plays a big part in life. I had arrived in Rhodesia by mistake. On leaving school, I wanted to go to university rather than work on the family dairy farm. My father was unimpressed and reminded me he had sent me to the most expensive private school in New Zealand 'and all you did was eat your lunch.' I went into a sulk, took a look at a map and headed for Canada, where I worked for a year as a wrangler on a ranch but it was too cold and I decided to head home.

"For some reason the air ticket I purchased included a stopover in Salisbury. I knew nothing about the country but gathered there were very few people travelling there. I was only in transit but had time so I decided to see if I could clear formalities and have a look around. "I wandered away from the arrival lounge, looking for officials but found myself on the steps of the building looking at traffic. I thought I must have bypassed someone so went back inside looking for an official and eventually found an immigration officer and explained that I had found myself in the country unexpectedly. He laughed, welcomed me to Rhodesia and wished me a happy day.

"I jumped in a taxi and asked the driver to take me to a pub. He dropped me at The Usual Place at the Jameson Hotel in the centre of Salisbury, and I ordered a beer. Before I had drunk it, a big bloke with a big smile sitting next to me picked up on my accent and asked me what the hell I was doing in Rhodesia. I explained what had happened and he bought me a beer. It turned out he was a farmer and wanted to go fishing at Lake Kariba and needed someone to take care of his place for a few weeks. He offered me the job. I thought, to hell with it, home can wait—I'll stay a while.

"I instantly fell in love with the country. The nicest, friendliest people, both black and white, the sun never stopped shining and the country was so well run. It seemed to me it almost didn't belong in Africa, and it didn't take me long to decide I'd not be going back to New Zealand for a while. I did not have to go to the army but when I found out there was a scrap on the go I volunteered, opted for a SAS selection course, and passed. And so I ended up on the Russian Front.

"At night we would lie dead still and strain our ears for the sound of frogs, which would give us some idea of where to look for water. There was great excitement when we heard a croak," says Terry. "There were times they brought dogs out to help run us down. The enemy was on our tracks the whole time, but whenever they got close we would invariably kill a few of them. Six weeks in Gaza was a long time. We were permanently covered in black-is-beautiful camouflage cream which made us sweat like pigs and I'm not sure how much it helped; everyone there knew we were white Rhodesians anyway.

"It was the most hostile place I've ever been in. We were permanently exhausted, hungry and thirsty. Early in the morning we used to tie a little '4×4' {rifle cleaning cloth} to a piece of string and trail it as we walked to try and absorb some moisture from the grass. If we were lucky, it would draw enough dampness for us to suck on. Just a little moisture on your lips was a big bonus. On a couple of occasions, I saw blokes mix their piss with the lemon-flavoured powder we were given to add to water and drank that. It was bloody desperate at times. Everyone's worst fear was not being able to carry on and having to be 'casevaced,' {Casevac is the abbreviation for casualty evacuation} bringing the operation to an end. That was almost a fate worse than death. No wonder we went berserk when we got home."

"The men would generally try to eat a decent meal mid-afternoon then lie up in the shade until dark," recalls Watt. "Those hours were sorely needed. Before stopping, even if it was just for a smoke, we would do a dog-leg: walk past the point where we were going to rest, then double-back and hide where we could see our incoming tracks. Anyone tracking us would follow the spoor past our position and the sentry would raise the alarm. This tactic saved many lives.

"Last light we would move. If we were going to set an ambush, I would give the men a quick briefing to remind everyone of their tasks then walk them to their positions. On occasion, we lay there listening to search parties approaching, sometimes over a hundred of them. We would listen to them tapping sticks together to keep their formation in the dark. We would hear the clicks coming closer and hope like hell they didn't find us. If they did, we opened up on them and ran like hell. I carried an RPK for most of this time but looking back I think the folding-butt FN was my weapon of choice.

"Map-reading was a real challenge at times. Much of the Russian Front was flat and featureless, while some areas were densely wooded, so one had to look for nuances in the landscape and keep a mental note of how far we had walked. On a cloudy day, with no sun to help you orientate, it was very difficult. Remember, we had no satellite guidance or global positioning systems to help us. Knowing one's position was critical to survival. If we didn't know where we were we couldn't call for help from the air force. An accurate 'locstat' was essential if pilots were to have any chance of finding us.

"In the field, the big day for us was the fortnightly resupply. The sound of the old Dakota's engines was always welcome. Quite often we had run out of water by this time so a missed supply drop could be disastrous. The drone of those engines coming closer in the dead of night never failed to bring a smile to our faces.

"The supply aircraft flew high, showing landing lights only. We controlled the drop from the ground. Corrections would be given to the pilot from the ground before pressing the pressle-switch on the handset that acted as a radio beacon which would beam him in. It was a huge relief when we heard the parachutes pop and knew the supplies we needed to sustain ourselves for the next two weeks were on their way. Resupply drops normally included one freshly cooked meal wrapped in tinfoil and if all went according to plan we could enjoy hot roast chicken and potatoes or steak and chips, some fruit, one tin of fruit juice, a solitary Castle beer and a miniature bottle of rum each to wash the food down. This was a huge morale boost but the nutrition was also badly needed because our bodies were so run down due to over-exertion. A small cut often got infected and turned ugly. Veld sores which could quickly become infected were a constant problem. Ticks were also a problem and we spent a lot of time picking them off. Tick-bite fever which brought a high temperature and a thumping headache was a constant threat. Also with the resupply would come water, batteries for the field radios, cigarettes, mail and anything else such as socks or boots that might have been asked for. By the end of our deployments we stank. You could see it on the faces of the pilots when they came to collect us."

Terry McCormick, then a young flight lieutenant, recalls one incident on the 'Front.' "I was sent to collect Grahame Wilson and his men after a long deployment. I had never met him but had heard he was one of the top SAS operators. We landed having just come under fire, so I was pretty tense waiting for a strike on the aircraft, when these faces came boiling out of the bush towards us. Bearded, clothes shredded and filthy, they looked like a bunch of tramps. I held steady and they dived in. The stench was terrible and I felt nauseous which did nothing for my state of mind. As I pulled the collective to get airborne, I heard firing behind me and lost my cool. It didn't matter who you were, no one was allowed to fire from a helicopter without the pilot's permission. I was pissed off and turned around and swung at the guy. Then I saw it was Wilson. I landed a blow he didn't seem to feel, which was a bit irritating, and he just carried on shooting, so I let him be. That was our first of many meetings. He was very good about it and we subsequently had many laughs."

"Amazingly," says Watt, "I never saw anyone throw in the towel despite the strain. Pride in the regiment and being part of this unusual brotherhood made them determined to stay the course. Incredible when you bear in mind some of them were barely out of school and others had not yet even started to shave."

THE 'WINGED STAGGER'

"First stop on return to Salisbury was invariably the 'troopies' pub, The Winged Stagger," remembers Terry. "Normal people would have had a piss-up then be gone, off to see families, friends or girlfriends, but a lot of the chaps didn't. I think we had become so dependent on one another that we could not face up to being apart for a minute.

"One group of four blokes decided no one was to leave the bar until they had drunk enough to surround the swimming pool with empty beer bottles. It was a big pool and it took them three days of hard work. When they could no longer stand they lay down on the floor and slept until rested, then got up and carried on drinking. Very sensible, thought-provoking stuff."

Sammy remembers 'The Stagger': "The barman had a torrid time. His name was Chipunza and he must have thought these white bastards had gone completely mad. Perhaps we had. If he was informing for the 'gooks', God knows what he told them about our behaviour.[34] In the midst of one of these binges I noticed he was hiding an 'AP' {anti-personnel} mine behind the bar. At first I couldn't believe my eyes. Then I looked again to make sure the booze hadn't got to me and saw I was right. I said, 'Where the hell did you get that?' He just gave me this vacant look and I lost my temper. I jumped over the counter and gave him a clout. Then we carried on drinking and just helped ourselves. The next morning Chipunza went and reported me to Captain Mike Curtin, the administrative officer, and hung over as hell, I was called to explain. Marched into the captain's office, I saluted and stood as smartly to attention as I could. There was brief, tense silence while he stared at me and I knew I was in big shit."

'Why did you fuck the barman up?' he asked.

'He had an AP mine in the fridge, sir,' I answered.

'Did you give him a chance to explain?'

'Not really, sir.'

'Well, now he's not looking too good,' he shouted, 'he's got a bloody great egg on his head, and he's off sick so there's no barman now!'

"Not knowing what to say I said nothing when Captain Curtin told me my punishment was to run the pub until further notice. It was the worst punishment I ever suffered," said Sam. "I never worked so bloody hard in my life as I did keeping drunken 'troopies' supplied with booze while listening to their crap till all hours of the night. Suddenly, the Russian Front didn't seem like such a bad place after all. At the end of our 'R&R' {Rest and Retraining} we were sent straight back there and, strange as it might seem, it was a bit of a relief. It never entered my head to hit that barman again. I think I called him 'sir' for the rest of my time in the army."

MOZAMBIQUE DECLARES WAR

In early 1976, Robert Mugabe's ZANU, along with its ZANLA military wing, was expelled from Zambia and left for Mozambique. There, Machel accommodated them and plans unfolded to intensify the war in the east on three fronts: Tete in the north, Manica in the centre and Gaza in the south.

By March 1976 President Samora Machel had had enough of the Rhodesians in general and the SAS in particular. In a vivid exhibition of the power of special forces units, their attacks had triggered a political reaction at the highest level that would have serious economic and political implications for the region. The Mozambican president closed the border with Rhodesia and declared his country to be in a state of all-out war.

Watt was promptly sent back into Mozambique. "Three troops were tasked to attack a camp near Chioco in Tete Province," remembers Johan Bezuidenhout. "We walked out of Rhodesia at night following the course of the Mazoe River. My section included Allan Hider, Rich Swan, and 'Horse' Greenhough. We were under Darrell Watt's command.

"It was going to be an all-night walk-till-you-drop scenario and we were heavily laden. But the 'Horse' was carrying more than anybody: triple rations, triple onions, tomatoes, potatoes, two gas burners, a pillow, ten books, five extra water bottles, two nylon shelters, spare clothes, raincoat, spare boots, five pairs of socks and extra ammo—hence the name 'Horse'.

"There was no moon, it was pitch-dark and Darrell was moving at speed. With 'Horse' lumbering along behind, we just blindly followed the man in front. Hider and Swan immediately seized the opportunity and led 'Horse' into a hole. I just heard a loud crash, cursing and then chuckling. 'Horse' knew he had been had and was shouting, 'Come here, you motherfuckers, before I bend ya two little bastards!' While they made good their escape, I levered 'Horse' out of the ant bear hole. But on his way down his rifle had gone flying so we had to scratch around in the bush a while, 'Horse' cursing furiously until we found it but we had lost time. When Darrell asked Swan where we were, they lied, said they had no idea.

"Eventually we caught up and 'Horse' asked me to stay in front because he couldn't trust Hider and Swan. We were barrelling along when I was struck full in the chest by a branch springing back into me, sending me stumbling back into 'Horse' and again down he went, shouting, 'Come here, you motherfuckers and I'll bend ya little bastards!' But again Swan and Hider trotted off into the night. 'Horse' eventually got himself and his massive pack vertical again and we hurried off to regroup with an angry Darrell.

"A few hours later they got bored again and I was told by Rich to lift my feet as there was a large tree-trunk ahead. I was going to warn 'Horse' but they pleaded with me to say nothing and watch the spectacle. I stood aside and watched this huge lumbering silhouette approach. Then his right foot hooked under the log, his rifle went rocketing forward into the bush, arms went up like flags in the wind and the pack went over his head dragging him head-first into a mean dive, head-first into the dirt. There 'Horse' lay, man-down and pinned to the ground by the weight of his pack. He was stuck but we heard him mumble, 'Come here, you motherfuckers, I'm gonna bend ya!' I then joined Hider and Swan and ran for my life.

"After walking all night we stopped in the morning on the banks of the Mazoe River but well into Mozambique. We were positioned and told to rest up till nightfall when we would walk to attack the target in the morning. A tired soldier could not have asked for more; it was like paradise. Tall shady trees, long green grass and cool, crystal-clear water running at our feet.

"It was about noon when 'Horse' decided he was hungry and started emptying his portable pantry. Out came the water for a brew, burners, potatoes, onions, tomatoes, bully beef and everything he needed for a super stew. Then while this cooked merrily away he took out his sleeping bag, pillow and book and lay back to relax and savour the moment with the sweet smell of stew wafting over him. The trees were full of birds singing. 'Horse' had finally found peace after a horrible night.

"Then I heard a familiar rumbling noise approaching and realised it was a hungry elephant's stomach. I alerted Rich and soon we all knew what was coming except 'Horse' who was buried in his cowboy book and had no idea that danger was approaching. We decided to evacuate fast so we packed and moved off about thirty metres away leaving 'Horse' oblivious to the danger: the noise of his two gas burners was such that he did not hear the elephant closing in despite the fact it was breaking branches nearby.

"We sat fascinated as it came closer to 'Horse' who did not stir until the elephant stood on a dry branch behind his head, making a loud crack. 'Horse' turned slowly and there was this elephant looking down at him. There was a loud bellow and he threw the book at it before booting his brew and stew in his rush to escape. He fled down the embankment, through the river and did not look back until on the other side. The elephant glared angrily at him, trumpeted in disgust and walked off. We stayed a long way away from 'Horse' while we waited for the sun to set. We attacked the next day but kills were few; the enemy was thin on the ground. This made 'Horse' even angrier."

ENTER HENRY KISSINGER

South Africa's foreign affairs minister, Dr Hilgaard Muller, in a bid to mollify the governments of Mozambique and Zambia, issued a statement saying his government supported majority rule in Rhodesia. It seemed what was good for the goose was not necessarily good for the gander. Apartheid would remain the bedrock of the South African dispensation but Rhodesia would be forced to accept black rule. Ian Smith braced for renewed pressure from his fair-weather friends south of the Limpopo and events would soon prove him right. A new political plan was already afoot. At the urging of Pik Botha, his ambassador to the United Nations, Prime Minister Vorster was plotting.

Botha was in close touch with the US state department, which was showing a growing interest in brokering a deal that would allow them to unleash Henry Kissinger, their diplomatic superstar. The master of realpolitik was in the employ of a president on the campaign trail. A triumphant foray into the 'Dark Continent' to end a racially charged conflict and bring peace to a tense sub-continent seemed like a fine idea. President Gerald Ford and Kissinger would be seen striking a blow for democracy and the eradication of white minority rule in one fell swoop. The big guns of the US State Department were wheeled into line.

It is now known that while Kissinger was the consummate diplomat, he was also well aware that the Cuban intervention in Africa with Soviet support was a major problem and he was ready to use American power to subdue them.

In an Oval Office meeting with President Ford on 25 February 1976, Kissinger said, "I think we are going to have to smash Castro." Ford agreed and a discussion followed on a whole range of options which included an invasion. A fortnight later at another Oval Office meeting Kissinger said, "Even the Iranians are worried about the Cubans getting into the Middle East countries. I think we have to humiliate them. If they move into Namibia or Rhodesia, I would be in favour of clobbering them."

Kissinger knew only too well that South Africa was the key to bringing Smith to heel. Without that vital ingredient his efforts would be a non-event. At his behest, the South Africans duly jumped into line and choked off fuel and ammunition supplies to Rhodesia even as the city of Umtali was bombarded by ZANLA from bases in Mozambique.

To compel the 'liberation leaders' to accept a negotiated settlement, Kissinger would have to solicit the support of the all-important, so-called Frontline State leaders, particularly, the presidents of Zambia, Tanzania and Mozambique. He took his plan to Nyerere and Kaunda and apparently received their blessing after convincing them that he would compel Smith to hand over power to a black majority government on the basis of a phased but short-term transfer. Then he headed for Pretoria.

The beleaguered Rhodesian premier was summoned south to meet his fate. With his head on Vorster's chopping block, it remained only for Kissinger to fly in and give the condemned man the good news: his life would be spared, but he would have to deliver his country to an uncertain future under black rule.

The stage was set, but Kissinger later conceded that his task became an awkward one on an emotional level. The man who had taken the US to the brink of nuclear Armageddon over Soviet backing of Syria in the 1973 war with Israel and who had forced the hard men of Moscow to buckle, took no pleasure in telling Smith to hand over his country. He acknowledged that he was looking into the eyes of a supreme patriot, a man whose face bore the scars of another war; smashed on the instruments of the aircraft he flew in defence of the country that now sought his destruction. Kissinger was in no doubt that Smith desperately wanted the best for his people and understood why he was fearful of black majority rule. He also knew that Smith was defenceless against Vorster's whim.

The American tried his best to soothe Smith's fears and promised financial assistance, along with a modicum of political protection. With a heavy heart, the Rhodesian premier asked again for confirmation that his agreement to surrender power to a black government would attract the unconditional support of the South African, US and British governments in honouring the letter and spirit of the deal. When this was forthcoming, tears welled in his eyes, he assented and left Pretoria to fly home and tell his countrymen it was time to lay down their arms. He would ask them to accept a harsh reality and endeavour to live with what Dr Kissinger had assured him was the best possible deal that the Rhodesians would be offered.

His broadcast to the nation on 24 August 1976 was met with understandable foreboding, but as always, the majority of Rhodesians simply looked to Smith to decide and if this was his decision, then so be it, they would knuckle down and try to make the most of what came their way.

General John Hickman recalls: "It was all too vague. The deal sounded like it might work but we had been down this road before with Vorster and been conned. We were going to do our damnedest to make sure it didn't happen again. It was obvious the South Africans wanted to dump us at virtually any price and as soon as possible. Vorster and Pik Botha were obsessed with black Africa. If they could get in there in return for ditching Rhodesia, that was good enough for them.

"The one South African politician who dissented was P.W. Botha, the Minister of Defence. He could see this was not a smart move from a strategic point of view and I think he empathised with the plight of the Rhodesians. I think most of the generals agreed with him. But he was well and truly outnumbered in that cabinet."

The operational soldiers wanted to believe that this was a positive development, but recent history had taught them a harsh lesson and they were determined to battle on with no respite, putting the enemy under maximum pressure until the political markers were cast in stone. With South African pressure relaxed following Smith's acceptance of the Kissinger terms, supplies and munitions began to flow again and controls on 'external' operations were loosened, pending final agreement.

CHAPTER 6

I am a warrior
Death knows my face
I have seen it mirrored in empty fly rimmed eyes
Smelt its sickly sweet perfume,
And held its cold hand.
—DAVID FOWLER

RUDE AWAKENINGS

From September 1976, with South African restraints on their operations lifted pending implementation of the agreement brokered by Henry Kissinger, the Rhodesians, using Mozambique as a springboard, adopted an aggressive strategy.

A furious Samora Machel went to the UN General Assembly to lament his country's fate and demand increased international intervention. Amid the rants, what Britain and the world chose to ignore was that Machel had managed to destroy Mozambique without any help from the Rhodesians. His ethnic cleansing and brutal nationalisation of the private sector had wiped out a functioning economy, impoverishing a nation and presented a begging-bowl to the world. But the international community rallied to his defence. Britain sent financial and material aid to Maputo {formerly Lourenço Marques} and the Americans weighed in with UN ambassador William Scranton announcing on a visit to Lusaka that sanctions against Rhodesia would be tightened and aid to "liberation movements opposed to the Smith regime" stepped up. It was a distressing reminder for the Rhodesians of how far they had strayed from the warm embrace of the motherland and their erstwhile allies in the West.

This all against a backdrop of authoritarian oppression as the Mozambican government, having outlawed Christianity, arrested 150 priests and confined them in concentration camps, while deporting 28,000 whites of Portuguese origin to South Africa with little more than they could carry.

In a statement at the time, Rhodesian Defence Minister P.K. van der Byl put it bluntly: "It is quite unbelievable and grotesque that a Marxist and terrorist regime should be financed by the British government to destroy a section of what was part of the British Empire."

RENAMO IS BORN

Meanwhile at CIO HQ, with enemy numbers increasing, the 'spooks' were looking for new ways to prosecute the war. News that dissatisfaction with FRELIMO rule in Mozambique was growing was music to military intelligence ears in Salisbury. Running the Mozambique desk at the time was Peter Burt who would be replaced in 1977 by Rick May.

Seeking to make contact with dissident Mozambicans, an unlikely figure emerged in Rhodesian farmer Chris Landon who, when not in Rhodesia, had run a tea-trading business in Mozambique where he worked with Portuguese Nationals, Americo and Antonio Felizardo until ordered out of the country by Samora Machel. He and Antonio knew potential role-players in the burgeoning resistance and facilitated contacts but Landon had another role to play. His brother Tim ['The White Sultan'] had positioned himself as a man with huge influence in Oman and the Omanis were watching the Rhodesian drama with sympathetic interest. Cash-strapped as always, May's resources were limited but thanks to the Landons and the Omanis, vital financial assistance was received and the RENAMO {Resistançia Naçional Moçambicana} ball set rolling.

To turn up the heat, Rhodesian Intelligence quickly established the Voice of Free Africa radio station, broadcasting propaganda into enemy territory urging the populace to rise against their Marxist masters. The search began for dissident Mozambicans to take up the cause and take the fight to the enemy.

THE SOUTH-EAST HEATS UP

With a growing threat coming out of Gaza Province in southern Mozambique, it was decided a stronger Rhodesian response was required and elements of the SAS were redeployed to base at Chiredzi in the south-east Lowveld. With the 'Tribal Trust Lands' {TTL} along the border being heavily infiltrated, the road and rail links from the port at Maputo to the border town of Malvernia constituted the insurgents' main supply route. Darrell Watt, now a colour sergeant, was one of those tasked to lead raiding parties into southern Mozambique in a bid to disrupt supply lines and tackle the enemy in what ZANLA had hoped would be a safe sanctuary. Initially, their orders were to refrain from engaging FRELIMO unless forced to defend themselves, but that changed as relations between the two countries deteriorated and Samora Machel issued a direct order to his troops to assist ZANLA in the field.

Sam recalls lying in ambush on the Russian Front alongside Billy Grant on the road and railway line near Malvernia. It was steamy and the days passed in a shimmery haze that caused their eyes to play tricks on them. On one occasion Sam looked down the track and thought he saw an elephant lumbering towards him "Billy, look! A fucking elephant!" he said.

. "Shit, you're right," Grant replied.

"Bloody sure it is too," Sam said, but then it didn't look so much like an elephant anymore and the two men heard a strange sound. "Suddenly, two 'gooks' wearing goggles emerged from the haze on a manually operated tram, going like the clappers. They looked like a pair of *Snoopys* in Red Baron guise. It was a bizarre sight. We got a hell of a fright then took them out. Soon a convoy followed with reinforcements to investigate the gunfire. We let them come in close then knocked the shit out of them. When we thought we'd pushed our luck far enough, we ran like fuck back into the bush. Don't know how many we killed.

"The 'gooks' became really skittish. The mines and ambushes were frustrating them, driving them crazy, and despite all their numbers, they couldn't catch us. Then we decided to try a trick and planted empty bully beef tins rather than mines, which we were running short on. It worked. Each time their metal detectors picked up the tins, there was a hell of a panic. They went to all sorts of trouble to secure the area before bringing in huge explosive charges to blow the tin.

"Wherever we left a bully-beef tin, they blew a fucking great crater in the road or railway line, making it impassable—which is exactly what we were trying to do, only they were doing a much better job. The Rhodesian taxpayer was getting real value out of us there. Nothing was being wasted— not even tins."

SHOOTING THE MESSENGER

Watt recalls another incident that yielded unexpected results: "We were lying in ambush on the road to Mapai when two FRELIMO suddenly appeared. We watched them and noticed they kept looking backwards as if they were expecting someone. Wanting them alive rather than dead, we tried to capture them but they would not yield and we had to shoot them both. On closer inspection it turned out the one was carrying a sack-full of mail and the letters inside were from ZANLA troops to their friends and family in Rhodesia and elsewhere. This was quite an intelligence bonanza and we handed it over to the people at 'PsyOps' {Psychological Operations} and Special Branch. A lot of the letters were great propaganda value because they were quite detailed in describing how hard life was being made for them by the Rhodesians.

"The contents of some of the letters were then broadcast from the army base at Vila Salazar on the border. The message to ZANLA was to avoid any further pain and suffering and to surrender, whereupon they would be well treated and allowed to get on with their lives. The plan was working and a large group of the enemy responded but there must have been a break-down in communications somewhere because someone on our side from one of the infantry companies opened fire at a critical time and they all ran off back into the bush and that was the end of that.

"The closest I came to dying there was one night waiting in ambush on the railway line south of Mapai in Gaza Province. There were plenty of enemy in the vicinity and I was very uneasy. About 03h00 in the morning, luckily I was wide awake and I heard movement. At first I thought it might be an animal but then I heard the leaves being trampled on and knew the sound was human and realised we were being hunted. They obviously knew we were there somewhere but not our exact position and had sent in a small reconnaissance group to establish exactly where we were. I whispered to the blokes to start packing and get ready to get out of there. Everyone reacted very calmly. We gathered ourselves and our equipment and crept away from the position then started walking at some speed. Just as the sun came up we heard the almightiest explosion coming from where we had been lying up. The explosion was followed by extremely intense fire and God alone knows how many troops they had mustered for that attack but we would not have stood a chance.

"From Gaza we went and did a number of 'external' camp attacks in Mozambique and Zambia. In most cases we found the camps ourselves and then did the attacks. In some cases, we brought the RLI in to do the actual attacks after we had identified the target. Some of them were very successful and I do think we were doing a good job of running the enemy ragged."

SAS Doctor Richard remembers this period: "It was my first incursion into Mozambique. It was a walk-in raid and we were walking in single file towards the terrorist camp just as dawn was breaking. Suddenly there was machine-gun fire at the tail end of the column. I remember this being a huge shock to realise that I had actually signed up for a real war. For a split second I was motionless like a deer caught in the headlights. Then I was knocked off my feet and dragged down behind an anthill. The person who pulled me down was Darrell Watt and he said, 'Doc, this is the real thing, you'd better get used to it.' On subsequent contacts I was more prepared but I never got completely used to it."

Johan Bezuidenhout remembers an unusual drama unfolding during one of these operations. "We had been deployed into Mozambique by chopper late one afternoon. Darrell was in charge, I was one of the NCOs and we walked until dark then up a hill which was just rock. Time for a brew, mash and some sardines then some shut-eye. Somehow I had inherited the wild Yank Rick Norrod and his best buddy Taffy Morgan; nobody else seemed to want them but they were two of the finest, most fearless soldiers I ever worked with. Also in my stick was Rich Swan.

"In the early hours I was awoken by what sounded like a very sick, bleating lamb. All I could make out was a feeble voice pleading, 'Sarge please help me' repeated over and over. I knew it was Taffy but he was behind a boulder so with Rich and Rick I moved off cautiously to see what the bleating was about. We had visions of someone with a knife to his throat.

"Well Taffy had company but there was no knife, only fangs. A big fat puff adder was curled up on Taffy's chest and a forked tongue was licking his nose. His eyes were like soup plates and he was understandably terrified but we could not help ourselves laughing when he was asked if his morning glory had softened. Taffy did not see much humour in this and we then attended to the delicate matter of getting the snake off him without him getting bitten. I told him to work his hands up slowly under the sleeping bag then flick it off but with his lips quivering he said he couldn't move anything. We encouraged him and eventually he struck and sent the snake on a quick freefall course as Taffy sprung up and out of his bag with a large wet patch showing in the crotch of his trousers where he had pissed himself. Norrod was laughing out of control so Taffy slammed into him and they went tumbling down the hill. It was one way to start a new op."

'OPERATION MARDON'

Out in the world of realpolitik confusion reigned as first Nyerere then Kaunda signalled they were backtracking from the Kissinger proposals. A furious Ian Smith demanded that the agreement be implemented in exact terms but his calls fell on resolutely deaf ears. Ever deferential to the Tanzanian and Zambian leadership the British government announced the convening of new talks to be held in Geneva, Switzerland under the chairmanship of Ivor Richard. Smith was livid but his options were limited; Vorster insisted the Rhodesians attend and do their best to salvage something from what was looking more and more like a débâcle.

To help strengthen Smith's hand and pressure Robert Mugabe, 'Operation Mardon' was launched at the end of October 1977 against ZANLA concentrations in Tete and Gaza provinces. This involved assaults of varying nature and intensity across a large swathe of Mozambique extending for more than 200 kilometres and included troops from the RAR, RLI, Selous Scouts and SAS. The Artillery Regiment provided fire support and the cavalry of the Grey's Scouts were used to ferry mortars and munitions to men on the ground.

In a pincer operation the SAS and RLI were tasked to attack targets in Tete while the Selous Scouts would raid enemy strongholds to the south at Jorge de Limpopo and Massangena.

The Scouts commenced hostilities at Chigamane garrison where they were initially welcomed by an enemy that mistook them for being friendly before paying for their mistake with their lives. The garrison was wiped out before the Scouts moved on to hit the large ZANLA camp at Maxaila. Continuing south a ZANLA troop train was attacked and destroyed outside Jorge de Limpopo which was then neutralised. Before returning to Rhodesia, Massangena was attacked and the enemy driven out.

Ron Reid-Daly was satisfied; "The aim of the mission, to destroy the logistics and disrupt communications between Jorge de Limpopo, Malvernia and Massangena had been achieved and achieved well."[35]

"We went into Mozambique near Mukumbura," recalls Watt. "The engineers cleared a path through the minefield opening up the route into Tete Province. We had horses from the Grey's Scouts to carry our mortars and heavy equipment but it was hard going. I had to get in the water and swim the horses through it. One of our guys put his boot down outside the cleared area while we were struggling with the horses and blew his foot off. We had to keep going so I put him on a horse after strapping his leg up. When the mine blew there was more pandemonium with horses bolting in all directions.

"We went on and attacked several camps, picking up lots of equipment but not many kills, and then we were called off. Most of the 'gooks' had run into Tete. I think the operation was compromised."

But the Rhodesians found themselves over a hundred kilometres inside the country with the enemy on the run. With a critical audience looking on from Geneva, the political implications of continuing the assault were deemed unacceptable and the troops were ordered home.

"The SAS achieved all its major objectives during 'Operation Mardon'," said Brian Robinson. "FRELIMO paid a heavy price in men and matériel for supporting Mugabe. Logistical and infrastructural problems which the SAS was instrumental in creating, significantly stemmed the flow of terrorists into Rhodesia's south-east."

CARTER WINS, RHODESIA LOSES

On 2 November 1976, much to the disappointment of many Rhodesians, Jimmy Carter from Plains, Georgia was elected president of the United States. To get there he had turned to Andrew Young, a sometime cleric and leading figure in the Civil Rights Movement, whose principal claim to fame was his proximity to Dr Martin Luther King on the day of his assassination.

In return for his support in attracting the black vote, Young was promised a seat at Carter's 'top table' in the event the presidency was won. In addition to a cabinet post, he was assured a special and powerful role in formulating US policy towards Africa. For a man whose only connection with the continent was his skin colour, this was a worry for the Rhodesians.

But for them there was more bad news. Robert Mugabe had already caught Young's eye and it was on his behalf that Young went to work even before the election results were announced. He had made contact with Tanzanian president

Julius Nyerere, to apprise him of political developments in the US and to explain that he, Young, would effectively be calling the shots on US–Africa policy if Carter won the election. Nyerere listened closely. Both he and Samora Machel were leaning towards Mugabe, but it was far from clear that their protégé would win an election in an orderly environment as demanded under the Kissinger proposals.

Young suggested they ditch the Kissinger accord, keep up the military pressure and await the arrival of a new Carter-led administration in Washington. He assured them the Democratic Party would be more supportive of their wish to see one of the guerrilla leaders appear as the new leader of the country that would soon be known as Zimbabwe. Unbeknown to Ian Smith, the deal that Kissinger had brokered with him was effectively stone dead and the optimism generated by the Kissinger proposals had been firmly laid to rest along with Kissinger himself and the Ford administration.

Young wasted no time in laying down his markers: he soon declared Ian Smith no lesser an evil than Uganda's Idi Amin and proclaimed his support for the Cuban intervention in Angola. For Young, the greatest menace facing the free world at the time was not the Soviets and their nuclear arsenal, but racism, and he would tailor US policy accordingly.

But Smith, unaware of what was going on behind closed doors in Dar es Salaam and elsewhere, soldiered on in the hope that the British government would support him in insisting on implementation of the terms of the Kissinger accord. Unfortunately, he was once again woefully out of step with the rest of the world. In an unusual show of unity Robert Mugabe and Joshua Nkomo announced the formation of a political alliance that would be known as the Patriotic Front.

It was now clear the ball was bouncing away from the Rhodesians. Kissinger had exited the scene and the British left-wingers who loathed the Rhodesians were back in the driving seat. Tony Crossland as Foreign Secretary and Ivor Richard, who was tasked with implementing the Kissinger agreement, were both going to be hard on Ian Smith. Kissinger seemed sincere in trying to give Smith an honourable way out; the British wanted to rub his nose in it.

FRUSTRATION

Heavy infiltration into the country from the Tete area continued and the SAS stepped up their mining operations on roads and paths. The Rhodesian commanders knew they had to attack, but political considerations bedevilled them. Smith had not given up entirely on a negotiated settlement and he did not want to be accused of wanton aggression, so military strategy was— not for the first or even last time— fettered by political timidity. The soldiers were told to steer clear of FRELIMO bases and target ZANLA only, a difficult proposition when the two forces were operating together. The instruction was not lost on ZANLA, who promptly sought sanctuary in FRELIMO strongholds.

"Around the beginning of 1977," said Ron Reid-Daly, "the fighting soldiers— and that certainly included me—very much wanted to take the battle to the enemy and hit them with everything we had. We didn't have much in the way of equipment, but we had some of the best soldiers and airmen in the world. All we needed was to be told the gloves were off, and I have no doubt the outcome would have been very different. It's a great pity that people like Majors Jeremy Strong, Patrick Armstrong and Nick Fawcett were not jumped up to the top faster and told to get on with it. Unfortunately, despite the fact that we were at war, the younger officers simply had to wait for the older ones to do their time and retire. If our commanders had been more progressive in their thinking I believe we would have brought Zambia, Mozambique and Tanzania to their knees quicker than anyone could ever have imagined. The countries that hosted our adversaries were not punished enough for their actions."

Brian Robinson, too, was disillusioned by the calibre of some military commanders. "On one occasion, I took an idea to one of the generals," he recalled, "and after I had explained the whole plan to him rather elaborately, I looked at him. He was as white as a sheet. I thought he'd seen a ghost. His mouth hung open and he was wide-eyed. He said to me, 'Jeepers, Brian— isn't that bloody dangerous?' I just had to hold my breath, but it was a pretty demoralising experience."

The SAS already had detailed plans in place to attack the harbours of Beira and Maputo in Mozambique, using divers to sink ships within the ports and render them unusable. There were also plans to destroy the main lines of rail and road communication, which would have caused the enemy a logistical nightmare.

Unfortunately, most of Robinson's pleas to be allowed to go after these targets fell on deaf ears.

"Frustrating our efforts here was head of the CIO, Ken Flower," recalls Robinson. "He was adamantly opposed to us attacking any strategic targets."

"From a source in Dar es Salaam we received the identity of a ship that was being used as a troop carrier ferrying trained terrorists from the camps in Tanzania to Beira in Mozambique prior to deployment in Rhodesia," Robinson recalled. "We wanted to sink it and kill in the region of 1,500 terrorists in one blow. One scenario was for us to go in with an attack-diving team. They would place a limpet mine on the ship's hull with a delay mechanism in order to sink it outside the harbour, where the sharks would take care of possible survivors. The alternative was to plant a beacon on the vessel, and wait. As soon as it put to sea, Hawker 'Hunters' were going to sink the ship. Unfortunately, neither plan ever materialised."

On the political front, there was no reason for cheer. To add to the Rhodesians' woes, it was apparent that a handsome, ambitious young medical doctor by the name of David Owen would soon replace Antony Crosland as the British Foreign Secretary. Known for his doctrinaire left-wing views, Salisbury could expect little empathy from Owen but an even more supportive approach towards Mugabe and Nkomo.

Somewhat frustrated by indecision at the top, the SAS went back to their classic role, operating in small, heavily armed four-man groups, harassing and destroying supply routes by setting ambushes and planting landmines. Playing a game of hit, run and hide, they caused considerable disruption, leaving an angry and frustrated enemy behind. Teams went in by freefall, static line and, in one case, on horseback. They were immediately effective and Andy Chait was at his lethal best. One ambush he laid saw him account for almost the entire group himself.

Ideally, Robinson wanted to use his men as much as possible in an 'eyes and ears' role: operating covertly, identifying targets, then calling in the infantry to deal with the problem.

"This was making the best use of specialist soldiers," Robinson recalls. "These were classical SAS operations. The aim was to strike in depth and terrorise the enemy who had no idea as to how we were able to attack them. Always frustrating us in the operational sphere was the perennial shortage of helicopters which sometimes made rapid deployment of shock troops impossible. When there was no support available the SAS simply had to finish the job themselves."

The sum of it all was that a handful of hard, dedicated soldiers were making life miserable for ZANLA and their FRELIMO allies in their very heartland, and at the same time severely curtailing their ability to cross into Rhodesia. A land mass the size of England had been infiltrated by no more than sixty SAS operators at any given time and they had gunned, mined and ambushed it into a state of confused disorder. Their aggression created a situation where the enemy had to be ever vigilant and defensive in territory it would have liked to call home.

Despite the war that raged so near, visitors were unfailingly astonished by the normality of life in the towns and cities. Soldiers back from the 'sharp end' relaxed at home with families and girlfriends. The white-gabled Salisbury Sports Club with its twelve separate bars and massive verandas and porticoes was a magnet for cricket fans at weekends. Big boisterous beer-swilling men caroused as if there was no tomorrow. Others went back to the bush to fish and hunt. All the while, pretty girls flirted.

Little more than a cover drive away from the Salisbury Sports Club was the pathetically insecure white-washed Prime Minister's residence. Rhodesian rugby lock forward Pete 'Lofty' Lombard remembers being the only guard on duty one Saturday night. He was told to "Go to the pub and leave us alone." With lettuces and leeks from Mrs Smith's garden to barter for beer, he departed his post.

Most, at some point during their leave, had paid at least one visit to the Khaya Nyama Steakhouse and enjoyed some of what was reputed to be the finest beef in the world.[36]

But terror was never far away. At Musami Mission on the western side of the country, seven white missionaries who had dedicated their lives to helping the black people were butchered. There was grim irony in this tragedy because it happened as two colleagues of the deceased were being jailed for supporting the organisation responsible for the atrocity. In the east, ten children were killed in a landmine incident, while on a lonely tobacco farm at nearby Odzi, two schoolboys fought off a large group of terrorist's intent on killing them and burning the farmhouse to the ground. Members of the security forces came upon a group of tribesmen whose arms had been hacked off before they had been left to bleed to death.

MINE EVERYTHING

Following a high level decision to increase the scale and frequency of crossborder raids, Rhodesian troops with air support had captured the town of Mapai, ninety-five kilometres inside southern Mozambique, in June. However, a Dakota had been shot down during the attack, killing the pilot, and enemy casualties were low with most of the enemy having vacated the town shortly before the raid. Once again there were rumblings in the ranks about an information leak.

In a bid to bring Mozambique military and logistical traffic to a standstill Darrell Watt was ordered to mine every available thoroughfare into eastern Rhodesia. "I was given all the aircraft and equipment I asked for and told to do nothing else for a month," remembers Watt. "Studying recently taken aerial photos I worked closely with the air force planners and we identified the areas we would mine. I was given twelve four-man 'call signs' and we went in by Dakota every night. We planned to lay twelve antivehicle mines every night. Pick-up in the morning was by chopper."

Gavin remembers. "We called it the Mtoko Mining Op and Darrell was in charge. It was intensive; I think I did seven jumps in fourteen nights. We used containers. It was jump–mine–uplift, all in twelve hours. Each 'call sign' put down two to four chocolate-cake mines per night then had a night off. I remember sitting down with Darrell and he showed us a map of 'Porkers' {Rhodesian slang for Mozambique, the Portuguese having been affectionately known as 'Porks'} and said we're going to shut the place down."

"The air force was short of pilots and was using older reservists to fly the night missions," remembers Watt. "We were working the roads all the way up to the Malawi border. We pissed the enemy off big time and the aircraft taking the men in started to come under very intense anti-aircraft fire. I normally accompanied the Dakota in a 'Lynx' {Cessna 337, ground-attack aircraft}. We flew in as low as possible using the moon as much as we could and then just before the drop zone the 'Dak' pilots would climb to about 800 feet, drop the men and head home. But it wasn't always easy and we were lucky not to have been shot down. On one occasion, with troops led by Phil Cripps standing in the door ready to jump, the 'ack-ack' fire was so heavy the pilot dived. The troops were completely taken by surprise and they went flying into the roof of the aircraft and in the process the plane almost barrel-rolled. Some of the troops were injured when they slammed into the floor and the drop had to be aborted. Back in Salisbury I went to the home of one of the pilots to see if he was alright. He was a Second World War veteran and he was laughing when he said, 'Darrell, this is worse than fighting the Germans.'"

Gavin recalls: "I remember being on early warning one night while the others were sticking a mine in behind me and an armoured patrol came past and then

Cecil Rhodes; planted
the seed of conflict.

South African Prime Minister
John Vorster; used Rhodesia as
South Africa's sacrificial lamb.

Ian Smith, Prime
Minister of Rhodesia
(right), and British Prime
Minister Harold Wilson
(left), 1965.

Foreign Secretary Carrington, Robert Mugabe and Prime
Minister Maragaret Thatcher. Ian Smith described
Carrington as 'the most evil man I ever met.'

Above: Zambian President Kenneth Kaunda.

Mozambican
President Samora
Machel; severely
pressured by the SAS.

British Foreign Secretary David Owen and Andrew Young, Jimmy Carter's UN Ambassador.

Queen Elizabeth; played a pivotal role in bringing Mugabe to power.

US Secretary of State Henry Kissinger; tried hard to end the war and earned Ian Smith's respect.

US President Jimmy Carter; determined to use US power to end white rule in southern Africa.

Joshua Nkomo; took responsibilty for the downing of the Viscounts.

Rhodesian military supremo General Peter Walls.

Darrell Watt (far left), early days.

Bert Sachse (left) and Darrell Watt (right) on operations in Mozambique
with Portuguese troops.

Watt (2nd from right) in Angola with Portuguese paratroopers.

Tracking Wing Kariba; Watt kneeling 2nd from right; Brian Robinson kneeling centre.

SAS on parade.

AIL, SEPTEMBER 29 1974

SOLDIER'S TREK FOR CHARITY KEPT SECRET

Sunday Mail Reporter

DETAILS of a marathon boating and walking trip by a Special Air Service sergeant are being kept secret — to protect the man from "troublemakers".

An SAS spokesman last week requested that details of the marathon route — 280 km on Lake Kariba, and almost the same distance between Kariba and Salisbury — should not be published.

The man who is to tackle the course is Sgt. Darrell Watt (24) of 52 Midlothian Avenue, Eastlea. He hopes to raise money for the Terrorist Victims' Relief Fund and St Giles, by completing the trip.

Some time during the next few months he will row single-handed along Lake Kariba, then walk from Kariba to Salisbury, also by himself. He hopes to complete the non-stop trip in about 20 days.

Sgt Watt said last week: "I'll be sleeping in the boat — probably rowing by night and resting during the hottest part of the day. I'll be in radio contact in case anything goes wrong."

He has got special permission to carry a rifle on the trip — although he is doing it in his own time as part of his holidays. He said: "I'll be carrying the rifle to protect me against wild animals or anything else. I shall not be shooting game for food though."

At the end of the rowing trip, Darrell will leave his boat at Kariba, then pick up an 80-lb. pack for the long walk south.

He already has considerable experience of roughing it in the bush, with the SAS. And at one time he spent several months game ranching near Beitbridge, "also living in the bush most of the time". He recently went on a hunting trip near Bulawayo and bagged an elephant and a few small buck.

Watt in the news following his journey for charity.

Chopper 'tech' Mark Jackson at his guns.

RLI Fire Force preparing for uplift.

'Sellout' with lips and ears cut off.

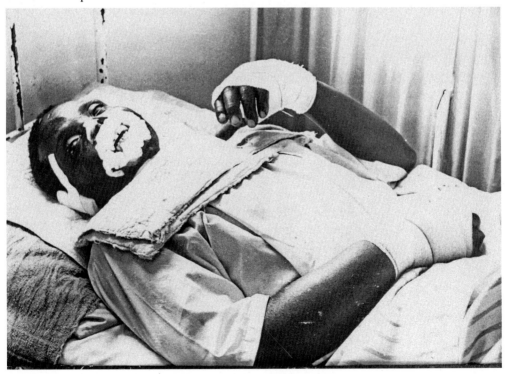

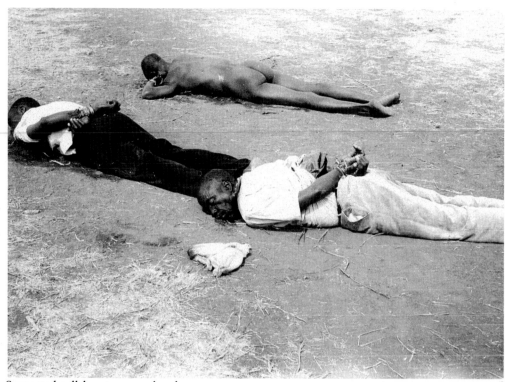

Suspected collaborators murdered.

ZANLA men killed in the north-east of the country.

SAS operators ready to roll.

Pilot Terry McCormick and 'tech' Mark Jackson; two
brave flyers who risked their all to save their soldiers.

Andy Chait, rated one
of the best NCO's.

Lt. Richard Stannard; feisty and fearless.

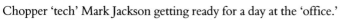

Chopper 'tech' Mark Jackson getting ready for a day at the 'office.'

Left: Frans Botha and
Dave O'Sullivan.

Center: Mother and child
slain at Elim Mission.

Bottom: Pride of the Rhodesian
Air Force, Dick Paxton.

stopped about a hundred yards away. Visibility was poor but I think it was called a BRDM {Russian, combat reconnaissance patrol vehicle} armoured car with a 14.5mm gun, and there was also bigger APCs {armoured personnel carriers}, I think BTRs' {Russian, armoured transporter}. I watched nervously then after a short while they fucked off again, thank God! I was heavily debriefed by the 'Brass' the next day about what the vehicles looked like because they then ascertained the FRELIMO had a motorized light armour company based nearby, and they were patrolling up and down at night looking for us. But by the end of the op we had stuck mines in every single road running for about 200 kilometres along our border. I remember much back-slapping when we finished because we had effectively closed off a long section of the border to any enemy vehicle traffic."

WALKING ON WATER

On the opposite side of the country, the resort town of Kariba was under virtual siege by late 1977. Insurgents were crossing from a nearby base to attack civilians on the main road into the town then vanishing under cover of darkness. Conventional Rhodesian security force units were frustrated; their efforts to come to grips with the perpetrators had yielded a nil return. Desperate for a solution, Ken Stewart, the Special Branch boss in Kariba, asked the SAS to intervene.

"We were sitting at the bar at Caribbea Bay having a good time when Ken appeared with a very worried look on his face," remembers Watt. "He told us something had to be done quickly because if the attacks continued they might have to close the road. He told us roughly where he thought their camp was and asked us to make a plan. I was happy to help."

Darrell Watt, Billy Heyns and two others wasted no time and took off in search of the enemy base.

"Picking up tracks, we had no trouble finding the camp in the mountains," says Watt. "Billy and I had a good look, all the 'gooks' seemed to be there and I formulated a plan of attack. I liked the look of the hills surrounding the camp. I could see what the lines of flight would be and knew it would be great for the stop groups. We went back to Kariba and I filed a report."

SAS HQ responded quickly and Bob MacKenzie was dispatched with his A Squadron to deal with the attack.

"I liked Bob," remembers Watt, "but I was a little wary of him. He was extremely aggressive. Back in Kariba I sat down with him, explained what we had seen and told him what I thought we should do. He then told me to give the orders which I did but then he said, 'OK, you do the attack but I want two sweep lines.'

"This struck me as very strange. And I asked him why he wanted two lines but he did not answer; just said do it. I refused point blank. I liked Bob but I don't think he liked me too much and I did not want him behind me when the bullets started flying. Eventually he agreed to do it my way. Bob and I had had words previously. I did not always agree with his approach to his men. On one occasion before embarking on a dangerous operation he ordered his men onto the parade ground. The task was a pretty daunting one and some of the men were very young and nervous. When they had formed up he then called the Squadron Quartermaster and asked him loudly how many body-bags had been made available. When the QM gave him the number he shouted at him angrily, 'We need a lot more fucking bags. A lot more of these fuckers are going to die tomorrow and they need bags.' I did not like this at all and approached him immediately after the men were dismissed and asked him quietly not to repeat that behaviour."

It was decided to cross the water at night in 'Klepper' canoes. The troops were divided into stop groups and assault sweep lines. The main group would sweep the position and the stops would cut down all those trying to flee.

Terry was in one canoe; alongside him was another foreigner, Murray 'Mo' Taylor, a former Welsh Guardsman who had also only recently passed selection and was on his first outing. The setting was entirely novel to Taylor who had not been in Rhodesia long.

"The day before the attack we went down to the river to have a look at where we would cross," Terry recalled. "Looking across the river, Mo asked what the 'grey-green things' were. Someone told him they were crocodiles. Being an Englishman, he looked shocked and said he wanted 'nowt to do with them fokkers.'

"On the night of the op, quietly nearing the opposite bank, there was a grunt and a splash and Mo was in the water, having been knocked out of his canoe by a hippo, losing his weapon and equipment in the process and being forced to swim to shore. He missed the attack. When we picked him up in the morning he was a pasty grey-white colour and he was furious. 'Fock this place for a joke,' he said. 'I didn't come all this way to feed the fokking animals. I'm fokking off back to England, and fock this focking place!' He claimed that after the hippo hit him the only part of his body that touched water was the soles of his feet, leading him to believe he might actually be Jesus Christ."

Despite the mishap, the rest of the men closed in on the camp successfully and took up positions to await the dawn. So confident was Watt of his force's tactical and fighting superiority that he arranged for his great friend Don Aylward, the District Commissioner at Gokwe, to be given a ringside seat on a nearby hill from where he would be able to watch the action. Perfectly executed, the coup de main went in as planned against an unsuspecting enemy. Shocked into action, they tried to run but could find no way out and the assault teams drove them towards where the stop groups lay in wait.

"There was pandemonium, screaming, shouting, some firing wildly," Terry remembered. "They didn't know where to run and ended up in total panic, running round and round a large baobab tree, but they were getting nailed from both sides and the group seemed to get smaller with every revolution."

"There was a very big man carrying a PKM machine gun and he fought back bravely," remembers Watt. "Eventually Gerry de Lange said, 'Fuck this for a joke' and ran out of cover right at him and killed him with his RPD {Soviet-manufactured, belt-fed, light machine gun} We counted twenty-nine bodies which I think was the full camp complement."

The operation had been an unqualified success. The raiders loaded up all the equipment in the camp, jumped into their canoes and paddled home to celebrate. Among the booty were recent photographs showing the enemy frolicking in the snow-filled streets of Leningrad. Their Soviet patrons had schooled them well in the art of killing civilians but in dealing with real soldiers, they had apparently been remiss. On their return to Kariba, District Commissioner Aylward insisted that all the beers were on him.

"Subsequently I discovered my attack plan from this operation was used as a model at the School of Infantry. Chris Schulenburg asked me to bring it to show him one weekend when we went spearfishing at Lake McIlwaine. I had to nick it because Chris was in Scouts and all hell would have broken loose if I'd been caught. I gave it to him and then forgot about it and went back to Salisbury. Chris had left it under his bed in the chalet and also forgotten about it. Luckily a game ranger found this Top Secret document, knew where it had come from and got it back to me."

In November 1977, Field Marshal Lord Carver arrived in the country as a prelude to filling the role of a sort of pro-consul who would, if David Owen's plan gelled, take over command of the Rhodesian armed forces. To make the point that he outranked the Rhodesian generals, he arrived in uniform. Carver had consistently downplayed allegations of terrorist atrocities in a bid to have the Rhodesian army disbanded. Ian Smith, warned in advance of the field marshal's leftist leanings, preferred to watch cricket at the Police Ground rather than meet him. With Carver was the UN-appointed Indian military supremo, General Prem Chand, who quickly became known as the 'Samoosa Scout.'

CHAPTER 7

Dazed, fleeing defendants
Break from their trenches
Into the shrapnelled wall which climbs
Where our bombers have passed.
We have returned, Rhodesia.
—CHAS LOTTER

GOING FOR BROKE

Ian Smith's hopes of finding an international political solution to his country's problems were fading. James Callaghan, the British premier was ratcheting up the pressure. David Owen met with John Vorster in South Africa and asked him to use his influence to force the Rhodesian government to hand over power. The US announced increased assistance for the Marxist regime in Mozambique and refused to pay any attention to that government's contempt for the basic human rights of its citizens.

Ian Smith could not find common ground with the British Foreign Secretary. "Like virtually all the English politicians I dealt with," said Smith, "Owen was unable to look at the Rhodesian problem in a genuinely objective way. More important to him than finding a solution, was his desire to punish us. The best way for him to cut our throats was to help Mugabe or Nkomo acquire power. By comparison, Henry Kissinger was a pleasure to deal with. He seemed very genuine in his desire to reach an understanding that took the interests of all into account. I have nothing but respect for him. If the British had approached our problem in the same spirit, I think our history would have unfolded with a great deal less tragedy, but they were terribly vindictive."

Andrew Young, the US ambassador to the United Nations, was in uncompromising mood demanding an immediate transfer of power. As far as Smith was concerned, the diplomatic initiatives had run their course; the world would settle for nothing less than a government dominated by the 'liberation leaders.'

Adding to Smith's woes he was in receipt of a report from CIO boss Ken Flower advising him the war was looking increasingly unwinnable as the financial burden on the fiscus increased. Seeking alternatives, he turned to black leaders within Rhodesia to find an internal political solution, and to his security forces to hit the enemy hard enough to bring their leadership to the negotiating table with constructive intent. However, still fearful of South African power and concerned about providing any additional pretext for further support to the country's adversaries, he again insisted that collateral damage to neighbouring government forces and installations be kept to a minimum.

The operational commanders and intelligence agents were busy. They were also worried. While many hopes had been pinned on the search for a political solution, they knew that the military threat was growing, with increased material, moral and tactical support from the communist bloc. And to everyone's dismay, civilian casualties in Rhodesia were steadily rising.

It was as a result of intelligence gathered from RENAMO operators, along with information gleaned following the Selous Scout raid on Nyadzonya camp, that the rapid growth of two very substantial enemy camps in that country was revealed. A capture retrieved to Rhodesia shed light on location and numbers before aerial photographs taken by an aircraft of 5 Squadron were studied along with first-hand reports from close-in field reconnaissance.

The worst fears of the officers tasked with defending Rhodesia became a startling reality. Experts from the photo-reconnaissance section concluded that the facilities were large in area and housed thousands of potential combatants. One prisoner let it be known that the bulk of the 'comrades' were ready and merely awaiting the onset of the rains, which would give them the cover to infiltrate Rhodesia. Even rough estimates of the numbers in the camps left operational commanders in no doubt that successful infiltration would be disastrous and, in all likelihood, could lead to the loss of the war and sacking of the country. The insurgency had to be stopped. The question was how.

The combative Colonel Ron Reid-Daly emerged, champing at the bit with a plan to use his Selous Scouts to demolish the bridges between the camps and Rhodesia, making it logistically problematic for the enemy to move to at least forestall their infiltration. However, the plan was not well received with Ken Flower outspoken in his opposition. It was felt that an attack on Mozambique's infrastructure would evoke more outside calls for intervention on behalf of the enemy.

Not for the first or last time, the generals seemed to be stumped. They turned to their juniors for ideas.

"When I was an officer cadet," recalled Brian Robinson, "I believed the generals made the plans and gave directives. Not so with us. Unit commanders and their intelligence staff did all the ferreting for information, prepared the plan and then had to sell it to the 'ComOps' {Combined Operations, the supreme security organ consisting of heads of all the services and headed by General Walls} commander and his top advisers. The first presentation of 'Operation Dingo' took place in November 1976. It was finally executed on 23 November 1977, after twelve revisions."

Intelligence estimates put the number of potential combatants in the camp that would become known as 'New Farm' at between 9,000 and 11,000. Also within the facility was a FRELIMO support group, armed with mortars and anti-aircraft weapons. At nearby Chimoio, apart from the FRELIMO garrison, there was a company of Tanzanian troops and more than one hundred Soviet advisers. Equipped with T-54 tanks, BTR-152 armoured personnel carriers and SAM-7 batteries, they would more than likely also have to be dealt with. Tembué, farther north, housed an estimated 5, 000 men under arms.

"The obvious plan would have called for a simultaneous hit on both targets," said Robinson. "However, we barely had sufficient resources to hit a single target, never mind both at the same time. We worked on a forty-eight- hour turnaround from Chimoio to Tembué, in the hope that even if the second target was forewarned, we would be able to hit them before they had time to get away. A major consideration was that all internal operations would be left without any form of air support, including 'casevac,' during that period. The rest of Rhodesia was going to be seriously vulnerable."

Apart from the potential loss of men, the logistical problems were enormous. This was an army and air force that relied on antiquated equipment which, by virtue of sanctions, was virtually irreplaceable. The stakes could hardly have been higher. The planners looked forlornly at the odds. One of the first fundamentals that had been drummed into them was that an attacking force should outnumber defenders by three to one. A generation later General Colin Powell, when weighing up the options for war in Iraq spoke of "the principle of overwhelming force as a necessary condition for waging war." Using Powell's mathematics 30,000 men would be needed. The Rhodesians would attack with one hundred and eight-five.

DO OR DIE

On the face of it, it was 'Mission Impossible' but the alternative was the possibility the county would be overrun by the enemy. If Rhodesia was to survive, there was no option. Quite simply, it was a matter of do or die. They had to strike, and it had to be soon.

Airborne was the only possible form of transport so the air force would have to provide the pre-emptive strike as well as the transport and support of the ground forces. Every single fixed-wing craft and helicopter in the Rhodesian Air Force would have to be used.

In his capacity as Commander 'ComOps,' General Peter Walls finally accepted the plan. After much debate and consideration of the political ramifications the green light was given.

'Operation Dingo' would decide the immediate future of the beleaguered country, and its successful execution was placed firmly in the hands of SAS commander Major Brian Robinson and Group Captain Norman Walsh, Operations Director of the Rhodesian Air Force. Using a huge papier-mâché model, they went to work and fine-tuned the plan.

"I have a vivid recollection," said Robinson, "of having to give a full verbal briefing to a sea of red-banded cobras and blue jobs dripping with gold braid, sitting on rugby stands around the model at New Sarum. Trying to look calm and totally confident in front of a very critical and discerning audience required some finely honed theatrical skills. I was followed by Walsh, who presented the air plan.

"The helicopters had a limited range, so a refuelling facility would have to be set up in enemy territory to enable the choppers to complete their tasks. This was known as the 'admin base' where fuel, ammunition, medics, first-line reserves and other back-up personnel would be positioned. It would also serve as a medical halfway house for the wounded who would be attended to prior to being ferried home to hospital.

"Setting up an admin area to refuel and re-supply in enemy territory must have been a first in modern guerrilla warfare," Robinson pointed out. "The idea came from Norman Walsh, a remarkable personality and original thinker who could have been equally at home wearing a SAS beret.

"It was all kept very quiet until the last minute," recalls Watt. "Only at New Sarum did everyone realise what was going on. A complete security blanket was thrown over us, but when the men saw the amount of ammunition they would have to carry, they knew something big was in the works, but they were simply told to pack, clean weapons and draw their ordnance, then jump onto the trucks to await transport to New Sarum air base. On arrival at New Sarum the troops had confirmation that something major was about to happen. They saw the rows of choppers, the Daks lined up and the RLI commandos kitted out and ready."

Chris Shields, one of the SAS troopers remembers the orders group. "At first I thought they were trying to be funny and I think most of us did. There were lots of blokes looking at one another nervously. We were all trying to make some sense of what they were telling us. It took quite a long time to realise this was no joke but we could laugh or cry so all laughed."

"It was a difficult time," Watt recalls. "Some were estimating 30% casualties, and expected worse. The odds against us were bad. But they were Rhodesians, and they were very brave. Some of them had just finished selection and were barely out of school, but if you had given them the chance to opt out, I don't believe a single one of them would have taken it."

The movement orders preparatory to the raid were exhaustive, with a huge translocation of men and equipment to points around the country. Intelligence estimates put the approximately 10,000 people at 'New Farm' in various stages of preparedness. It was assumed that most of those in residence would be armed and dangerous, though some might be wounded and recovering, while others could be en route to Tanzania and China for training. Women and children were expected to be among the inhabitants. Women, it was agreed, were known combatants and fair game; children were to be spared.

The camp was situated on a farm abandoned by a fleeing Portuguese farmer and covered approximately five square kilometres. Some of the buildings, consisting of the old homestead, offices, sheds and tobacco barns, had been converted into military facilities, turning 'New Farm' into what was effectively the administrative centre for ZANLA. There were rooms and offices for Robert Mugabe, Josiah Tongogara, Rex Nhongo and the rest of the organisation's top echelon, raising hopes of 'celebrity kills.'

A labyrinth of trenches, revetments and defensive lines had been constructed, anti-aircraft weapons and other heavy weapons were dug in and an early warning system of sentries in towers with whistles was in place. Tethered baboons were strategically placed and watched by sentries. It was believed that their senses were better tuned than those of humans, and any restive behaviour from the animals was to be considered a possible indication of imminent attack.

Surprise was absolutely vital to the success of 'Operation Dingo', so the sound of approaching aircraft presented a major challenge. The man who would have to deal with that particular problem was the indefatigable Jack Malloch. Malloch was already a Rhodesian legend. Flying Spitfires in the Second World War as a pilot in 237 Rhodesia Squadron, he was shot down in Italy. Hidden by nuns, he was flown to safety in a captured German aircraft. After returning to Rhodesia he flew in support of Mike Hoare's mercenaries in the Congo and then flew missions on behalf of Biafran secessionists in Nigeria. After Ian Smith declared UDI Malloch set up Air Trans Africa to fly cargo in breach of the international economic embargo on the country. So successful was he that the British government asked the UN to intervene in halting his operation. With the war and the demand for aircraft Malloch put his small fleet at the disposal of the air force.

As part of the plan he would fly his DC-8 jetliner over the camp on the morning of the attack as a decoy, mere minutes before the raid. This shrewd ploy, it was hoped, would provide the vital time needed to mask the sound of the approaching air armada. The big jet would pass over 'New Farm' at 07h41 when the camp inmates were expected on parade. The military strategists banked on them scrambling for the trenches at the sound of jet engines, only to discover it was a commercial aircraft, relax and return to their previous positions. No sooner would they have done so than the fighter planes and bombers would be upon them.

Hawker-Hunters of No 1 Squadron would initiate the attack with bombs, rockets and cannon. They would be followed immediately by the Vampires and finally, the Canberras, which would keep the enemy heads down while the paratroopers deployed by jumping into action from the ageing Dakotas, while some forty RLI commandos were ferried in by helicopter. The vertical envelopment would cover three sides of the target 'box,' while the gap would be closed by 'K-Cars' armed with 20mm cannon. Coordination of the airstrike and the para-drop had to be perfectly timed. If the helicopters were too close to the target, the noise would give the game away. If the Canberra strike was too early, the paras would be shot while still in the air. If the Canberras were late, even by minutes, the paratroopers could hit the ground among exploding bombs.

Once the escape routes were closed, troops in sweep lines would advance to flush the trenches and gun pits and kill anyone who appeared before them. Those choosing to flee rather than fight would run into the stop groups. Machine-gunners were loaded with as many belts as they could carry, with instructions to replenish with looted ammunition when they needed more.

John Ngwenya, one of those who survived the attack, said of the period leading up to it: "I had just arrived from Nachingwea in Tanzania and was awaiting my first mission to Zimbabwe. Our commanders told us the Rhodesians were not to be feared, that they were fearful of us and that because of sanctions, their equipment was old and unreliable and our bases were too far inside Mozambique for them to strike.

"We were very tightly monitored and spreading any alarm within the ranks of the fighters was a serious offence, punishable by death, so we were all careful of what we said, and to whom. Despite this, I did hear some talk that did not concur with what we had been told by our seniors and instructors. Some of the comrades had been involved in action against Rhodesian soldiers and they had not liked it. The Rhodesians did not run, as we were told, but were aggressive and accurate with their weapons. One told me that the Rhodesian riflemen did not use their weapons on automatic fire as we did. Instead, they fired one or two shots at a time, and they were very accurate, even over a long distance. As a result I was a little apprehensive about what to expect, but there were so many of us and we had so much weaponry at Chimoio that we were mostly of the opinion that they would never attack us there."

In addition to their own forces, ZANLA had its FRELIMO comrades close by, and they had tanks and other armoured vehicles as well as artillery and mortars. Ngwenya: "We were agreed our numbers and equipment would dissuade the Rhodesians from attacking us. As a result, I think we were not well prepared when they did come, because most of us just believed it would not happen.

"Our leaders told us the Rhodesians were tiring and we would be victorious, because our cause was just. We were told Marxism gave the power to the people, where it belonged. I studied my book containing the thoughts of Chairman Mao and believed strongly that the communist system would triumph over capitalism, which was another form of colonialism."

On the eve of the operation, across the country at Thornhill Air Base outside the central Midlands town of Gwelo, the crack pilots of No 1 Hawker-Hunter Squadron, who would initiate the attack, had been closely studying their 'Air Task.' Led by Squadron Leader Richard Brand, they were all experienced combat pilots, but they knew the morning of 23 November would bring with it their most challenging mission. Awaiting their arrival were batteries of 23mm anti-aircraft guns, RPG-7 rocket launchers and Strela heat-seeking missiles, along with thousands of AK-47s and RPDs. The ground fire was one thing; they would also have to be mindful of interception by the MiGs of the Mozambican Air Force.

They studied the details: the target description and position, the 'TOT' {time on target}, the armaments and weapons systems they would be carrying, and copied all the frequencies and 'call signs' they would need to maintain vital communications. Ground crews were briefed on fuel and armaments, time for take-off and the number of planes. The crews would work into the night to make sure all aircraft were 100 per cent serviceable.

Then the aircrews went back to the aerial photographs to study the target more closely, with particular reference to the position of the 'ack-ack' guns and the likely prevailing winds, which would affect their weapons delivery. They could only hope that cloud and poor weather would not make the task at hand even more difficult than it was already expected to be. Taking all external factors into consideration, they plotted their attack patterns and 'IP's' {initial points}, those all-important coordinates at which each aircraft would commence the final run-in' a mere fifty feet (little more than fifteen metres) above the ground, prior to pulling up to the 'perch' from which the pilots would turn in for the attack. Satisfied that they had done all they could, the aircrews went to bed, after telling the duty orderly when to kick them out of the covers.

At New Sarum, the Vampire and Canberra pilots went through the same preparations. There were six of the old wooden Vampires left, but only two had ejector seats.

Steve Kesby remembered: "Our squadron was to fly two Vampire T11s and four FB9s. The briefing was held in the parachute hangar and was the most comprehensive for any target to date. The enormity of the strike filled us with excitement and not a little apprehension. The FB9s with no ejection seats were to be flown by Varkie Varkevisser, Ken Law, Phil Haigh and me. The northern part of the Chimoio target, comprising the training element, was allocated to the Vamps. Varkie and I were to suppress flak by taking out anti-aircraft weapons, while the others were to take out barrack blocks and other targets."[37]

When they and the "Hunters" had completed their initial strikes, the Canberra bombers would pound the camp with a mixture of explosive ordnance.

While the pilots plotted their strikes, there was excitement among the ground crews at New Sarum. Coming from posts all over the country, the operation had brought many of them together for the first time in a long while, and they relished the moment. The Corporals' Club was designated the meeting place, and after completing their checks they congregated to drink a few beers and catch up on old friends. But at 22h30, the shutters came down and the men in blue went to their billets to await the dawn.

Brian Robinson and Norman Walsh took themselves to the air force officers' mess to have a drink that evening. They were mentally drained and physically exhausted, but confident that the planning and coordination was in accordance with their wishes. Robinson was especially mindful of the fact that the battle for 'New Farm' would be only the beginning. "We then had to extract the men, equipment and parachutes post haste for the next phase of the operation," he said. Both men felt a natural anxiety that the unexpected could upset the entire plan, but the stark fact was that they had done all that could be expected of them; 'Operation Dingo' was now in the lap of the gods, the 'troopies' and the weather. They drank a toast to the success of the mission then had another drink. After that they went to bed, but sleep proved elusive.

At 03h00, Robinson and Walsh stirred and dressed before joining their officers to see their men in the hangars as they prepared for battle. They did not like what they saw overhead: it had rained and the sky was overcast. Bad weather would dash the best plan and that seemed a distinct possibility.

Troops checked weapons and equipment, fitted their parachutes and strapped rifles into place, then checked one another. Ready to go, most smoked cigarettes while waiting for the order to board. Bad weather notwithstanding, they were going to go for it; the survival of the country as they knew it lay in their young hands and youthful eyes showed some of the strain. The banter of the previous day had been stayed and men went quietly about their business, each alone with his thoughts and fears.

Andrew Standish-White, a farmer's son from Sinoia, vividly recalled that morning: "The hum of voices, the snapping of clips being tested and fitted, that funny sweet smell of the parachutes, the nausea of one too many the night before . . . the morning chill causing shivers that were desperately suppressed, lest anyone watching thought it was from nerves . . . needing to take a bloody pee after being fitted and checked—what a pain it was to get to the necessary apparatus. Collapsing in a heap on the jump mats to wait . . . and wait . . . and thinking that maybe, very soon, you would be 'jumping to a conclusion.' Everyone was thinking about dying but trying not to let on. Fiddling with your weapon—was the gun tight enough behind the shoulder? Was the pistol well secured but still easily accessible? Should you stow the metal feeder strip of the RPD belts in the webbing pouch or have them protruding for instant access? The smokers all had to bugger off outside once fitted—no smoking in the hangar. Heaps of them stood outside, puffing hard on their cigarettes."

At Thornhill, Richard Brand's pilots entered the crew room to sign off their individual aircraft before he led them across the tarmac to the waiting jets, poised and primed like steel predators of the night.

Brand was continuing a proud tradition. The scion of a venerated family of fliers, his uncle Sir Quentin Brand was a pioneer of African aviation who had been first officer on the first aircraft ever flown to Rhodesia. In March 1920, the converted Vickers Vimy bomber named the Silver Queen II had landed on the racecourse at Bulawayo, introducing commercial aviation to the young colony.

Now, fifty-seven years later, a heavy burden lay on the young shoulders of Sir Quentin's nephew. His squadron's strike had to be precise and devastating. His point of impact would be the marker that the other pilots would follow. It was on Brand that the planners were relying to hit the enemy very fast and very hard, putting them to flight from which they would be given no respite. If his aim was off, the enemy would have the chance to brace and fight, and that eventuality could prove calamitous for the ground troops. The pressure to perform had never been greater.

Brand greeted his ground crew and they wished him luck. After completing a thorough pre-flight check, he climbed the ladder and lowered himself into his cockpit, secured his helmet and microphone, carried out his final checks and fired up the engine. As always, the feel of bridled power gave him strength and confidence. He taxied out to the runway threshold with the remainder of Red Section in tow. As he requested clearance for take-off, he noticed a little light in the east as the sun sought to break the day and give them the visibility they would need to fly and fight and kill the enemy that threatened their country.

At New Sarum to bid his pilots and crews farewell was Air Marshal Frank Mussell, the air force commander. General Peter Walls climbed aboard the Dakota from which he would monitor radio traffic and remain in contact with the prime minister on a teleprinter. Ian Smith wanted to be kept informed and would make decisions of a political nature. Of concern was what to do if Mozambique committed troops and armour and how to deal with the MiGs of the Mozambican Air Force if they were scrambled from their base in the port city of Beira.

Darrell Watt stood on the runway smoking a cigarette and looked anxiously skyward, searching for a break in the wet, grey gloom. He knew better than most how critical timing was, and that if the weather was overcast when they reached the target, the operation would probably fail. He tried to hide his concerns, kitted up and chatted briefly to his troops, then ordered them into the waiting Dakota. They moved quietly to their positions on the hard metal bucket-seats that lined the fuselage. Final permission granted, virtually the entire Rhodesian Air Force roared into life while soldiers and airmen strapped themselves in and girded themselves for battle.

The helicopters were airborne first, flying almost due east in waves of five for security reasons. The bush telegraph among the local population was known for the speed at which information was conveyed by word of mouth, and the sight of an aerial armada would trigger a quick response from hostile observers that might be communicated to the enemy in time to warn them of approaching danger.

The Dakotas, laden to the maximum with fuel and heavily equipped men, used up all the distance the runway offered before lumbering slowly aloft. Soon they were all airborne, following carefully selected flight paths to avoid, as best they could, being noticed by too many on the ground.

The further they flew, the more Watt's apprehension deepened. "It was just cloud and more cloud. I could only hope the navigators were on the ball; they certainly had their work cut out for them, and I did not envy them their task."

Breaking the silence in one of the Dakotas, Sam, unable to control himself, started to sing 'Happy, Happy Africa!' which soon caught on and the pilots were treated to a raucous chant to their rear.

At the same time, seated quietly at the controls of his DC-8 was the stocky figure of the old warhorse, Jack Malloch. Headset straddling a balding pate, he listened closely to the radio traffic for any indication that his unauthorised incursion into Mozambique airspace was being challenged. If that happened, he was utterly defenceless against the MiGs; but that, he knew, was the nature of the game.

Squadron Leader Harold Griffiths led the formation of thirty helicopters flying line astern, map-reading his way down the valleys leading to the target. All of a sudden they were in cloud, and his heart must have stopped as he realised that he had to backtrack and map-read a new route to the target area, without losing a second. In a remarkable feat of airmanship, he did just that, handling his controls while reading a 1: 50,000 map in an open cockpit. Behind him was the command chopper, flown by Norman Walsh with Brian Robinson sitting next to him.

Estimating that he was over the target at 07h41, Malloch opened the throttles for maximum power and lowered the flaps to increase the noise factor. The ruse worked. Unseen by him, blinded by cloud, the occupants were on morning parade and the sound of the aircraft triggered an air-raid warning, sending the entire camp scurrying to the trenches and bunkers. Realising soon thereafter that it was a false alarm, they relaxed and returned to their stations, a little warily, but relieved.

THE ATTACK

Approaching the target, paratroopers were pleased to look out of the windows and see Hawker-Hunters and Vampires racing past them.

Red One initially flew at low level, with the pilot navigating to his IP before setting course for the target. At the designated pull-up point, he pulled the stick back until reaching his perch height, when the desperate search for the target began. Through a break in the clouds, Richard Brand was relieved to see the barracks at the westernmost side of the camp, called, "Target visual" and screamed in out of the sun, his four 30mm cannons blazing, before launching two fifty-gallon napalm bombs that cascaded like a blanket of fire over the buildings housing troops convalescing after forays into Rhodesia.

Behind Brand, the second 'Hunter' deposited two 450kg Golf bombs[38] on the headquarters and a third bombed Chitepo College, where 250 ZANLA recruits and staff were about to immerse themselves in a lecture on why Marxism would dominate the world. None would live to learn the truth. Brand and his 'Hunters' had found their mark.

At H-hour, Norman Walsh looked nervously at his watch. Unable to bear the tension, desperate to know if the 'Hunters' had indeed been successful, he broke radio silence.

"Red One, are you on target?" he asked. He waited nervously, then smiled and sighed with relief.

"What a question!" replied Richard Brand in a languid air force drawl.

Following the 'Hunters', the Canberra pilots were overjoyed when they emerged from the clouds into clear sky below. Banking slightly in a shallow dive at low level, they saw a mass of dark faces looking up at them as their bomb doors cranked open and thousands of pounds of high-explosive homemade Alpha[39] bombs thundered down on the target.

The lead bomber carpeted the smoking remains of the convalescent camp and the second did the same on the administrative complex. The third Canberra hit Chaminuka, Mugabe's billet on his visits and also home to 500 Chinese-trained guerrillas. A fourth obliterated Parirenyatwa Camp, with approximately 1,200 trainees in residence.

Waiting quietly, Watt was ready. "I couldn't wait to get out the door; it was a very exciting time."

Ten minutes out, the 'Prepare for action!' command was given by the dispatchers, seatbelts were unfastened and it was time to 'Stand up! Hook up!' and everyone came to their feet. The jumpmaster gave the order to 'Tell off' for equipment checks, starting with 'Twenty OK then all eyes were fixed on the red and green lights above the door. Two bells rang for action stations.

"I was hanging on the static line looking out the door, and it was quite spectacular watching the leading aircraft drop their troops into the battle below," remembered Watt.

Finally, out the door at just over 500 feet Watt looked down. The picture that unfolded before his eyes was "like nothing I had seen before. There were 'terrs' running in every possible direction and plenty of smoke from the bombs. The 'K-Car' cannons were hammering on, blowing buildings and people away. The place was strewn with bodies before we hit the ground and no sooner had we got out of our chutes than we were in the middle of a very heavy engagement."

For Sam, the high-spirited troubadour, the action got off to a rollicking start. "I hit the ground hard and off balance. A 'gook' running at the speed of light smacked straight into me, sending me sprawling, arse over kettle. My rifle was still strapped in behind my shoulder and I couldn't get to it fast enough. I was fumbling behind my reserve chute for my 9mm pistol to shoot him, when Merv Jelliman let fly and smoked him. Merv just looked at me and smiled—gave me that you-owe-me-one look. I felt a real prick. I quickly dusted myself off and tried to look like I knew what I was doing."

For Watt the scene in the camp was a revelation. "My orders were to cut off part of the camp then assault the position. Bruce Fraser was next to me. We just ran into one contact after another. Most of them just ran blindly in complete panic and we could hardly change magazines fast enough to cope with the numbers coming at us. There was no command and control. With thousands of them and less than 200 of us, all they had to do was take up their defensive positions and fight and we would have been in very serious trouble, but they just ran in a confused panic. The assault groups included one machine-gunner for every two rifles, so the Rhodesian firepower was hugely enhanced. With bodies fleeing everywhere our firing had to be disciplined and controlled. I have no idea how many we missed in the long grass and how many more we wounded, but our weapons were boiling hot."

Captain Colin Willis had landed in a tree. While trying to extricate himself from his parachute entangled in the branches, ten ZANLA cadres ran past him on the ground. Grabbing his 9mm pistol, he fired on the group. One man went down with a bullet in his head. The rest were milling around trying to make some sense of it when Willis's sergeant shot them.

Terry's jump into battle had also proved complicated. "We were loaded down with all the ammo we could carry. In our stick of four we had two RPDs and two FNs. It all happened so fast. As we neared the target, the aircraft descended rapidly and the next thing the lights were flashing, I was in the door, then I was airborne and before I knew it, I was hanging from a tree while below me the other blokes were on the ground and getting busy. I eventually released myself but I came out at an angle and almost went head-first into the dirt. I fell hard on my shoulder and the side of my head hit the ground, but I managed to get up. The enemy was everywhere I looked, running in all directions at a furious pace. We fired at them for all we were worth. They were dropping like flies. If they had known how few of us there were, they could have taken us on and won, but they were panicking and there seemed to be no leadership at all to speak of."

Jimmy Swan, a stick commander from 2 Commando RLI, describes a typical encounter: "We went to ground and watched in absolute silence facing the camps we had clearly seen prior to landing. Then it happened as predicted—the bush in front of us opened up and they were running in the crouch. All hell let loose as we fired into them from approximately thirty to fifty metres and they reeled back, shouting and screaming in shock and panic, some firing at us without effect . . . as we took them out with volleys of fire from the gunners and riflemen on both sides of me. All riflemen used the economical but effective double-tap which is accurate and always kills. They started dropping like flies and the bush was alive with movement and screams. The sounds of automatic fire from the MAG gunners and those methodical double-taps from the riflemen filled the air. They tried to run back but they were being annihilated. We threw HE {High explosive} and white phosphorus grenades and it was a massacre. We ran through their position and then went to ground awaiting the next wave. Other 'gooks', hearing their comrades making contact, headed off in another direction and straight into the 2 Commando sticks on the left flank. It was full-on killing."[40]

In desperation, some of the enemy shed their ZANLA uniforms and fled stark naked, hoping that their lack of identification through Rhodesian gun sights would spare them, but they were wrong. All adult males were to be dispatched, no matter how they presented themselves. Mrs Teurai Ropa ('Spill Blood') Nhongo[41] jumped into a pit latrine and submerged herself in human faeces. Quite correctly, she surmised, it was one place in the camp the soldiers would not want to investigate too closely. Others were less creative and paid the price.

Bob MacKenzie, the irrepressible American officer, led his men through innumerable engagements to a point on the edge of a tree line. Seeing a trench complex ahead, they charged and overran it, killing those within. They relieved the dead of their ammunition and recharged their belts and magazines before Robinson ordered them to push on and wipe out the remaining resistance. Moving up a dry riverbed, they found ZANLA men hiding in hastily dug holes. They were flushed out and killed. Then MacKenzie resorted to stealth as he and his men crawled through the long grass towards an anti-aircraft position. The gunners, engrossed with the task at hand, heard and saw nothing until MacKenzie's men opened fire, killing them all. The guns they could not use or plunder were blown up. Then they found the support party, and killed them too.

Moving on to the Intelligence Centre, they found it devoid of life but not loot, and the troops were happy with their bonus of cameras and watches. In one of the lecture rooms lay more than sixty dead, some under the blackboard they had been facing on which Mao's teachings were scrawled. Inside the old farmhouse, they found four prisoners, their hands tied behind their backs, who had been executed earlier that morning. It was a chilling reminder of the type of justice Mugabe's followers would dispense if and when they acquired the power they sought in Rhodesia. Finding a Peugeot station wagon, MacKenzie and men started the car up and jumped aboard to increase their mobility.[42]

Within five minutes of the battle being joined, every aircraft had been holed by ground fire. The command chopper flown by Norman Walsh and carrying Brian Robinson was shot down when a 12.7mm round hit the main rotor. Walsh nursed the stricken craft skilfully to the ground and no one was hurt, but the battle lost direction while he and Robinson were incapacitated. Another helicopter was hastily detailed to recover them and take them back up into the air to continue managing the proceedings.

"This was a very bad planning error on our behalf," Robinson acknowledged. "The ground forces were leaderless for about thirty minutes. That was the last time we made that mistake. From then on, as many as three alternative command aircraft were designated for major operations. It was imperative that the sweep lines be controlled from the air, but fortunately, the stop lines held their positions by coordinating movement using A63 radios and waited for us to get airborne again. It was the longest thirty minutes of my life, during which I cursed myself for making an error that could have had serious consequences."

Choppers landed regularly for fuel and repairs at the admin base, where technicians worked feverishly, and all damaged aircraft were soon back in action again. At one point, an engine hit by a missile was rendered irreparable. Technicians from 7 Squadron effected a complete engine change in the middle of the bush, using two fuel drums as a stepladder. For the enemy, there was to be no relief. Ageing aircraft manned by remarkable pilots and crews, working with some of the most aggressive and best trained bush-fighters in the world, wreaked havoc on an enemy bereft of the will to stand and fight.

In his old Vampire, Steve Kesby's weather worries had dissipated as he closed in on the camp. "We left our IP on time and on pull-up I searched frantically for my target and experienced a huge feeling of relief at finding it exactly as depicted in the photographs. On turning into the attack, I saw vast numbers of 'swastikas' {people on the run, arms and legs flaying, making a 'swastika' profile} bomb-shelling in all directions. I called to my number two to concentrate on the parade square.

"We had been briefed to re-attack from different positions so as to confuse the anti-aircraft gunners. As soon as I had fired my rockets and positioned for a re-attack with the front gun, I heard Phil Haigh report that his aircraft had been hit. I formatted on him climbing through the cloud. Phil said he had a very high jet-pipe temperature. I did a close-formation evaluation of his aircraft but couldn't see anything untoward, so we continued to Salisbury. I crossed back into Rhodesia and informed them we were 'feet dry' but Phil did not check in."[43]

A worried Kesby went down to a lower altitude to look for Haigh and found a pall of smoke where his wingman, trapped in the cockpit, had crashed. The Englishman, who had left the Royal Air Force and the relative safety of his homeland to fight in an unpopular war for Rhodesia, had flown his last mission.

For Terry and his fellow soldiers, the battle continued at a relentless pace. "Trying to conserve ammunition, we fixed bayonets and went at them with steel. As we swept inwards we barely took a step without flushing someone. The firing was constant. There were children in the camp and it was not a pleasant sight. We were careful to let the kids run to whatever safety they could find through our lines and beyond."

After clearing the trenches, his group entered an old barn to clear it of possible hidden dangers. Against one wall there was a large clay pot. It looked pretty innocuous to Terry and he gave it little thought, but another soldier to his left had a hunch and banged off a round into it.

"I shat myself when up popped a female 'terr' like a Jack in the Box," said Terry. "Her eyes were like white saucers and her mouth was open, but she made no sound. Another round was pumped into her head and she dropped back into the pot, gone again as if she had never appeared. I had to shake my head to make sure I wasn't dreaming. Not a very glamorous place to die, I suppose. I sure as hell would never have seen that if I'd stayed on a farm in New Zealand."

There were piles of thatching grass in the barn and, having been told to destroy everything they could not take with them, Terry and the other men torched the structure.

"I couldn't believe my eyes. The enemy came scurrying out of the barn like rats from a sewer. Behind the smoke they looked like grey ghosts in the wind. We shot them through a fiery haze and left them to burn."

Continuing their sweep, Terry went into a larder filled with foodstuffs, the likes of which had not been seen in Rhodesia. "It was a personal blow to see dairy products from New Zealand. It looked like these chaps were much better fed than we were," he remembers.

WATT SHOT

Watt's sweep line moved with determined aggression as they charged, skirmished, ran, stopped, fired, all the while wielding their weapons with lethal precision and leaving piles of bodies in their wake. They swept up to and over the trenches in their path and with a combination of small-arms fire, grenades, bunker bombs and bayonets, cleared them of all life. Swift progress was being made towards their objective when Watt went down.

"We were clearing a series of trenches and I came over a small rise and then ahead a deep, dry riverbed. As I came over the rise I saw this guy aiming at me and then a bullet slammed into my leg. I tried to move but struggled. I kept going a while helping the blokes clear the lines but then I could not carry on and told them I was hit and needed help. They went into the trench and cleaned it out, then a medic came, put a pressure bandage on and a 'casevac' was called."

Sergeant Phil Cripps was leading a 'call sign' under the command of Lieutenant Ken Roberts which landed atop a gentle ridge: "'Terrs' were running through us and seemed to have little desire to fight. We settled in and then started to fire away from the standing position because of the long grass. Not much passed us and if they did they got nailed by the other stop groups. We retained this position for about four hours before we were ordered to advance into the centre of the camp.

"We were going well through open ground when we approached a *donga* {deep ditch} and there was a long burst of automatic fire. We went to ground and I heard on the radio that Trooper Cranswick to my right had been wounded. Later it transpired he had been shot in the chest by a 'terr' in the donga but saved by his chest-webbing.

"Lieutenant Roberts ordered me and my section into the donga to flush and kill the enemy. It was narrow so we were in single file but we cleaned it out and killed eight 'terrs' in the process. We then returned to our position and awaited the 'casevac' of Trooper Cranswick, then continued our advance.

"Coming upon an open *vlei*, Lieutenant Roberts instructed me to take my four men across while the rest covered us. Frans Nel was on my immediate right with an RPD. We were about half way across and I could see a rise in the ground again about 200 meters away. Suddenly a single shot rang out and out of the corner of my eye I saw Frans clutch at his right elbow and fall down. We all went to ground and one of the guys crawled to Frans who was slightly to the rear of me. Single accurate shots continued to be fired at us that pinned us down but I could not determine the direction. I thought Frans had been hit in the arm but when I crawled over I saw he had a wound to the head and was only being kept alive through mouth-to mouth resuscitation. We just had to lie there with accurate incoming fire laying us low but we had to stay with Frans. I then remembered we had been briefed about a sniper-training facility in the camp and concluded these guys firing at us were probably from there. "I realised I would have to sort things out as Lieutenant Roberts informed me he could not see where we were or what was going on. I got on the radio and asked for a 'casevac' but I was informed there was none available right then but one would come as soon as possible. I then asked for a 'K-Car' as by now I was certain the enemy had moved to the rear of us as they continued firing at us. It wasn't long before a 'K-Car' appeared overhead. I was lying on my stomach facing our axis of advance with my map on the ground in front of my face. The map was mainly to indicate to the K- Car pilot and gunner where we were. When he had us visual I told him to 'stonk' {blast} the thickly wooded area about 200 metres to our rear. I remember the pilot questioning this action but I told him to just do it as we were still taking fire from that area. He opened up with a long burst right on target and with that all firing stopped. The 'casevac' took about twenty minutes to come and pick up Frans. We loaded him on but he died soon afterwards.

"Lieutenant Roberts then ordered me to take my section and assault a tented camp in amongst a clump of trees. We charged forward and put down heavy fire. As I was peering into a tent, a shot blasted my eardrums and I thought one of my blokes had loosed off a round at my head but that was not the case. I am certain a sniper was at work and I had been narrowly missed."

Meanwhile a stricken Watt waited patiently until a helicopter flown by Mark McLean landed in a hail of fire. "It was mayhem when the chopper landed and I was tossed inside. We were barely airborne when the chopper seemed to lurch. I heard an explosion and I saw that the pilot was hit. A round went through the Perspex and through his helmet above his eye, leaving a hole. I didn't know if the hole extended into his brain or not. If it did, we were obviously done for.

"Fortunately, he was merely stunned and I watched him closely as he fought to regain his senses and control of the aircraft. For a brief while, I was convinced we were going in but he did a great job of landing. Another helicopter came to pick me up and we managed to make it back to Rhodesia, where the doctors were waiting. For me the war was over for the moment, but I knew we had won the day and that was a great relief."

At dusk, an SAS trooper scaled a tree and raised the 'Green and White,' the flag of Rhodesia, amid cheers from tired soldiers. The day was theirs; the biggest battle in the history of the bush war had been won in spectacular style. With darkness upon them, some troops were assigned to lay ambushes and others to move gingerly through the night in search of stragglers. Sporadic contacts took place and tracer regularly lit up the sky.

Radio intercepts indicated 3,500 dead and approximately the same number wounded. The Rhodesians had lost one soldier and one pilot. It was a feat of epic military proportions, possibly unequalled in history. Never before had so few battled so many. On the ground, less than 200 had taken on 10,000, and scored a decisive victory. When news of the routing of Chimoio reached Mugabe, he reportedly came close to throwing in the towel. Commiserating with his close confidant Edgar Tekere, he confessed he was "beginning to wonder if this armed struggle is worth pursuing."[44]

In a letter to The Times following the raid retired British General Sir Walter Walker wrote of the Rhodesian Army: "Their army cannot be defeated in the field either by terrorists or even a much more sophisticated enemy. In my professional judgement based on more than twenty years' experience from lieutenant to general, of counter-insurgency and guerrilla type operations, there is no doubt that Rhodesia now has the most professional and battle-worthy army in the world for this particular type of warfare."

CHAPTER 8

People talk
Of the gulf between our races
Which must be crossed
To mend these times of ours.
What gulf? By now
The community must be rare
Where families have not mourned.
—CHAS LOTTER

THE MADNESS CONTINUES

War-weary men, missing their dead and wounded, arrived back at New Sarum in time for a hot meal and a wash, then they replenished their stocks of ammunition, replaced grenades, flares and bunker bombs, filled water bottles, drew rations, checked radios, cleaned their weapons. With meticulous diligence they stripped them down, checked the components for wear and tear, oiled the smallest details, then reassembled, checked the actions to make sure they were smooth and fluid. They knew that if the breechblock failed to move, first backwards in response to expended gas from discharged rounds, then forward to drive the firing pin into the next cartridge case, the tool that gave them life, purchased with the lives of others, would be useless in their hands and death would come knocking. It was their metallic, mechanical link to life.

Orders were given. There was bad news and good news.

The morning would see them going a lot farther into the heartland of the enemy, making insertion and extraction riskier and difficult, but when they arrived there the odds were better. Intelligence estimated an enemy force of only six thousand. For the pilots and their crews, the attack would demand every ounce of stamina and skill they could muster; for the old machines they flew they could only hope they would stay the course.

There was nothing more to do. Beers were brought into the hangars in crates and although tired no one could rest. Cricket bats and a ball were found, beer crates were turned into wickets and teams picked. Hours away from the fields of slaughter the contrast was not lost on them. Gone was the clatter of machine guns, here was the light crack of leather on wood, laughter, banter, good cheer. The smell of freshly cut grass softened the psyche of men with the smell of dead flesh and stinking entrails fresh on their senses. From whence they had recently returned, violent death or disfigurement, mutilated bodies; here the worst that could happen was a lost wicket or banishment to fine leg for bad bowling, a round of beers for a dropped catch—a sublime, surreal transition from the agony of war to the joy of the gentle game. Being healthy and alive had never felt so good.

When bad light stopped play and the rays of a sinking sun cast a crimson light on the waiting helicopters, soldiers sat on the grass outside the hangars, cooled to a brisk winter breeze from the east and bade silent farewell to their friend Frans Nel. He would be avenged in the morning.

The plan for Tembué was principally the same: airstrikes followed by six 'Paradaks' dumping paratroopers augmented by over forty heli-borne RLI commandos. But the distances were daunting and the first stop would be at Mtoko near the Mozambican border. Then it was on to Tembué 225 kilometres away. The choppers would refuel at a prepositioned admin base on the range of mountains south of Lake Cabora Bassa known to the troops and airmen as 'The Train,' so called because when viewed from afar it had the appearance of a train complete with loco in front steaming off into the distance.

The problem for the planners once they arrived there was that reconnaissance reports indicated the camp regimen involved muster parade in the dark at 04h30, after which the inmates dispersed, denying the attackers the opportunity of catching the enemy concentrated on the square. Of even more concern to the planners was the fear of early warning. Did they know the Rhodesians were coming?

Incredibly, Tembué was just as ill-prepared as 'New Farm' had been. The 'Hunter' pilots dived onto an unsuspecting mass of humanity. The first to die heard nothing. The survivors heard the thunder of the bombs and the blast of the rockets, then the clatter of 30mm cannons, the strikes sending dust and sand flying all around them. Running into the trees to escape, they caught sight of green parachutes landing.

One SAS man made it to the killing fields but only by the grace of God. After a count to four on exit, he saw his parachute billowing like an overstuffed bra. By the time he pulled his reserve he was convinced it was too late and resigned himself to a bone-crushing end when he felt his body snap violently to a halt, saw his feet hanging above the ground and looked above in relieved wonderment: his parachute was snagged on the lower branches of a stout tree; his prophecy of doom had been misplaced, he was intact and ready for action. His only problem was that having fallen faster and straighter than anyone else he arrived on the ground first, very much alone and in a different alignment to his stick. Severing his lines, he was quickly into action and feasting his shooting eye on targets that were running at terrific speeds through the woodland. Johnstone's 'Jungle Lane' training kicked in. Estimating speed and distance, he led the fleeing figures of the enemy precisely and dropped the targets as they came to him.

Men swept through flushing and shooting in a rhythm that took on a lethal momentum all of its own. Moving swiftly, they kept the momentum, giving the enemy no relief and no chance to stand and fight. Supporting them low overhead were the 'K-Cars', their 20mm cannons providing a thumping staccato over the whine of the turbines, a reassuring sound that comforted the men on the ground.

MacKenzie, commanding A Squadron, slowed in a gully as a sense of danger unseen cautioned him. A stone rattled down a cliff face and he looked up to see six of the enemy waiting in ambush. In a flash he brought his AR 15 to bear from the hip and gunned them down as their bodies rolled noisily down the cliff face and came to rest at his feet.

Proceeding further into another gully, the four-man stick walked into scores of men fleeing in all directions. Two of the SAS men carried RPDs and they knew how to use them. The quartet consolidated in a back-to-back huddle covering a 360° radius and poured fire into an enemy that was panic-stricken and shocked into a state of almost pathetic disorder. All that limited their killing ability was the need to change belts and magazines. When they were finished ammo, barrels were burning and bodies were strewn all around them.

But for ZANLA more hardship would follow. Special Branch officers were quickly onto the prisoners who revealed the location of another base thirty kilometres north to which a thousand of their number had been moved the day before. Walsh immediately ordered the Canberras back in Salisbury to be armed with Alpha bombs and just before sunset they made direct hits on the target.

Spirits were high in the morning as the troops prepared for uplift and home but the weather was poor en route and progress was slow. The distance meant the helicopters had to refuel twice before the border and it was late afternoon when they crossed, too late to make it to Salisbury so the pilots decided to land at Mount Darwin.

There, congregating in the local country club was what remained of the Mount Darwin farming community with wives and in some cases their small children. Many of their number had been killed on their farms and in their houses by the terrorists over the previous three years and life had become a dangerous day-to-day existence. The news of success across the border brought them great cheer.

One of the first to condemn the raids was David Owen. "A savage and pretty brutal attack," he said, "which threatened peace and security in southern Africa." The truth was the Rhodesian strike probably did not sit well with his plans: the side he was backing had taken a terrible beating.

In Salisbury the following day a drained soldier finally complained to the troop medic about a pain in his neck that refused to ease. He was sent to the consulting rooms of Mike Standish-White {Uncle of SAS soldier Andrew Standish-White} an orthopaedic surgeon of considerable renown who had, throughout the war, provided selfless service to wounded warriors. Arriving at the rooms, Terry was put under an X-ray then told to go and take a seat in the waiting room. Minding his own business there, he was startled by the shouts of a sister hastening towards the awaiting patients loudly calling his name.

When he raised his arm in some alarm she shouted to him: "Sit still, sit still! Don't move!" Then she told him he had broken his neck on falling out the tree at 'New Farm' on the first day of the fighting.

WATT TO BOTSWANA

Once over his injuries, Watt was soon back in the fight. "In February 1978 Special Branch passed information to us of a growing ZIPRA presence at a camp in Botswana not far from Kazungula. Mike Howard, a Special Branch officer, was driving along the Botswanan border fence with our SAS doctor, John Topping, when he was ambushed by a group of ZIPRA. One leg was smashed but he kept driving and came through, saving both their lives. I was sent in to find the enemy camp it and recce it. I found tracks and had no problem getting into an area where I suspected there was enemy activity. We lay low for two days watching people move about when suddenly about twenty men in uniform appeared and we knew the camp was close by. Moving in closer, I gathered the information we needed and returned to Rhodesia.

"The captain in charge had orders to attack the camp but with a very clear instruction to use all possible means to avoid inflicting casualties on members of the BDF {Botswana Defence Force}. The Botswana government was trying hard to stay out of the Rhodesian conflict in the face of pressure to be more involved from Zambia and Mozambique, and Ian Smith did not want to antagonise them which was very understandable.

"I led the assault group back into Botswana and positioned the men on some high ground before the captain and I went in closer. Watching the area of the camp through binoculars, we noted BDF trucks arriving and they began loading the ZIPRA men. The order to prepare to attack was given. I protested loudly, warning the captain that we would be disobeying orders because we risked harming BDF personnel. He refused to listen, reminded me that he was the senior officer and we returned to where the main party waited. He then ordered the attack to commence. The assault was a complete success from a military point of view but it had severe political consequences. Botswana closed their border at Kazungula and the matter was referred to the United Nations."

DOMESTIC PROBLEMS

"By this time there were some real problems in the SAS. From 1977 onwards bad blood crept into the regiment with the growing number of foreigners," recalls Watt. "The Rhodesians did not always mix well with them and dangerous divisions were emerging. This was a pity because there were some excellent British and American soldiers and we had enough problems without fighting amongst ourselves. The problem was made worse by the suspicion that some of the foreign soldiers may have been placed there by foreign intelligence services. This is one of the reasons why Grahame Wilson drew most of his operators from the ranks of the born-and-bred Rhodesians. They became known as 'The Club Tomorrow Gang,' after the Salisbury nightclub, and they were a very good outfit."

"I did not feel the Squadron commanders were doing enough to suppress the internal dissent and went to see our commanding officer, Colonel Barrett," remembers Watt. "I always felt comfortable with him because we had known each other for a very long time. Aged five we used to play Cowboys and Indians together in Gatooma. He listened carefully, acknowledged the problem and assured me he would deal with the issue. Unfortunately, the problem was never really resolved and it caused a great deal of unhappiness. Eventually most of the men from the UK left the Squadron and went to Special Branch to work under Mac McGuinness. I was sorry to see them go.

"Just who was passing information to the enemy remains unknown to me," says Watt. "After a series of externals, I was summoned to a meeting in Kariba by senior officers. I was surprised to hear that I was accused of carrying out missions without authority. I flatly denied the charges, telling them that I had sent details of my daily plans in my daily 'sitrep' {situation report} to HQ but this was not readily accepted and the signaller who should have received my messages was summoned and asked to produce all the relevant 'sitreps.' When they looked they discovered I was right but then noted that I had deleted the Special Branch commander and the representative officer at 'ComOps' from the list of intended recipients. I was told this was unacceptable and I was asked to explain myself. Bluntly I told them that I had done so because I believed our command echelon was riddled with spies. This raised eyebrow but no rebuttal: there was just a silence. Subsequently I noted my precedent was followed in the field by other officers. The fact that we never got to grips with who the traitors were was one of our biggest failures."*

---

* On the vexed issue regarding which government CIO boss Ken Flower was serving, former Foreign Secretary David Owen threw some light on the subject in an interview with Mike Thomson of 'Radio 4' where the subject of discussion was a search for an answer to the question as to who had forewarned Joshua Nkomo of the SAS raiding party that was coming to kill him in Lusaka in April 1979. Thomson reported that days after the raid, David Stephen, an aide to Foreign Secretary David Owen, penned the following note to the Foreign and Commonwealth Office.

"Dr Owen told me this morning that he has been considering how to respond to Mr Nkomo's request that Dr Owen's request to Mr Nkomo should be made public. Dr Owen sees difficulties in such a course of action."

So what message had Dr. Owen, sent to Nkomo? More than 30 years later, this was his answer:

"I think it was connected to whether or not we had tipped him off about an assassination attempt. It seems to be a pretty sensible thing, a pretty clear link. I think he {Nkomo} wanted to put a spin on it as our favourite candidate." Owen goes on to add, "The head of Rhodesian Intelligence, Ken Flowers (sic),

CAMP ON THE ZAMBEZI

"In March 1978 we attacked a ZIPRA base in south-eastern Zambia," remembers Roger. Having finished school he was selected for an officer cadet course when he asked to be excused and given an opportunity to test for the SAS. "I was very anxious to get into action. I did not know it then but I was not to be disappointed.

"I was still new to the SAS at this stage and keen to prove myself. My first operation had been horrible. Our troop had been sent in to the Russian Front to cause chaos and we ended up in a friendly-fire incident in which American Sergeant Dick Biederman was killed. I was the fresh *poes* straight out of Training Troop and still trying to earn my colours so I was told to look after the body. This involved strapping the corpse high in a tree away from the ants. Choppers only came days later by which time the body was in a bad way. We still had some big punch-ups there and in one Gerry de Lange loosed off too many RPG-7s, bursting both his eardrums. I remember seeing blood coming out both sides of his head and I thought he had been shot. Eventually we were pulled out but our chopper was shot down and crash-landed. Luckily the 'gooks' never came looking for us and a new chopper gearbox was delivered the next day and we made it back to safety."

Another new arrival in the SAS at this time was South African Mike West who had come from the RLI. "Every young man who joined the Rhodesian Army had visions of glory, of charging into battle with guns blazing and destroying the enemy. This dream became a reality when I joined 2 Commando RLI and fought alongside some of the bravest young men who gave their all and often their lives to protect their beloved country. Fire Force was the name of the game and battle-hardened

---

was also on our side. So I was well aware of what Ken Flowers was claiming was being done, and I used to read the reports."

Asked by Thomson if he would have stopped the killing of Mugabe and Nkomo, Owen is forthright: "Yes because it was not justified . . . we believed in what Robert Mugabe and Joshua Nkomo were fighting for."

The Foreign Office quickly condemned the attack as a 'major and deplorable step' and Robin Renwick, then a member of the Foreign Office team working on the Rhodesian conflict adds: "We did at the time have a colleague in Lusaka who was in almost daily contact with Nkomo, and a colleague in Mozambique who was in daily contact with the Zanu leadership too," he said.

Peter Petter-Bowyer told Thomson in the same radio programme about a meeting he had years later with Zipra commanders Dumiso Dabengwa and Lookout Masuku who indicated Nkomo was tipped off only an hour before the SAS arrived and by none other than Zambian President Kenneth Kaunda himself. According to Petter-Bowyer, this information could only have come from someone very intimately involved with the operation who knew the 'Kermit' code-words.

Choppers ready for raid into Mozambique.

Dave Berry
(right) with
Renamo
trainees.

Lt. André Scheepers and 'Chunkie' Chesterman in Mozambique.

Pensive troops ready for battle.

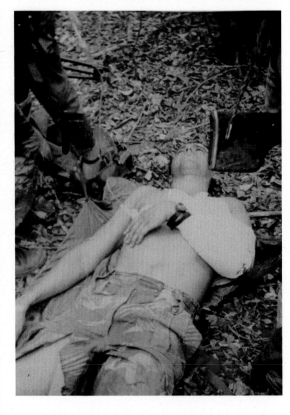

Scheepers wounded.

Watt (far right) on the firing range.

Watt (seated centre) ready to deploy.

Watt's men in southern Mozambique.

Scheepers about to be awarded
'Wings on Chest' by General Maclean.

Mike West (right) after Mozambique resupply.

Green Leader, Chris Dixon (3rd from right) and his navigator Mike Ronne (2nd left)—two fearless flyers who caused havoc in enemy ranks.

André Scheepers (second from left) looks on anxiously as Rob Johnstone (2nd from right) and Garth Barrett (far right) study a map before a long range reconnaissance mission.

Darrell Watt's headquarters in southern Mozambique.

An exhausted Scheepers prepares to enter the trenches at Mapai.

Below: Watt (2nd from left) and a Super Frelon from the South African Air Force before camp attack.

Choppers on their way to Barragem.

Below: Luke Muhlangu (centre) at flag raising; earned the respect of his SAS allies.

Scheepers (at right) preparing for Mozambique deployment.

Below: SAS prowl the streets of Salisbury looking for the trouble that never came.

Watt's men before bridge-blowing operation

5 RUSSIAN OFFICERS DIE IN CLASH

Anti-Frelimo success in Mozambique

By AIDA PARKER

THE USSR has suffered its first military casualties in Southern Africa.

In a face-to-face firefight with anti-Frelimo forces near Metuchira (district of Nampula), five senior Russian officers were recently shot and the bodies burnt in the vehicle in which they had been travelling.

This is the latest known incident in a rapidly deteriorating internal security situation in Central Mozambique, where intelligence reports indicate that more than 50 percent of the population now supports anti-Frelimo resistance movements.

Both the Russians and the Machel Government have gone to extraordinary lengths to keep the Metuchira incident under wraps.

It is now known, however, that the bodies of the dead Russians were air-freighted to Moscow by Aeroflot from Maputo Airport on July 7th.

The fatal shootout has caused intense concern in the Russian and Eastern Bloc forces now stationed in Mozambique. The resident Russian Ambassador has stoned all senior Russian officials throughout the territory to Maputo for discussions on security arrangements and the increasing strength of the resistance movement on July 26.

Cotton

According to reports leaking back from Mozambique, the incident occurred when sugar field workers were instructed to help with the reaping of cotton.

Local cadres of the Mozambique National Resistance advised the workers to tell Frelimo to do it themselves.

[handwritten note:] A. Scorra — Russians definitely have increased enemies wherever they move in Moz. CW 01 Aug

Scheepers makes the press.

Consecration service at the wreckage of the 2nd Air Rhodesia Viscount airliner shot down by Zipra.

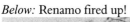

Below: Renamo fired up!

SAS men resting after attack on Barragem.

Below: SAS men and their Renamo allies.

Watt (left) with Renamo leader Luke Muhlangu.

Below: Final ceremony; the end of the Rhodesian SAS

young men were routinely dropped at low altitude from the old Daks. Those chutes could not be steered so we went with the wind and often crashed hard into trees, thorn bushes and rocks. On one occasion I landed so hard I snapped the butt off my machine gun. The 'gooks' were pouring fire onto us and the cordite smelled strong in the air but we managed to get into a skirmish line and attack them with help from the choppers. We were too aggressive and they panicked and we nailed them. Only afterwards, when the adrenaline had settled, did I realise that I had been firing my gun by holding the pistol grip and bipods. Everything I hoped for had become a reality but I wanted more so I went to the SAS.

"I left a fantastic fighting unit to join an even better one. I thought I was tough but that selection was pure torture but I wanted that beret so badly I was ready to go to hell and back for it and I did. The SAS turned out to be everything I'd hoped for and more. Just when I thought I had done everything that a man can do in combat, Darrell Watt arrived and I was in another world. He was in a league all of his own and with him in command, I felt we were utterly invincible."

"The ZIPRA camp was large and A and B Troops went in with the RLI," recalls Roger. "Over forty of the enemy were killed but our 'call sign' found the biggest arms cache I ever saw. It was the first time we found heat seeking missiles so it was quite an event. RLI engineers blew it and it was the loudest bang I ever heard.

"We were in an extended line when we encountered an early warning post," remembers West. "We leopard-crawled forward and one of the 'gooks' was taking a dump on an ant mound. He became suspicious and pulled up his pants and moved towards us, AK at the ready. We remained very still hoping he wouldn't see us and return to his original position as shooting him would alert the 'gooks' in the base and they would gap it. We dropped him with one shot and we immediately moved at a half-running pace to engage the 'gooks'. There was one hell of a commotion and they were hightailing it in the opposite direction but as we were firing at such a rate they were dropping like flies. Those that escaped our assault were cut down by stop groups. In the base we found tents with medical supplies from Switzerland and other European countries which made us realise that our enemies were scattered worldwide."

"Chris Schulenburg had done the recce with Martin Chikondo," says Roger. "I talked to him afterwards and he showed us the ant bear hole he had been living in for two weeks while watching the camp. It was right inside the perimeter.

Unfortunately, the camp was very spread out so many of the enemy escaped and we were told to form a stay-behind party to catch them if they came back.

"We went to a feeder road. Steve Donnelly and I were told to man the one early-warning position. Two days later, sitting at our post I saw Steve's eyes widen. He said, 'Roger, they're coming straight for us, off the road, but if I move they'll see me.'

"I managed to slither round a tree and reverse position. Just in time because they were then upon us and I opened up, killing three of them. The rest ran. Then it was quiet and we assumed we had scared them off when the same situation unfolded, except this time it was I who saw them and too late to move without being seen. I told Steve they were coming again and he did what I had just done and opened up, killing another three. Incredibly they had walked right past the bodies of the ones we had shot earlier."

"It was crazy," recalls Mike West. "We kept ducking and diving and nailing the 'gooks' sneaking back to either loot or collect their gear they'd left behind. We were positioned on a hill and from there we were sent down in pairs to wipe them out. On one occasion we dropped two 'terrs' in long grass. It turned out they were carrying a wounded guy on a stretcher but the wounded bloke hit the ground running and gapped it to safety like an Olympic sprinter."

INTERNAL SETTLEMENT

Meantime there had been political developments. Having despaired of an accommodation with the rest of the world following the Geneva debacle, Smith set about finding what would later become known as the 'Internal Settlement." Reaching out to leaders on the black political landscape who shared his desire to find a solution to the country's troubles, he attracted all the main players bar the leaders of the Patriotic Front. In March 1978 a deal was announced which included Bishop Muzorewa's ANC, Ndabaningi Sithole's local ZANU (not to be confused with Mugabe's external ZANU [PF]) and Senator Chief Chirau as head of the traditional leaders. Henceforth the country would be run by a governing council. Each faction would be permitted appointees. It was swiftly condemned by the United Nations and recognised by no country, but it was hoped it would be a new political beginning that would eventually lead to a lessening of internal tensions and reduction in violence.

RENAMO RISES

With efforts to create an effective armed resistance within Mozambique continuing, fortune had struck with the arrival in Rhodesian hands of the charismatic figure of one André Matsangaissa in October 1976. A former FRELIMO officer who had distinguished himself in the fight against the Portuguese, disillusionment had set in with the excesses of the Machel administration. Matsangaissa had made his feelings known and been incarcerated. After managing to escape from Sacuze re-education camp, he was on the run and Rhodesia offered sanctuary.

Deeply suspicious of him at first the CIO debriefers eventually warmed to the man and his story was music to their ears. He confirmed the fact that there was massive political dissent in Mozambique and that the populace would respond positively to, and be supportive of, an armed resistance movement. The question was how to raise a viable fighting force and Matsangaissa had the answer: he planned to sack Sacuze and return the inmates to Rhodesia to form the new army. When the young rebel told his mentors he would do this with three men they were incredulous but he was as good as his word.

The first effort failed but on the second attempt he successfully freed over fifty prisoners and brought them back to what became known as the 'Funny Farm,' the CIO-run secret base on an abandoned farm in the Odzi area close to the town of Umtali. The Rhodesians sensed they had found a man of steel and they were right. It was May 1977, a new phase in the war had begun and RENAMO was about to make an impression.

The initial RENAMO operations were of a short-range hit-and-run nature, with the rebels making sporadic attacks and sabotaging lines of communication while trying to attract recruits to return with them to Rhodesia. In this they were moderately successful and by the middle of 1978 the operational zone grew to include parts of Sofala Province and successful attacks took place on the Beira–Umtali railway line but the real impact was to be made later in the year following the establishment of camps in Mozambique with a small but potent permanent SAS presence.

MURDER MOST FOUL

On 23 June the country was shocked by the chilling news of the slaughter of eight British missionaries and four of their children at Elim Mission in the Eastern Highlands close to the Mozambican border. Formerly an elite private facility for boys known as Eagle School, the mission lay in a setting of mountainous magnificence.

On that cold winter's night, shrouded in low cloud and light rain, the killers had emerged from their forest lair and roused the African children from their dormitories. While half the group harangued them, telling them that the school must close because the fees were being used to support the racist government, the rest of the group dragged the terrified whites from their bedrooms.

The youngest victim was three-week-old Pamela Lynn. She was found wearing her white smock with large sock-shoes; a bayonet had been rammed through the side of her head. Her left hand was raised, frozen in a fist. Her mother Joyce lay next to her, her head pulped, her arm around her child in a last vain attempt to hold her safe. Alongside them lay another child, her face disfigured by the pounding of heavy boots which had left their prints on what had been a pretty face. Catherine Picken, a survivor of the 1960s Congo massacres, lay with a long-handled axe embedded in her head, her blood-stained curlers splayed out next to her. Two women and two children, one in pink pyjamas, the other in a floral nightdress, lay in a huddle next to what had been the cricket pavilion. They had all been raped then bayoneted to death. Reverend Evans, his face split with an axe, lay face down, his hands tied behind his back.

Sadly, it was revealed that only days before, an army officer from 3 Brigade in Umtali had come to the mission to convey his concerns for the safety of the missionaries and their children but had been impolitely rebuffed. He was told that they had no problems with the guerrillas and that the sentiment was a mutual one.

Challenged by Conservative MPs in the Commons to comment on the atrocity, Dr Owen was resolute in his refusal to condemn the perpetrators before railing against the intransigence of the white Rhodesians and hinting strongly that the Selous Scouts were the possible culprits. Few observers were surprised by Owen's position; after all, the people who had committed the murders were the same people he was calling for the Rhodesian government and people to surrender to.

Recent revelations explain why. Minutes from a cabinet meeting on 29 June of that year record Owen saying: "It seemed more probable that those responsible were guerrilla fighters who were out of control. Whoever they were they had evidently gone to ground in the country and had not fled across the border. But it was in any case not possible to place responsibility on Mr Mugabe as many people in the House of Commons had wanted him to do."[45]

On 11 August two opposition Conservative MPs were taken to Grand Reef Forward Air Field and shown the bodies of two dead ZANLA men. A diary with a detailed account of their involvement in the atrocity along with a list of looted property was exhibited. "We killed twelve whites," it read, "including four babies, as remembrance of Nyadzonia, Chimoio, Tembwe [Tembué] and in Zimbabwe massacres (sic)."[46] This evidence failed to evince any comment from Owen who had, by this time, gone quiet.

BACK TO TEMBUÉ

"We heard that there was the possibility of another big camp attack happening and there was quite a lot of excitement about it but details were vague," remembers Watt. "Then I heard it was a camp in Mozambique and there were a few thousand ZANLA there that we would be sent to take out." To do the reconnaissance two pairs of Selous Scouts including Chris Schulenburg were para dropped to two positions north and west of the camp on 10 July. The target area was widely scattered and with a time frame imposed, the Scouts were under pressure to complete the task timeously. Schulenburg then split from his partner Martin Chikondo as was his wont. Initial estimates of the enemy numbers were disappointing and the attack was delayed. Three weeks later a decision was finally taken to attack but plans went awry following communications problems and most of the paratroopers were dropped off target.[47]

Gavin remembers the disappointing aftermath: "It was as big as the previous Tembué raid but after all the hype it was a bit of lemon, a waste of time. We were expecting more 'gooks' there than there had been at Chimoio but there could not have been more than a few hundred and there were a lot of pissed-off people. Darrell was angry and we were watching from our stop position when Schulie emerged from his hideout prior to him being choppered home. Darrell had words with him but I'm not sure what was said.

"A decision was then made for our group under Darrell to stay behind and attack when they came back to try and regroup. After all the rest were flown home they brought in Bergens for us with seven days' rations. We did not know it then but we were in for the time of our lives.

"We loaded up and Darrell immediately marched us to the top of an inselberg while anti-tracking the whole way. Every night thereafter we would ambush the paths and roads at night and watch them from the mountains by day. Incredibly, the enemy were always behind us and could never catch up because we kept moving and anti-tracking. But all this time we were really anxious because the whole Squadron went back to Salisbury so we had nobody within striking distance to help us if we got into trouble. This was the deepest penetration most of us had ever done and we knew no chopper could get to us without a refuelling station and the last-used refuelling station had been packed up, so we knew if we got in the shit it would be days before they got to us. I remember Darrell was talking direct to someone outside of SAS HQ and was getting orders from him which worried us all because we were well aware we were out on a limb trying to make the most of their mess.

"Then we were told to make the seven days' rations last ten, but only received this order on day four, so we had already eaten more than we should have and had to stretch three to six. Then they told us to stretch it to fourteen days so we were fucking starving all the time. As it turned out, over the following weeks only a handful of ZANLA showed up but a battalion of FRELIMO came hunting us. They seemed to know we were there and were determined to find us but thanks to Darrell they really never even came close."

"We had been waiting and hiding for about ten days and I think the 'gooks' must have thought we'd left because a big vehicle convoy suddenly arrived at night," remembers Watt. "I signalled Salisbury and at first light 'Hunters' arrived to bomb the column and they were right on target but by this time the enemy were very spread out and the jets had to keep running in and strafing targets. I had hoped they would be able to do a big single hit. But there was total panic and the 'gooks' ran like hell into the bush. I don't know how many were killed and wounded. We could see the survivors running from the hill. I waited a while then said to the guys, 'Let's go down and have a look.'"

"I'll never forget going down that mountain," remembers Gavin. "We got to one of the abandoned trucks amid the carnage from the airstrike and found it stuffed with imported food. There was canned Dutch chocolate milk, canned pear juice, hams from Denmark, sardines from Portugal and we were starving. We could not hold back and launched ourselves at this food but our stomachs went into shock I think and I immediately commenced vomiting: our stomachs couldn't deal with it. Mike West, our big man from South Africa, always looking for loot, took a big toolbox with state-of-the-art spanners and sockets which he later sold in Salisbury for money for his daughter."

"I said to my guys that these 'gooks' are also hungry and they are not going to be able to resist this; they're going to come back," remembers Darrell. "We put two landmines under the food and set a trip-switch then put everything back nicely and closed the doors. All the other undamaged vehicles we placed charges on then went back to our mountain to watch. Sure enough, the next day, they started to appear out the bush, moving very cautiously at first on foot. Then when it looked safe enough to them they brought in vehicles and parked near the food-truck ready to start loading. They were obviously very hungry. I said, 'OK, sit back and watch the show.'

"Quite a few boxes came out and all was quiet when I became concerned. I asked the bloke who laid the charges if he had done it right and he said, 'Oh yes, sir, don't worry.' No sooner had he finished speaking than there was the most incredible explosion and stuff was flying everywhere. I thought I could actually see the shockwaves such was the power of the blast. I don't know how many were killed because they had been crowded around. We went down to look later. There were bones, blood and meat everywhere. Even in the trees there was meat hanging from branches."

"It was the most incredible time," remembers Gavin "We also booby trapped bodies then mined the roads. We sat on the inselberg watching their vehicles detonate the mines. By the time delay from when we saw the smoke from the mines detonating to the time it took for the sound to reach us, we realised how high and far Darrell had moved us.

"One of my best memories of Darrell during this time was taking over OP watch from him one evening on the mountain. He was sitting quietly on a rock watching the sun go down. The view was stunning; we could see forever. I sat down and instead of him going back into cover to take his rest he seemed to want to talk. He told me it had just occurred to him that he had been on this mountain ten year previously when he was attached to the Portuguese Army. I thought about how much he had seen and done and it made a massive impression on me. Then he went quiet again and we both watched a black-breasted snake eagle flying right by us. It was a surreal feeling: all was so quiet, peaceful and pretty with Darrell reminiscing, and knowing that that night we were going to go back down that fucking mountain and lay more mines while trying to avoid being killed by all the fucking 'Freds' {FRELIMO} and ZANLA 'gooks' that were crawling all over the place trying to find us. Darrell was such a machine and I was in such awe of him; it was nice to know he had feelings and thoughts like the rest of us lesser mortals.

"'ComOps' kept telling us we were going home and then postponed it. When they finally did come to uplift us we'd been running around that fucking country for almost a month and our uniforms were shredded, leaving us with really not much more than our webbing and packs and our dicks hanging out. Naked and starved, covered in black polish, we were a stinking mess concealed in a ring around the landing zone. When the first chopper came in our spirits soared; we were finally going home. I was with John Barry and Taffy Morgan when we ran out to get in the chopper but when the pilot saw us he shat himself and started to take off again because he thought we were 'gooks'. We nearly burst into tears and screamed at him to come back. We had to refuel twice before we got back to the Rhodesian border.

"After we landed we were loaded onto a Dakota and flown back to Salisbury, cussing our peers all the way. We were so fucked we didn't go to town that night and that never happened when we came back to town.

"For all of us who stayed behind on that operation it was the toughest time of all our days in the SAS. It was fucking scary and fucking tiring and thank fuck Darrell was in charge because if it had been anybody else I firmly believe we would have all been killed. I think the decision to leave us behind was the Brass trying to salvage something from their cock-up. The only reason we did the damage we did and survived was because of Darrell. He was aggressive but so careful and skilled we were probably never in very much danger. He was the perfect man for that particular job; everything he made us do was for a reason and he never made us do anything he didn't do himself. I don't ever remember seeing him look like he was worried or scared or lost. Most of us 'troopies' never got to know Darrell because he talked so little which is why I'll never forget our chat on the mountain and my chance to get to know him a little better."

CHAPTER 9

Turn back the years.
Pick through the bones
We left behind
Examine our few remains
In vain
The search is useless.
For the raw, rich stuff of life
Has long since fled us.
—CHAS LOTTER

MONKEY BUSINESS

In June 1978 Brian Robinson handed over command of the regiment to Lieutenant-Colonel Garth Barrett. "Commanding C Squadron was the high point of my life," writes Robinson. "Popularity was never my strong suit. In fact, after I was involved in a near fatal aircraft accident, it was rumoured that I had visibly raised the morale of the men until they realised I had survived."[48]

By July 1978 C Squadron Rhodesian SAS had its own home at a converted tobacco research station which was named Kabrit Barracks after the small town outside Cairo where the SAS first housed itself during the Second World War. Conveniently close to New Sarum Air Base, the new facilities were positively salubrious compared to Cranborne and the change enhanced an already powerful esprit de corps but problems loomed.

"Our base, if set on a beach, would have been one of the best holiday resorts in the world," remembers Johan Bezuidenhout. "We had an all-ranks' pub made out of thatch and stone, serving every drink known to man. There was a large fireplace which separated the bar from the lounge. Facing north was our pool and then the dam which provided a lovely view.

"Being soldiers who travelled to all sorts of wild places, we inherited a few animals that needed a home and brought them to our barracks. We had Enoch the baboon, Stripes the zebra, 'Torty' and Billy the two warthogs and Jack and Jill the two goats. Despite not having much in common, these six formed a close family and would wander around the base in file led by Enoch who had assumed command and who would go up and down the line pinching those who lagged behind or broke ranks. The order of march was disciplined; Stripes behind Enoch, trailed by the warthogs and then the goats.

"At exactly 4 p.m., pub opening time, Enoch and his gang would form up outside the bar at their respective saucers and Chapunza the barman would pour them their daily tipple of Castle beer and they would relax a while. Then soon as the pub door opened Enoch would swagger in and take his stool in the corner and mutter a few grunts which became louder if he was ignored or if the beer didn't flow fast enough. Then he would sit quietly with his hand under his chin watching us making fools of ourselves. Eventually drowsiness would set in and his hand would slip from under his chin which annoyed him and he would slap it with the other hand before placing it firmly back where it was supposed to be. But eventually he would fall asleep and there would be a thud as he hit the floor. This did not even cause him to blink and we would put him to sleep for the night on one of the couches.

"Early morning Enoch would be found under a tree holding his head battling a hangover along with the rest of us. This was always a bad time to go near; if you did he would scream and attack but then become friendlier during the day.

"One day Billy Heyns had been given extras for being late for parade by Snake Allen, our RSM. Billy was pissed off with Snake because he had just been to DB {Detention Barracks} for having had an AD {accidental discharge}.

"Snake by this time had a new office made out of wood which he was very proud of and nobody was allowed near the place. Billy wanted revenge so he put carrots in Snake's office, took Stripes inside and closed the door. Then he dashed off to the pub where Enoch was sleeping off his hangover and jumped on him. Enoch screamed angrily and there was a hell of a commotion with much shrieking and swearing before Enoch attached himself firmly to Billy's leg while biting, snarling and grunting. While screaming at Enoch to stop biting him, Billy hobbled quickly to

Snake's office and flung Enoch inside. Then he shut the door and ran to hide behind the main office block.

"As expected, Enoch furiously jumped onto Stripe's back in a rage, scratching and pinching. Loud whinnying and bucking ensued, sending Enoch flying onto Snake's desk, landing with a flop and a loud fart. Thoroughly unsettled, Stripes reared onto his back legs, whinnying like a stuck pig, and crashed his front hooves onto Snake's carefully organised desk which collapsed to the ground. This was too much for Enoch who decided to have an emergency bowel movement over Snake's papers and floor. It was a war zone when Snake came strutting to work. When he heard the commotion he broke into a sprint, tripping over the kerb and adding to the entertainment. Looking around threateningly, he spied no perpetrators as we were well hidden. When he opened the door there was a look of disbelief and horror as Enoch and Stripes bolted for freedom."

"'Fucking hell, what the fuck was that!' Snake shouted before quickly regaining his composure, adjusting his beret and straightening his uniform. Then he looked anxiously to see if anyone had witnessed him seeing his arse but there was only silence. Then we saw his cheeks go crimson, his eyes bulge and his chest heave as he drew a deep breath. 'Heyns, you little cunt, come here before I find you and kill you, you fucking cunt!' There was silence followed by, 'Heyns, you cunt, come here noooow!' There was another brief silence before Billy's head peeped around the corner and an innocent voice asked, 'Are you looking for me, sir?'

"Snake, barely able to stop himself attacking Billy, roared, 'Yes, you little fuck-head, did you put those animals in my fucking office?' Billy, with choirboy eyes, said, 'Who me? No never, sir.'

This only increased Snake's decibel range: 'Don't fucking lie to me, you little cunt!' he yelled before moving menacingly towards Billy who knew real danger when he saw it, decided to run for it but sadly for him he slipped on the grass as Snake struck, catching him on the ground before lashing out with his pace stick while raging on, 'I've got you now, cuntie! I'm going to fuck you up, cuntie! Now you are fucked, cuntie!'

"All the while there were loud 'ooohs' and 'aaahs' from Billy pleading for mercy. Eventually Snake exhausted himself and stopped to regain his breath. Then he told Bill to stand and Billy seized the moment to escape, running like hell for the kitchen with a panting Snake yelling after him, 'Come here, cuntie! I'm going to fuck you up!'

"Billy got six weeks of extras but not before cleaning 'Snake's office with Snake standing over him: 'Here cuntie, there cuntie, here cuntie.'

"After this incident we felt we owed Enoch for pain suffered so he was sent on a parachute course under Billy's watchful eye. The special chute was made by Mike Mingay and Taffy Morgan. Every morning, as soon as Enoch was over his hangover he was taken to the squash court for jump training. They would get on the roof and follow the correct procedures. The first jump Enoch did not know what was going on: 'Stand in the door, head up, red light on, stand by, green light on, go!' Billy yelled before giving Enoch a firm push on the bum and off he flew with arms and legs splayed, mouth wide open, saucer-like eyes and amid much squealing, he glided down into the welcoming arms of Mike and Taffy.

"On his second jump he knew the plan and gave Billy hell, biting and screaming, but Billy swore back, 'Come on, you little fucker, you're not getting out of this!' And off went Enoch again. His third jump went better and he was given the rest of the day off. Training progressed and Enoch so enjoyed it he started waiting for them at the squash courts. After eleven jumps he was given his wings and we had a celebratory piss-up for him. Enoch got stuck in to the booze and the next morning slept until 12h00."

'TINY' ROWLAND

Meanwhile, in August 1978, there was some excitement on receipt of rumour that Ian Smith was in Lusaka trying to cut a deal with Nkomo. Silent in the shadows was the wily figure of 'Lonrho' {London-Rhodesia Corporation} boss 'Tiny' Rowland.

Of Dutch/German/British parentage, born Roland Fuhrop in an Indian internment camp in 1917, he became a member of the Hitler Youth before moving with his parents to England where he was schooled. After the outbreak of war, Fuhrop changed his name to Rowland and served briefly in a non-combatant role in a service corps. Hostilities over, Rowland visited Southern Rhodesia and laid the seeds of an African conglomerate that would grow exponentially and soon wield enormous influence the length and breadth of the continent. Keen observers of this meteoric rise insist it was achieved only with solid financial and diplomatic support from the British government. It has also been suggested that the multinational was in fact a front for British Intelligence and for the projection of British influence by corporate means. Having selected Nkomo as 'his man' to rule an independent Zimbabwe, Rowland was grooming him for the top job, but then it all went quiet and the gambit fizzled.

The irony was not lost on Rhodesians. While Smith was talking multiparty democracy to Nkomo, Kaunda, the president of the host country, was announcing himself as the sole candidate of the only party legally entitled to contest the upcoming elections. All Zambians had a vote but there was only one name on the ballot. Buoyed by the arrival in Zambia of batteries of new surface-to-air missiles from the Soviet Union, secure in the knowledge it was constitutionally impossible to remove him from power, Kaunda was in firm control. Although initially positive and forthcoming in his talks with Smith, it seems a call from Nyerere warned him off the course he was on and brought the proceedings to an end.

In Mozambique the government of Samora Machel, under pressure from the Red Cross, belatedly admitted it was holding over 20,000 religious dissenters—many of whom were Jehovah's Witnesses—in concentration camps. Despite protests Machel refused to accede to demands for their release.

From Dar es Salaam there was more good news for Mugabe and Nkomo. Julius Nyerere told a press conference that he was insisting that an absolute prerequisite for a political settlement in Rhodesia was the disbandment of the Rhodesian Army as currently constituted, to be replaced by the 'liberation armies.' The Tanzanian president was pleased to report that Dr Owen seemed sympathetic to his demands.

On Saturday, 2 September Rhodesia's rugby-mad supporters tuned their radios to Pretoria where the mighty Northern Transvaal lay in wait. Boasting Springboks Ray Mordt, Ian Robertson and David Smith plus the insanely brave fullback Leroy Duberley and the long-haired flyer Danny Delport, the Rhodesians gave themselves half a chance. Despite getting no lineout ball off the towering Northern Transvaal locks and having two tries controversially disallowed, the Rhodesians came close to upsetting the Currie Cup champions. But then tragedy struck.

VISCOUNT HUNYANI

On Sunday, the following day in the resort town of Kariba, holidaymakers assembled at the small country airport and awaited their flight back to Salisbury.

They had all enjoyed their time on the banks of the water wilderness. Some had fished, some had spent their time watching elephant on the islands and a lucky few had seen a lion-kill on the floodplain alongside the Umi River. They were tanned and happy and the war seemed a world away.

It was hot in the airport building and the men found themselves a cold beer in the bar and talked rugby and fishing. In the concourse children kicked balls and played. Then they heard the familiar drone of one of the 'ladies' of the local skies: the approach of the ageing but much-loved Vickers Viscount. As the engines wound down outside, the men took the last gulps from their glasses and made their way from the bar to the departure gate. Shimmering in the afternoon heat was the welcoming sight of the trusty aircraft in its shining silver and blue livery.

At the controls were the recently married Captain John Hood and his co-pilot Garth Beaumont. The passengers made their way to the aircraft and were met by two pretty, fresh-faced flight attendants with cheery smiles. In their simple lavender frocks, Dulcie Esterhuizen and Brenda Pearson stood at the top of the stairs and welcomed their guests aboard. Brenda was a much-loved member of the staff. Convent-educated, an excellent sportswoman with dark hair and lovely soft eyes, she was vivacious and seldom lost for a smile. She was also in love with SAS soldier 'Spike' Lemmer and looking forward to seeing him back in Salisbury.

Her parents were tobacco farmers in the Mtepetepa area of the remote north-east. Hanging on to their livelihoods with resolution, they were prospering in spite of being firmly in the firing line of the enemy campaign to kill or dislodge the entire white farming community. Her brother Ashley was with the SAS. As usual, she had no idea where in the world he was.

Ignoring the dangers, she had recently spent the weekend at home and had loved every minute of being back with her parents. It had been the normal routine: travel on the farm roads was done in a mine-protected vehicle, and weapons were carried at all times; at sunset 'Agric-Alert' calls were made on the local network, grenade screens checked, dogs sent outside and weapons readied.

Aboard the packed aircraft, passengers took their places while children bounded to the rear in search of the pre-flight treats they knew were hidden in the galley. Seated, the propellers began to whirl while the crew welcomed everyone aboard. Boisterous men pleaded with the girls to waste no time in rolling the drinks trolley down the aisle.

Captain Hood introduced himself, gave the flight details and asked his passengers to sit back and relax. Taxiing, he turned into a light breeze and halted, did his final checks then opened the throttles and released the brakes. Surging forward, the passengers watched the trees flash by as they gathered speed, felt the runway leave them, and then airborne, they said goodbye to the great lake below. As they banked over the basin, elephant and buffalo came into view on the shore but soon the animals were out of sight as the aircraft climbed and set course for Salisbury.

One of the first to get a drink was Robert Hargreaves who was sitting next to Shannon, his wife of one week. A vodka and tonic was quickly before him and he sat back to relax and savour a happy, recent memory. Beside him was the girl of his dreams. Meanwhile the two hostesses were moving quickly down the aisle, plying people with refreshments amid the banter and the thrum of the turbines.

Then, suddenly, there was a thunderous explosion and a burst of flame from one of the starboard engines as the plane lurched wildly, shuddered, swung violently around in the sky and dived towards the ground. Standing passengers and crew went crashing to the floor and screams reverberated around the cabin. One passenger tore out of his seat shouting for a fire extinguisher. The hostesses, bravely back on their feet, regained control and ordered everyone to their seats. Captain Hood told the passengers to brace themselves and prepare to crash. A mother, Sharon Cole, clutched her four-year-old daughter Tracy to her and said to the man sitting next to her, "I don't care if I die but please get her out of here for me." Tears streamed down her face.

Shannon Hargreaves remembers the soft, gentle voice of Dr Cecil MacLaren, a dental practitioner who had just completed a locum in Kariba. He said, "Shannon, I'm very sorry. Let's just hold each other very tight." And he pulled her towards him. The last transmission from Captain Hood heard by air-traffic controllers was, "I can't . . . Mayday, Mayday, Air Rhodesia 825, I've lost both starboard engines, we're going in."

The two hostesses, stoic in the performance of their tasks, checked all passengers were belted and braced with heads between knees, prepared the doors and were last to their seats. Captain Hood's final words were to his passengers were ". . . to be brave."

With remarkable skill and accuracy, he directed the doomed plane into a space in the trees, and but for an unseen ditch all may have survived but it was not to be. The aircraft ploughed into it and burst into flames, leaving a scalded path in its wake.

Buckled and burning, wings torn asunder, inside the cabin it was dark and momentarily quiet with most passengers dead, the survivors shocked and speechless. Then people started shouting. Both pilots were dead at their posts and the two hostesses were badly hurt.

Passengers Tony Hill and Hans Hansen kicked a hole in the side to make an exit. Then Tony, Hans and his wife Diana started moving people out, including one of the hostesses, until the inferno made it impossible to continue. Within the fuselage passengers fought the flames with their hands. One woman sat helpless, holding her baby tight while her clothes burned before a hand came through a hole and grabbed the child.

Dr MacLaren found himself hanging upside down looking at the flames that threatened to engulf the plane. He tried a window but the handle snapped off in his hand. Struggling through the wreckage, he reached Sharon and Tracy Cole and along with the Hargreaves managed to exit the plane through a hole in the fuselage. Diana Hansen tried to comfort one of the hostesses who drifted in and out of consciousness.

Having exited the plane, the heat was stifling as Dr MacLaren left the crash site, leading a small party including Tracy and Sharon Cole along with the Hargreaves to look for water and seek help. Finding an African village, they requested assistance but received a hostile response. Whether through fear or malice the mood of the people was unsympathetic; however, they persisted and finally acquired some water.

Outside the wreckage a few sat silently trying to make sense of it all while terrified children clung to their parents. Some asked for water and bandages. Passenger Cynthia Tilley, who had just lost her fifteen-year-old brother when terrorists had attacked the family home, was one of the first to go to the aid of the survivors. At this stage, forty were dead with eighteen survivors. Those with broken limbs groaned in the fading light when suddenly the starboard wing exploded and smoke filled the air. Out of the haze appeared figures moving and hopes that these were friendly forces were quickly dashed when AK-wielding terrorists appeared.

They ordered the survivors forward following a warning burst of fire. Having struggled to the assembly point, the children embraced their parents in terrified silence beseeching the men with the guns through wide, innocent eyes to be merciful. They would be ignored. Those capable of standing were ordered into a row while the maimed lay on the ground. Satisfied all were in place the commander unclipped his 'pig-sticker' bayonet and addressed the condemned.

He was to the point: "You have stolen our land, you are white, now you must die."

With that the firing started and bullets tore into the bodies of the defenceless. With all prostrate and dead or writhing in pain, the commander ordered the firing to cease. In order to conserve ammunition, he led his men onto the bodies with their bayonets fixed. Brenda Pearson was struck five times by bullets but lay there alive looking into the eyes of the man who stood over her with a blade glistening from the muzzle of his carbine. She looked for mercy but found none. She was white, she was to die. Seventeen thrusts from his bayonet ended a life which only moments ago seemed set so fair.

One little girl of four had escaped the firing unscathed. She was stabbed to death hanging on to her dead father's leg. Then it all went very quiet. Behind the smoke-filled sky, beyond the woodland silhouette, the sun moved to set in a blaze of orange, closing out the final day for the victims and ending another violent day in a troubled land on a turbulent continent.

Hiding a short distance away in horrified silence was Dr MacLaren's group. The killing over, the ZIPRA men came looking and the survivors trembled at the sound of the stomp of heavy boots as the terrorists scoured the bush in search of them.

MacLaren kept little Tracy close to his chest. One noise from the child would have given their position away and meant death. The four-year-old held still within metres of the killers as they came in close, shouting to them to show themselves immediately. All this time, unbeknown to MacLaren's party, Tony Hill, another survivor who had escaped through the flames earlier, was also in hiding not far from them. He had armed himself with a rock and was going to go down fighting if discovered. Mercifully, they all remained unseen. Finally, the killers left.

In Salisbury relatives and friends waiting at the airport were told to go home. SAS CO Colonel Garth Barrett was relaxing at home when he received a call advising that a Viscount was "missing." He was instructed to prepare a reaction team.

Quickly assembling twenty men including doctors, he was ready to move but with darkness approaching the men would have to wait till dawn.

Watt recalls the day of the downing. "I'll never forget. We were in our barracks when we were told a plane had gone missing. At first I thought they must be talking about a military aircraft then discovered it was an Air Rhodesia Viscount with a full complement of passengers and crew. I felt a shudder run through my nervous system. I had no idea then what lay ahead, but the events and the images that confronted me that day are burned into my memory."

Near the crash site, dressed in her white cotton dress Tracy Cole slept through the night on MacLaren's chest. Through the hours of darkness, the good doctor and his wards shivered in silent fear while he talked their spirits up with constant encouragement. "It was the longest and most terrifying night of my life," he recalls. Eventually bright sunlight greeted them but with it sheer terror at the thought of being discovered.

But help was trying to reach them. Airborne from New Sarum before first light, the Dakota with the SAS contingent aboard was flying a grid pattern. "The pilots were trying to plot the search area looking at the aircraft's projected line of flight and the estimated time after take-off when last contact was made. Part of the problem was that no one had any idea how far the captain had kept the aircraft aloft after losing his engines so there was a lot of guesswork going on," remembers Watt.

"We sat at the doors and windows straining our eyes to see what we didn't want to see: the smouldering wreckage of a downed civilian airliner. I knew that was the reality but it did not stop me hoping for a miracle. Of no help was the turbulence which was unrelenting and many of the troops were sick. We flew for what seemed like forever. Tracts of the area were unpopulated wilderness but the rest was Tribal Trust Land which was fairly heavily settled. Most of the dwellings were thatch but not all, some were tin and the flash of metal in the bright sun kept catching my eye and every time I hoped I had them visual it was not to be. I was feeling very frustrated when suddenly someone shouted and the plane banked sharply. There below were the unmistakable blue lines on silver of the Air Rhodesia livery and I knew we had found Viscount *Hunyani*. It was hot and I could see the heat waves distorting the light off the mangled fuselage.

"The wind outside was blowing too strongly and normally we would not have jumped in those conditions but this was different. I watched the dispatcher and soon we were in a tight orbit over her. Hooked up, the CO Garth Barrett was out first. As I flung myself out the door I knew I was in for a difficult landing with the wind gusting as it was and I landed awkwardly, almost on the fuselage, breaking a bone in my foot. Having dumped my chute and checked to see if all the rest of my blokes were on the ground, we started looking.

"The medics rushed to see who was dead and who was alive. Then my eyes filled with the worst sight any civilised man could be asked to bear. Death was not new to me; I had been involved in it for a long time but nothing I had seen or done prepared for me what was in front of me. I think it was the dead children that destroyed me emotionally.

"Then I heard a soft voice and looked into the bush. Out of it appeared a pretty lady, naked but for her underwear, covered in blood and dirt but she forced a nervous smile as our eyes met. 'You can't believe how pleased we are to see you,' she said. It turned out to be Mrs Hansen. I said, 'How can I help you, ma'am?' and went to comfort her.

"She explained that she wanted to look for her wedding rings. Fearing the 'terrs' would cut off her fingers to steal them, she had taken them off and lost them. I went with her husband Hans and found them.

"Then I returned to the accident scene and all was silent. The dead were grey from all the ash that had settled on them. None of the men were talking. They were hardened soldiers but were standing around looking broken. We were all in a bad way seeing our countrymen and -women slain in this fashion."

Sergeant Phil Cripps remembers: "On the tip of the port wing lay something that looked like a baby doll lying on its back. On closer inspection I saw it was a human baby with dried blood leading out of its mouth. In front of the same wing was a black shoe with a foot still in it. The shoe was of the black leather type worn by pilots at the time. I looked into the beautiful face of Brenda Pearson and recognised her as the girl who had been with us in the Winged Stagger the weekend before." [49]

"I struggled then as I still do now to come to terms with the mentality of the people who did this," says Watt. "I could not stop looking at the pretty little girl who could not have been more than four years old. She was wearing a pink summer frock and her hair was still in two plaits. Her eyes were open almost as if in disbelief at what was happening to her. She was lying on her side with her arms clutched tight around her father's leg. Next to her were her mother and her brother in the same position. I struggled to control myself. Just who could find their way to kill innocent holidaymakers with their children after they had survived a plane crash left me lost. Some of the dead were not even from Rhodesia. And the people who had done this did so with the support of the churches, the missionaries and the leaders of the Western world. It was a moment of despair in my life.

"The choppers came in with more troops. I did a check and found the tracks but we were refused permission to follow; another tracker team was to come in and do the follow-up. I was very upset; I know I would have got them, even with a broken foot, but we were told we had other tasks to attend to. I'll never stop thinking about that day and will always regret the fact that I never got to go after them. If there is a hell they deserve a place in it."

Dr MacLaren's group of five had remained in their hiding place in the riverbed until after ten o'clock in the morning when they saw the search aircraft loaded with paratroopers but their frantic waves went unseen. Emboldened by the sight of help at hand, they moved out of their hideout with MacLaren in the lead, heading for where he thought they would eventually cross the main Kariba road. With the Hargreaves' bare feet cut and bleeding, Tracy in his arms and sullen locals glowering, it was not a happy party. Having walked close to fifteen kilometres, they were rescued by a police Land Rover before being placed in an air force helicopter and flown to Karoi.

The night following discovery of the wreckage a coded message was received by an SAS 'call sign' on a harassing mission in Zambia. It was to tell one of the operators to stand by for uplift in the morning. Flight lieutenant 'Bud' Cockroft arrived at first light to recover Ashley Pearson. On his return to base, Captain Martin Pearse had the unpleasant task of telling the young trooper that his sister had been murdered. With the family unable to face the horror of bearing witness to her mutilated body, they turned to Ron Reid-Daly, an old family friend, and asked him to do the identification and certification.

THE DEAFENING SILENCE

Back in London, on news of the atrocity, Dr Owen was asked to comment. He expressed reluctance to do so while awaiting confirmation as to the identity of the perpetrators. He was holding out the possibility the Rhodesians had shot their own aircraft down then bayoneted the survivors to death. He refused to condemn the obvious and never did. It was an awkward situation in which he again found himself: the killers had acted on behalf of a leader who the British government refused to criticise.

In a BBC interview, Joshua Nkomo, the ZIPRA leader, after admitting responsibility for the atrocity, laughed awkwardly. The British press, in the main relentlessly critical of the Rhodesian stand were somewhat lost for words and unsure how to spin this woeful story out without being too critical of the culprits and their supporters. The mind-set of the Fleet-Street men sent to report on the war is well summed up by one of their doyens. Writes Sir Max Hastings in his memoirs, "I felt not the smallest sympathy for the Salisbury regime. Ian Smith and his cohorts were near-fascists committed to . . . suppression of the black majority by ruthless use of force."₅₀ Rhodesia mourned and listened in sombre silence to the sermon delivered by the Very Reverend John da Costa, the Anglican Dean of Salisbury at a memorial service for the victims attended by the prime minister, service chiefs and most of his cabinet. Explaining that the enormity of the crime and the desultory response from the leaders of the civilised world compelled him to break with diocesan protocol and venture into territory that bordered on the political, he said, ". . . times come when it is necessary to speak out against "murder of the most savage and treacherous sort." He went on to say:

"This bestiality, worse than anything in recent history, stinks in the nostrils of Heaven. The ghastliness of this ill-fated flight from Kariba will be burned upon our memories for years to come. Nobody who holds sacred the dignity of human life can be anything but sickened at the events attending the crash of the Viscount *Hunyani*. The horror of the crash was bad enough, but that this should have been compounded by the murder of the most savage and treacherous sort leaves us stunned with disbelief and brings revulsion in the minds of anyone deserving the name 'human'. . .

"One listens for loud condemnation by Dr David Owen, himself a medical doctor, trained to extend mercy and help to all in need.

"One listens and the silence is deafening. "

One listens for loud condemnation from the President of the United States, himself a man from the Bible-Baptist belt, and again the silence is deafening.

"One listens for loud condemnation by the Pope, the Archbishop of Canterbury, by all who love the name of God.

"Again the silence is deafening.

"I have nothing but sympathy with those who are here today and whose grief we share. I have nothing but revulsion for the less-than-human act of murder which has so horrified us all.

"I have nothing but amazement at the silence of so many of the political leaders of the world. "I have nothing but sadness that our churches have failed as badly to practise what they preach."[51]

CHAPTER 10

When the war drums rolled and the dark clouds gathered.
Through the smoke as it rose from the burning huts.
A brotherly band of hard dangerous men
Who held the fire in our hands
And the storm in our souls.
—CHAS LOTTER

As had become usual, Ken Flower argued strongly against further attacks on Zambia, suggesting it would alienate the country's friends and lead to an escalation in the conflict.[52] There was also some concern among the political and security chiefs about a full scale attack on a Commonwealth country. Mozambique had already been similarly dealt with, but that, some argued, was a Marxist dictatorship and never part of the Empire. This was not so of Zambia. President Kaunda, heading a Commonwealth country, held a special place in the affections of the Queen, and British policy on Africa was profoundly influenced by the views of the Zambian president. He was in a sense a favourite son and his country's welfare was of great concern to Whitehall.

At a political level there was no change in London's position. In an open response to a letter from a woman aggrieved by Britain's tepid response to the massacre at Elim Mission, David Owen stubbornly defended Britain's support of the Patriotic Front and the leaders of the Frontline States. Ian Smith, responding to an invitation from the United States Senate to visit Washington and explain the changed political dispensation, was told he would be arrested if transiting through the United Kingdom.

CHRIS DIXON

Back in Salisbury at 'ComOps,' General Walls, tiring of Flower's obduracy, finally flared, accused the CIO boss of trying to sabotage the country's security and insisted it was time for the faint-hearts to stand aside. Walls had decided to attack

Zambia as a matter of urgency. "If we worried about what the West says, we would have had our necks wrung a long time ago," he remarked.

Flower stormed off to see acting PM David Smith to seek his intercession and thwart the planned attacks but failed to get the desired response. The political hierarchy gave the go-ahead and the planners went hard to work.

An area of pressing concern for the air force was the status of the British-supplied Rapier air-defence system in place in Zambia. Kaunda had recently torn a strip off Prime Minister Callaghan during a meeting in Nigeria following publication of the Bingham Report implicating both BP and Shell in sanctions-busting. Anxious to sooth the Zambian leader, concerned about potential Rhodesian revenge attacks following the Viscount downing, Callaghan promised to boost the Zambian air defences with batteries of anti-aircraft missiles which would be installed by British technicians and operated by British advisers. Not lost on officers of the Rhodesian Air Force was the fact the missiles were mobile and could be moved to the Rhodesian border for possible use against aircraft inside Rhodesian airspace.

The Rhodesian commanders decided on three targets after studying aerial photographs, hearing reports from agents on the ground in Zambia and information gleaned from captures.

The main ZIPRA camp in Zambia sat only fifteen kilometres north of the capital Lusaka. Known as FC, or Freedom Camp, it was situated on an abandoned farm known as Westlands. Both the Zambians and the ZIPRA leadership were confident its proximity to the capital would be an effective deterrent against a Rhodesian raid. It was estimated the camp contained 4,000 inmates in various stages of operational preparedness. The second target, 125 kilometres north-east of Lusaka, was known as Mkushi and it was thought to contain 1,000 of the enemy. The third target, known as 'CGT-2' {Communist Guerrilla Training}, was located 100 kilometres east of the city and was believed to house over four thousand.

The air force hierarchy, fearful of a British plant within their ranks, maintained tight security with only three senior officers having detailed knowledge of what was being planned. Pilots and crews were not to be briefed until the evening before the attack. The strike was given the code name 'Operation Gatling' and the brief was to bomb a parade expected to be held at FC Camp at 08h30 on the morning of 19 October 1978.

The main strike force would consist of four Canberras and eight 'Hunters' with back-up supplied by four Alouette 'K-Cars' fitted with 20mm cannons. The Canberras would be carrying locally produced Alpha or 'bouncing bombs' designed to hit the surface before rebounding and detonating approximately three metres above the ground causing extensive horizontal damage. The Canberra flight would be led by Squadron Leader Chris Dixon. Like his friend Darrell Watt, he was not liked by many of his senior officers. Often outspoken, almost to the point of insubordination, he was openly critical of over-promoted 'desk-jockeys' and adamant there was an enemy 'mole' in the air force and wanted the hierarchy to do more to address the problem. Gripes notwithstanding, he responded with courage and skill to the demands placed on him and flew some of the most dangerous missions of the war.

"The Tanzanian tasks were a bloody long way away," Dixon recalled. "In some cases the distance meant we only had minutes over the target so any navigational errors would have been disastrous. We would not have had the fuel to get home and would have had to ditch. There was also the real likelihood of being intercepted by MiGs or shot down by SAMs. Of course we in Canberras had no way of defending ourselves. I asked the Brass once what they thought we should do if we ran out of fuel, had mechanical or other problems and had to jump for it. I can't say I warmed to the response. The answer was that we best head out to sea and parachute into the shipping lanes of the Indian Ocean in the hope we were rescued by a passing freighter. I reminded them most of the sea traffic in that neck of the woods was Soviet or Chinese and they probably wouldn't give us Rhodesians a tumultuous welcome. They just shrugged their shoulders. Times like that I had the distinct impression that the hierarchy did not have a clue what we were up against.

"Mike Ronne, my navigator and I were given the handsome sum of US$20 each to buy our way home if we had to bail out! I managed to squeeze another hundred for the two of us from a pal at Special Branch so we each had US$70 in our pockets to get home from Tanzania or northern Zambia. I once asked Mike what his plan was if we were shot down. He said it was simple. He was going to take out his 9mm pistol, shoot me in the leg, leave me for the wolves and fuck off as fast as he could."

The strike on FC camp would be entirely from the air but Mkushi would be attacked by a combination of air and ground forces. An airstrike by Canberras and 'Hunters' would be followed immediately by airborne troops.

Every single SAS man on the nominal roll was summoned to Cranborne for the attack. With reservists called up, 270 men made muster including Stan Standish, a Second World War veteran who had seen action with the British Paras at Arnhem. Colonel Garth Barrett wrote the operational orders while Grahame Wilson planned the movement orders.

Anxious to maintain security the troops passed the time leading up to the attack ignorant of what their mission was. On the afternoon of the 18th, the squadron commanders travelled to their new barracks at Kabrit near Salisbury airport and received their briefing. They then returned to Cranborne and presented their orders to the troops. The plan called for a vertical envelopment of Mkushi by paratroopers, followed by the helicopter insertion of forty-four men under Captain Bob MacKenzie who would have an 82mm mortar team under his command.

Just as the sun climbed the horizon on the morning of the 19th, General Peter Walls and Group Captain Norman Walsh stepped into the command Dakota, 'call sign' Dolphin 3. At the same time two 'Hunters', four Canberras and four 'K-Cars' flew across the Zambezi River and entered enemy airspace. Maintaining radio silence, the pilots dived to 1,600 feet and under the Zambian radar. Not lost on any of them was the presence of MiG-21s that might be sent to intercept them. Looking down at the ground the airmen noticed a heavy haze obscuring the ground and concern set in: would they be able to find their targets behind the smoky veil?

Tony Oakley, one of the 'Hunter' pilots remembers, "Since our strikes were often the precursor to bigger airstrikes followed by a ground assault, the timing was critical. I can still recall the tension that ran through my body as I got close to the target area and nothing seemed to fit the photo— then just as that sick feeling started rising in my throat—there it was. The elation was unbelievable and the photo got stuffed in next to the seat while you got your wits about you for the long, almost vertical dive. Then you had to remind yourself to keep calm and make the right switch selections so you didn't bring your bombs home again. I often wondered what the pulse rate got up to at times like this."[53]

Precisely on time and on target the two 'Hunters' broke from their formation with the Canberras and accelerated on to the target. Their prayers were answered and thousands of surprised faces looked up in shock and horror as the unthinkable happened. Like avenging angels, the 'Hunters' streaked down, loosed their bombs and explosions rocked the ground spreading chaos and carnage below. But there was no respite. The Canberras followed suit immediately and Green Leader, leading Green Section, could hardly control his excitement as he shed his load and banked to bear witness to the carnage below.

"Yes, fucking beautiful!" he exclaimed. Breathless he continued, "Beautiful! Jeez! You want to see all those bastards! The fucking bombs are beautiful!" Then, his work done, he climbed to a higher altitude and prepared to deliver an instruction to the Lusaka air-traffic controller, ordering him to tell the Zambian Air Force not to interfere. En route the navigator carried on, "That was lovely! Fucking hundreds of the bastards. It worked out better than we could have . . . they ran straight into the bombs."

One of those who narrowly survived was ZIPRA military supremo Dumiso Dabengwa who remembers the day well. "I looked up at the sky and couldn't believe it . . . I failed even to run." Hiding at the base of a tree he marvels at the narrowness of his escape from death. "All the branches were cut to six inches above me."[54]

Brave Matavire, another survivor, remembers surveying the subsequent carnage. "Never before had I seen so many dead bodies. I could not believe it. I thought to myself if I blow a whistle surely they must wake up."[55]

PARA ATTACK

Meanwhile, back in Salisbury soldiers were restless. "We were listening on the radios and anxious to get stuck in," remembers Lieutenant Andre Scheepers. It was not long they would have to wait. The 'Hunters' arrived home and news of success spread fast. With morale buoyed the SAS men filed out to the aircraft to board the six old Dakotas that would take them to Mkushi. In the Zambian capital a pall of thick black smoke towered over a city in turmoil as panic spread. Sirens screamed and women wailed as people fled to safety while trucks and buses poured into Lusaka loaded with dead and wounded. To the dismay of the ZIPRA survivors some of the Zambian onlookers cheered as the body-laden trucks passed. The Zambian public had become increasingly disenchanted with the growing body of foreign fighters in the country who they saw as arrogant and ungrateful despite the hardship they were causing their hosts.

Radio traffic was thick with recrimination as Zambian security commanders scolded one another for the disaster that had befallen them. While they ranted they had no way of knowing their problems were far from over. Quietly watching the

Lusaka Hospital was Selous Scout operator Chris Gough who was anxious to see what sort of numbers were arriving so he could report back to Salisbury. He was shocked by what he saw.

At the same time, crossing into Zambia, at treetop level, the Dakotas carrying the paratroopers headed north but they were like ovens inside and the hot air brought turbulence that had the planes bucking and bouncing in flight. "It was very uncomfortable inside the aircraft," remembers one soldier. "Some of the blokes got sick and we were all looking forward to getting out the door."

Andrew Standish-White remembers, "It was like the domino principle. The first guy vomiting set off a couple of others and the malady spread; it got really ugly. Then trying to keep steady on your feet in the queue was tough with our heavy packs on our knees while the plane bounced all over the place sending us slipping and sliding in all the puke."

But despite the problems all was proceeding according to plan and the airstrikes found their targets just before noon when, following closely, the Dakotas zeroed in on the objective, changed course sharply to drop their troops at the correct angle of attack and disgorged their men. Unfortunately, some flight crews erred. Struggling with poor visibility from all the bushfires below, the pilots struggled to find their drop zones, leaving some of the attackers too close and others too far from the camp.

"My fond memory of this attack," recalls Scheepers, "was jumping in the company of Stan Standish whose last operational jump had been at Arnhem with the British Paras. What a wonderful man. After landing we swept along a river line and took fire from mainly women. Bruce Lang, nearby me was shot in the jaw. Vern Conchie, the tough little Australian, got busy with his 9mm pistol."

"Getting to the door was a problem," Standish-White recalls. "Eventually we jumped, there was a brief silence with the rush of air then the sight of the attack jets diving in and the rattle of gunfire from below got the adrenaline going nicely. We landed fine but the bush was dry, fires were burning and smoke obscured our view, making it a little difficult to orientate. On the ground we regrouped but soon were under fire."

Mike West remembers: "When we jumped in we were between the female and male camps and 'gooks' were running all over; I was firing my 9mm downwards at them as we were being fired at from all angles. I hit the deck and had to move fucking quick to get my weapon ready as it was tied down to my shoulder with para-cord. It was a hell of an attack with plenty of targets."

Bob MacKenzie was immediately frustrated on landing. Accidentally dropped eight kilometres away from the target, he and his men wasted valuable time waiting for helicopters to refuel at the prepositioned administrative base before moving them closer to the action.

Sweeping towards the defenders, Jeff Collett was hit and went down, blood pouring from a leg wound. Grahame Wilson rushed to rescue him but his femoral artery had been severed and he died of his injuries. To the surprise of the attackers the fatal shots had been fired by a woman.

In a day of intense close-quarter combat assault troops skirmished through a multitude of enemy positions. Some of the defenders lay low and had to be winkled out from various forms of cover. Hundreds of foxholes sprinkled around the complex had to be individually cleared. Those that chose to run had to risk a gauntlet of waiting stop groups and ever vigilant machine-gunners in orbiting helicopters. The number of women involved in the action came as a surprise as did the steadfastness of the resistance of some of them.

"I think I saved Colin Willis's life at Mkushi," remembers Mike West. "He stepped around a large broken-off branch while we were in a sweep line through the base. I was about five metres behind him due to some broken ground. I spotted movement in that huge branch still covered with leaves and approached carefully. I pulled the branch to one side and sure enough a female 'gook' was positioning herself with an SKS aiming towards him. I jerked the weapon out her hands and shot her twice in the head with her own weapon. Colin at least had the decency to say thank you."

"Captain MacKenzie had given us our briefing," recalls Roger. "I was an RPD gunner and we initially were on the outskirts of the camp. Captain Wilson and his blokes were doing the hard work sweeping towards us. Wave after wave came at us at speed, running over the mounds of burning bush. We lay still in a long spread-out line and let them come right onto us before we blasted them. It was amazing as every ten minutes a new group would appear running out of the camp and, despite seeing the piles of dead and wounded in front of them, they just kept coming and suffered the same fate. After a couple of hours of non-stop killing we went forward to clean up, deal with the wounded and sort out the prisoners.

"I remember guarding a group of about thirty prisoners when a 'K-Car' flew overhead, did a big circle and appeared to be lining us up for a burst with his 20mm cannon when I shouted to one of the other 'troopies' to take his shirt off so they could see the white skin and see we were the good guys and hold his fire. Covered in black grime and dirt from all the smoke and fires, we must have all looked the same from the air. We then marched the prisoners to an area and left them with some troops detailed for the task of looking after them.

"That done, our task was to move forward in an extended line, sweeping towards the camp centre and in the process clear out the foxholes and trenches where 'gooks' were still hiding. I remember our officer was in the centre of the line issuing orders and keeping the line straight as we moved forward. Because I was a gunner I was furthest away at the end of the line and I knew that I had to be fully alert as I had a wide arc to cover while moving forward. What happened then was quite scary and obviously I had my guardian angel looking out for me. As the line was approaching a gully obscured by thick green foliage, I noticed slight movement in a bush to my one side and immediately let rip at it before rushing towards the movement. As I got there another bush moved to my left and being left-handed, I had my RPD aiming to the right. I pulled the bush to the one side with my left hand and there was a woman with a SKS pointed some ten inches from my face. Without thinking I slapped the weapon out of her hands, spun it around and pulled the trigger. It went off in her face and as she dropped backwards into the gully, I followed up with my RPD. I think I got such a fright that aggression just kicked in and I launched myself into the ravine rather recklessly, emptying an entire belt into the enemy hiding in there.

"It all went quiet and I remember our commander coming over a minute or so later and surveying the carnage. There were about twenty dead and dying sprawled all over the place. He looked at me and said, 'What the fuck's going on here, Rog?' I wasn't sure what to say. I got a big fright that day and will go to my grave not knowing why that woman never pulled the trigger and sent me to my maker.

Another man who narrowly missed his meeting with his maker was André Scheepers who walked into a POMZ {a Soviet stake-mounted antipersonnel fragmentation grenade}. Eyes focused on the enemy, he missed the trip-wire and went down in a hail of shrapnel which ended this fight for him but he recovered quickly from his wounds and was soon operational again.

"It was a time of madness in that camp," says Roger. "In the centre of the camp I remember all the piles of charred bodies curled up from the airstrikes. It was a big victory but the news of Jeff Collett was bad. He and I had been on the same selection together and I kept thinking that should have been me. Captain Wilson took it very badly. He was very fond of Jeff. Jeff used to shadow the captain on his gambling forays into the casinos. When Captain Wilson wasn't looking he'd pocket some of his winnings. End of the night when the captain had lost everything Jeff would appear with the stolen stash and much to his boss's relief, announce he had escaped bankruptcy."

Designed by Soviet advisers, it was the most elaborate enemy complex the Rhodesians had visited. Spread out with well-organised defences, there was an underground headquarters and armoury. Above was a large administrative block, huge communal kitchen, several parade grounds, a clinic and even a library bulging with communist propaganda.

Standish-White remembers the day. "People often ask me how so few could win over so many. I know it's hard to believe but I think it was our aggression that terrified them, causing them to panic and then they were like headless chickens. Their leadership must have been hopeless. All it would have taken was one good officer to rally his troops and retaliate with sustained and accurate fire and it could have changed the outcome drastically for us, but thankfully that never happened."

With the fighting dying down, a Soviet troop carrier was commandeered and Mac Macintosh left the camp to mine all the incoming roads.

Alarm followed with the appearance in the sky of a circling MiG-21 and wary eyes on the ground watched the circling jet. A 'Hunter' pilot, itching for the chance, asked for permission to engage but was told to maintain a close eye and react only if he detected hostile intent. The Zambian fighter did one more circle, reported being low on fuel then left the area without incident.

Eavesdropping Rhodesian signallers chuckled as they listened to the storm of invective that filled the Zambian military net as accusations and counter-accusations flew fast and furious. Once again their radar and missile defences had failed to make any impression. Some in the Zambian defence hierarchy blamed the British technicians for not maintaining the systems adequately. It seemed the British, no matter how hard they tried, could not please their African allies.

The following day, after a night of sporadic night-fighting with survivors stumbling into ambushes, the camp was cleared of danger and the international press was flown in. Previous raids had been misreported as attacks on refugee camps. This time the Rhodesian authorities wanted their critics to see for themselves. Zambian officials fulminated over the brazen violation of their sovereignty. Attacking an enemy camp was a staggering affront. Flying in a press corps was the height of insolence.

AMBUSH

On day three Grahame Wilson took his weary men to a high feature on the outskirts of the cantonment to watch over the extraction phase of the operation.

"We were tired and the action was over when we moved to a position outside the camp to await uplift but to still keep an eye out for movement," remembers Gavin. "We were on high ground overlooking a burnt-out *vlei*, about a hundred metres broad in the brachystegia woodland that was to be our LZ for the choppers later in the day.

"Not long after sunrise we were brewing up when suddenly there was a chorus of hisses and finger clicks. On the opposite side of the *vlei* approaching over the high ground came first one sweep line then a second and also a third probably about 400 metres away. I'm not sure when we realised it but the first sweep line were ZIPRA dressed rag-tag in browns and civvies and rice-fleck camouflage, the second Zambian Army in their camouflage and the third, somewhat strangely, were Zambian police in khaki and pith helmets. We were all hunkered down letting them come closer and closer and it was only when some of the ZIPRA were so close that they were in the dead ground below us, less than a hundred metres away, when we were seen and Sergeant Cripps initiated.

"The beauty of it was that we now had the ZIPRA troops turning back up the facing slope completely exposed in burnt open woodland and running into the Zambian Army, and then the police frozen at the back maybe 250 metres from us. I remember that completely exposed slope being covered by running, crouching, crawling figures while we were stretched out in the prone position with our RPDs on their bipods with spare belts lying ready in pouches; it was everything you imagine a turkey shoot to be.

"I saw a ZIPRA man in a bright red shirt sprinting up that slope, hit repeatedly as he zigged and zagged to escape the rain of fire. At this time Grahame stood calmly behind Barry and me picking out targets for us with a stick, giving us clear target indications as we methodically picked them off one by one. He stood there fully exposed with his folding-butt FN propped against a tree behind him, calmly giving orders. This was command and leadership at its best.

"For the enemy there was no escape and even when they dived behind trees we shot the trees down. Some of it was longer range than what we were used to but again Wilson gave us range indications based on our strikes that he could see through his binoculars. I moved my sights up to 300 metres at one point, something I'd never done before.

"The return fire, as usual, was high, showering us with leaves and bark and for some reason I decided to come to my feet. This brought a swift response from Wilson who whacked me with his stick and said, 'Get down, you dumb cunt.'

"Following a lull, Captain Willis and his troop swept through the position, flushing out survivors. It was then that two captures were made, one of which was Mountain Gutu, a very important ZIPRA commander based in Francistown, Botswana. Later handed to Special Branch, he was a mine of information.[56] We counted forty-nine bodies.

"I remember when the 'shoot' was over we swept through the position and the Zambian Army folding-butt FNs were snatched up by the officers and NCOs. We helped ourselves to the .303 Lee Enfield bolt rifles of the police and the pith helmets were much sought-after for clowning around as colonials.

"Later that morning when the choppers finally arrived I jumped into a 'G-Car' {troop carrying Alouette helicopter} whose gunner had an unusually long, droopy moustache. I think he might have been from the South African Air Force. As we climbed over that *vlei*, he became very excited, pointing his twin Brownings at all the corpses dotted across the landscape. I spied his water bottle in his webbing and being as usual very thirsty, I signalled to him my need for some water. He quickly obliged and passed it with a big smile. I took a good pull and my head nearly exploded: it was full of neat brandy. He thought it was hilarious."

Standish-White remembers: "We left the camp looking at our watches, anxious to get back to Salisbury for the rugby where Rhodesia was set to play the Orange Free State in a Currie Cup match. Transferring from the helicopters to a Dakota at

Mukumbura, we put some pressure on the pilot to put his foot down. Cleared to descend to low level, it was a wonderful feeling of pride when the waiting crowd cheered as we flew over the rugby field with the Rhodesian flag flying out the door. The crowd below, having heard the news of the attack, gave us a loud cheer. We quickly ditched our battle gear and raced to the ground for the game. Rhodesia won a thriller of a game 29–27.

"After the rugby all ranks were invited to the Winged Stagger. Everyone suitably fired up on a lot of beer—the post-operation adrenaline dip—comparing notes and talking louder than necessary. Then on comes the television RBC {Rhodesian Broadcasting Corporation} report—they had been withholding most of the details until the guys were back. It was the first time reporters had been allowed to inspect a battle site immediately after an operation and we were all a little surprised. It was weird for us to see such detailed reporting on our work, but what really hit us was watching this story on the screen, cold beer in hand, surrounded by mates, only two and a half days after it had occurred. It was a major morale booster and made the death of esteemed Winged Stagger member Jeff Collett that much more poignant. They estimated we killed over a thousand 'gooks'."

CHAPTER 11

Times change, wars change
The very things we fight for change
But, at the bottom is still the common soldier.
—*CHAS LOTTER*

Following the raids on Zambia, the British Council of Churches issued a statement saying it was supporting its sister body, the World Council of Churches, and would be giving financial, materiel and moral support to the forces under Robert Mugabe and Joshua Nkomo. The government of the United Kingdom announced it was stepping up aid to Zambia to help the country deal with "unprovoked aggression" from Rhodesia.

When rumours swirled that it was a British-supplied Rapier missile fired by the Zambian Army that had in fact downed the Air Rhodesia Viscount, President Kaunda forced Joshua Nkomo to clarify the situation. Nkomo duly stated that it was men under his command using Soviet supplied missiles that had accounted for the airliner. In October it was announced that a new weapons consignment from the UK had arrived in Lusaka and that this included surface-to-air missiles which the British government said would be deployed to protect ZIPRA facilities in the country. Some months later two Zambia Air Force aircraft were shot down in a friendly-fire incident. Unconfirmed reports indicated the British-supplied missiles had been responsible.

PRIVATEERS

Provision was made within the Rhodesian Army for serving soldiers to receive incentives for fighting on during their leave periods but with the understanding they would be acting outside the formal logistical and support structures, so while they were quietly encouraged they were also warned they could not expect any assistance if plans went awry.

"Some of the younger soldiers came and asked me to join them on one of these forays. I agreed to give it a go," remembers Watt.

"I was greedy for combat," remembers Mike West, "and would volunteer for any mission regardless of the fact that I had just returned from an operation. I somehow could not get enough. I went out on one of the first bounty hunts in Centenary. John Barry was killed there and I was put on a military trial. It was one of the worst days of my life. John was my best friend and godfather to my daughter. We had been in the best of barroom brawls but John was a man of few words, a real quiet operator. In this contact it went wrong in poor visibility and John was hit above the waist. We did not have the medic pack with us and all I could do for him was give him my 'Sosegon' {morphine substitute} to dull the pain but it did not help much and John asked me to knock him out because he could not deal with the agony he was in. I tried to keep his spirits up but he passed on and I miss him very much.

"I was only a trooper at that time, but had combat experience from my days with 2 Commando RLI. I was placed before a team of senior officers who listened to the facts and found me not guilty. I was promoted shortly afterwards to lance-corporal. From then on doors opened for me and I had a war-happy-filled life."

"Their plan sounded doable so I went to Garth Barrett and Grahame Wilson," remembers Watt. "I told them what our thoughts were and they gave me permission to do it and said the necessary weapons and equipment would be made available so we started getting ready. I then went to Andy Samuels who was the 2 Brigade Intelligence Officer. Andy was a great guy and very helpful. I was blunt: I told him we wanted to know which part of the country was the most heavily infiltrated because that was where we could make the biggest impression. He quickly pointed to an area in the north-east of the country near Marymount Mission in the Hurricane operational area. 'The place is swarming with 'gooks',' he said.

"There were six of us and we left for Mount Darwin the following day. There we heard the area we were going into was a virtual no-go zone and heavily subverted. Some people thought we needed our heads read. One of the guys, Keith Cloete, watched the police station near Marymount and actually saw the police exchanging pleasantries with the 'terrs.' We gathered a deal had been done: the 'terrs' did not interfere with the police and the police did not interfere with them. It was quite a revelation to me that the situation had reached that point.

"I knew some of the chopper pilots and two of them agreed to give us a ride in but reminded us we were on our own after that because we were unofficial. We rested for the rest of the day then walked hard through the night to get right into the middle of the designated area. At first light we were on top of a hill and we looked down on a large training camp. Such was their sense of security they even had a flag flying. For a while we watched them training and looking at the numbers I knew we were in for a serious punch-up.

"Maintaining their security they had *mujibas* {youthful collaborators who reported hostile activity to the guerrillas} out looking for any sign of Rhodesian soldiers and one of these guys walked up the hill so we grabbed him. The *mujibas* normally worked in pairs so if something happened to one the other would report back and that is what happened, because suddenly the activity below changed and I could see they now knew where we were. I told the guys to get ready for the fight of their lives because we were outnumbered at least ten to one and very much on our own. We knew not to expect support from the air force or anyone else so we were literally going to have to fight or die.

"We watched them form up into assault lines ready to move on our position, then they opened up on us with mortars, machine guns and rockets. The incoming fire was intense but we hid amongst the rocks and I told the guys to hold their fire. Then the barrage subsided and they started their attack. There was a lot of shouting and blowing of whistles as the commanders worked to keep their men in line. I said to my blokes, 'They think we're done; let them close in till we can see the colour of their eyes then we'll hammer them.' I don't think those 'terrs' realised the level of professionalism that awaited them. I think the line that reached the top of the hill must have thought we were finished when there was no firing from us and they did not see us. When they were no more than ten metres away I pulled the trigger on my FN. All the others had RPDs and they let rip. At that range the 'gooks' did not know what had hit them and there was carnage. There was a lot of screaming and we kept firing until they abandoned the attack and it went quiet, but I knew they would return and told the blokes to ready themselves for a counter-attack which soon came and was done very professionally, while they carried their dead back down the hill before launching another assault. One of the dead was the overall commander."

"I remember a few of us launched a downhill assault into the advancing 'gooks' as they were trying to attack us on that little hill," remembers Mike West. "I had the radio in one hand talking to the chopper pilot and my RPD in the other firing at the enemy. The pilot said it was a good Audie Murphy act.

"I could see we were probably not going to have enough ammo to see this through and called Mount Darwin to say we were in big trouble. The pilots were great and took a bit of a chance but they came and when the 'gooks' saw the 'K-Car' they fled."

Flight Lieutenant Terry McCormick recalls: "I remember having to pick up Darrell and his guys when they were legging it after their mercenary venture had gone a little awry. Bastards got me off my precious inner sprung mattress while I was trying to have a nice kip."

"Thanks to the choppers we had the opportunity to get out of there and we went far and fast that night. In the morning we were told to get to a road where we were met by Police Support Unit troop carriers," remembers Watt. I knew we had stirred a hornets' nest and warned everyone to expect an ambush. Not far down the road the vehicle behind me was hit by rockets and machine guns, killing the driver and wounding Mike and 'Mo' Taylor."

"That ambush they caught me in was hectic," says West. "I lost my right eardrum and my RPD was battered from the RPG rocket that hit the driver's cab right next to my head. They had a Goryunov heavy machine gun lined up on us and shot the shit out of us. A real lucky escape. Darrell had us in full view. Thank God, because he saved us."

Watt recalls. "Anticipating the attack, I had a 60mm mortar ready and I jumped to the ground and fired several rounds. The 'gooks' did not like the sound of that and took off. The dead driver was a mess: eyes blown out and both arms severed.

"When I arrived back in Salisbury I was reprimanded by Colonel Barrett and told not to do it again but I reminded him he had given us permission and he acknowledged that. More importantly I told him the bad news: despite what everyone said there were indeed 'liberated' areas and I told him that as far I was concerned we were losing the war inside the country. I asked to see General Walls and was given an appointment.

"I went into his office and did not mince my words. I told him what we had discovered and told him our own forces were now siding with the enemy. I said, 'We're losing the war, sir.' He looked at me and said, 'I think you're right.'"

WATT FINDS THE KILLERS

Late November '78 a battle-weary Darrell Watt arrived back in the farming town of Karoi in a rush to make the bar at the Twin Rivers Inn and have some cold beers with the proprietor, Rufus Snyman. Rufus was something of a Rhodesian legend. Solidly built with a barrel chest, his sharp-set eyes sparkled behind a rakish smile buried in a thick black beard; given a patch and a peg-leg he would have been a cinch for a pirate.

Born in 1937 in Beaufort West and bred in that vast expanse of arid country in South Africa known as the Karoo, few people were allowed to slip him by without being bombastically informed that the world famous heart surgeon Dr Christiaan Barnard was a son of the same town. "There was Christiaan Barnard, his brother Marius and then there was me: Rufus Snyman!" he was wont to pronounce, "and I was the cleverest."

As a businessman he was famous for being reckless and for exasperating bank managers, sheriffs and bailiffs alike. As a hotel manager, wildly incompetent, running the country inn known as the Twin Rivers Inn in the style of a Wild West saloon where bad behaviour was actively encouraged and patrons and proprietor alike were frequent guests of the Karoi constabulary. A keen hunter of big game, his forays into the nearby Zambezi Valley invariably attracted the attention of the wildlife authorities whom he constantly irritated. His loyal and omnipresent black factotum was Bosman. Of light complexion, slender with a bullet-shaped head, he was shy, somnolent, almost despairing. It was as if he understood and forgave the insane patrons, accepting it was a situation beyond his remit.

But for the war-weary patrons of Twin Rivers, Rufus was golden. Some questioned the lack of security at the hotel and it was rumoured he was a marked man with the terrorists. "No one will make me put up a fence. I'm here if the fucking bastards want me." One night as Karoi was attacked from a hill behind the inn, Rufus asked Bosman to place chairs on the lawn to give everybody a better view as tracer bullets and rockets screamed overhead. The post office, the fuel depot, the police camp and the Karoi Hotel were all hit.

Ross, a visiting farmer from the Eastern Highlands, remembers that night. "It was quite frightening watching the incoming fire and I wasn't as relaxed as Rufus and some of his pals were. I took up a position behind a tree with my FN ready. I was looking somewhat apprehensively into the night, expecting a ground assault when I heard a whisper and felt a nudge from behind. I got a hell of a fright and then felt like a fool when I heard a voice and the words. "A beer for you, baas." Then I saw Bosman standing behind me with a tray and a cold Castle beer.

Watt continues: "We had had a rough ten-day deployment and we were looking forward to a beer and a fat steak with Rufus Snyman at the Twin Rivers Inn. What had happened in the weeks before was as a result of a discussion I had had with Grahame Wilson. The SAS was badly in need of more officers and I told Grahame I thought the best way for me to evaluate the candidates would be a sort of live-firing exercise where I would take them into a heavily infiltrated area and draw fire. He agreed and mid-November we drove to a drop-off point near the Urungwe TTL, then we walked hard through the night. With me was Rich Stannard who I knew well but one of the newer guys was André Scheepers whom I had heard a lot about. Soon I could see he had all the makings of an excellent officer."

Scheepers came from the Rhodesian Midlands and was the son of a farmer. "I was motivated to join the army by Stretch Franklin and did so out of a sense of patriotic duty more than anything. I was an average student, but a good athlete and won five Victor Ludorums on the track. My parents were committed Christians, they were strict but fair and took special care of the poor. I grew up with values that imbibed love, care and justice for all people which I have always cherished.

"Holidays I spent hunting on our farm near Gokwe and I used to spend much of my time in the bush looking for rocks because I wanted to be a geologist. Some of my best times were with my African friends whom I used to hunt and play with. We used to collect snakes, crows, eagles, rodents and find and eat mopani worms. I learned to love the Rhodesian bush and will never forget those days. Then my father was ambushed by terrs and seriously wounded and we were forced off the farm. I went off to the army in 1974 as a member of Intake 137. I passed the SAS selection but later spent one year in 3 Commando RLI as OC 13 Troop after completing my officers' course at the School of Infantry. It was primarily the specialist side of the SAS that interested me," recalls Scheepers.

"I was on the same course with André," remembered the late Dave Greenhalgh. "I was the youngest and he was the oldest. We were commissioned together and both of us were posted to 3 Commando as troop commanders. No sooner had André got there than he was in some major Fire Force punch-ups and was shot up in the one. He said to me, 'Stuff this for a joke; I'm going back to the SAS" and off he went. He was lucky to come under Darrell's wing. Darrell would have helped him a great deal in finding his feet."

Another officer under evaluation was Joe du Plooy and he was not happy with Watt. "Joe got pissed off with me after a long hard walk in to the target area. I told him to wind his neck in and do as I said: I was in charge for the duration of the exercise and would decide who to recommend for an SAS commission. He shut up but was not very happy. I wanted to teach these officers the value of anti-tracking," says Watt, "and how easy it was to compromise yourself, so I deliberately left clear sign for the 'gooks' to follow to make sure they came after us. And it worked. We were eventually attacked by a large ZIPRA group led by a *mulatto* {mixed-race} who was well organised and used whistles as command signals. They used mortars and rockets and gave us a good stonking. I was very impressed with them. Later we stumbled onto a lone 'terr' strolling along with his rifle slung and a beat-box on his shoulder blaring into his ear. I waited then shot him through the beatbox, breaking both the machine and his head.

"At the end of the exercise we returned to Karoi where I did the reports at the local police station. I met with the senior security force commanders in the area. I had just finished briefing them and was getting ready to relax when I walked out the door and there was an anxious face that I recognised."

The man Watt was looking at was Keith Nell and he badly needed help. Nell was from the SAS but he had been seconded to work with a newly formed militia known in the vernacular as *Pfumo re Vanhu* or 'Spear of the People.' Officially named SFA's, {Security Force Auxiliaries} they were effectively the military wing of the United African National Council led by Bishop Abel Muzorewa who was destined to become the first black prime minister of the country. The fighting core of the SFAs was made up of former ZANLA and ZIPRA fighters, supplemented by rudimentarily trained young men and some women who were supportive of the UANC. Poorly equipped, undisciplined, loosely led and fractious, Nell's first task on assuming his duties had been to quell a simmering mutiny in the militia ranks at a camp on the Angwa River north of Salisbury.

A daunting task, a lone white man, facing down a mob of over a hundred armed and angry men, he had used a carrot-and-stick approach. "I had to be firm but fair with them," remembers Nell. "They did have legitimate gripes which I acknowledged and offered to address. But then I warned them, the price they would pay for mutinous behaviour was a high one; I would make one radio call to the RLI Fire Force which would be acted on immediately and they would be annihilated. That got their undivided attention. They knew all about the RLI and did not like the sound of that option at all. Thereafter we settled down well and the retraining exercise proceeded quite smoothly.

"With trust in me and in the Rhodesian support personnel growing, their confidence improved and this company-strength group of men became increasingly effective at gathering solid information and then reacting to it, culminating in successful contacts and kills." It was in the process of gathering intelligence that Nell went looking for help.

"He looked very worried and said he needed to talk to me privately," remembers Watt. "I then recognised Keith from the SAS and immediately felt comfortable. Having said that, I was planning on some time in the pub and in no real mood for any serious stuff but I said okay and we made for a quieter spot. Keith, with a very determined look on his face, said, 'I've got some very hot information for you.' I listened and he said, 'I've got information about 'gooks' in a village near here and my informants insist this is the group responsible for the Viscount. I trust the chaps who have passed on this information.'

"I looked at him unconvinced because this was too good to be true but this guy was no fool. He was adamant that the information suggested they were carrying a launcher and heat-seeking missiles. I asked him how he could be sure. He said the local headman was angry with the 'gooks'. They had abducted two of his daughters and were holding them as sex slaves while eating all their food and drinking all their beer. The headman was terrified that they would kill his daughters very soon if they were not dealt with. I told Keith I had just finished a training exercise and was going home, that I would report it but he was adamant. He grabbed me by the arm and shook me—he was dead serious. 'No,' he said, 'Darrell, you must come now if we're going to get these bastards. I can't risk going after this group with my guys, it's too valuable a target and we can't afford to cock it up. I need the best and you are the best. We must move quickly.' I asked him again if he was certain these were the 'gooks' and I could see from his reply he meant it when he said yes. I decided to move on this.

"With no other means of contacting Colonel Barrett, I had to use the phone so I chose my words carefully but he quickly got a handle on what I was saying. He asked if I was sure the person supplying me with this information knew what he was talking about and I said I was. He thought for a while then he said, 'Okay, go for it!' I went and told Keith we were on and he was elated.

"Early next morning we left for the area and then walked through the night with one of the SFA men to guide us in. We arrived near a village and watched for a while. I was pleased we had managed to get close without causing the dogs to bark; then I tasked André Scheepers with going into the village to see if the 'terrs' were indeed there. Taking an infrared night sight with him, he slunk off into the night while I waited. About thirty minutes later André returned. He was excited. 'They're there!' he whispered. 'They're definitely there and they're definitely 'gooks'. I saw a weapon by one of the huts.'"

Scheepers: "We approached the huts quietly and I gave the arcs of fire and positioned the men because I had just done the recce and knew the lay-out better. Darrell went to my right a few hundred metres to the rear to cover an escape route. I remember the leading 'gook' coming to two metres in front of me for a pee and I had no option but to shoot. Rob Slingsby was on my immediate left and covered that side of the kraal because I wasn't certain that Darrell would be able to cover the back if a 'gook' ran out to my left away from where he was positioned.

"With that more 'terrs' came running out of their respective huts and we took them down. I remember Darrell coming in on my right and quite a few women running into view. I remember feeling guilty because I shot a person running away in the back who turned out to be a female witchdoctor."

"We then walked to a small hill next to the village," recalls Watt, "and I asked Rob Slingsby to put up an aerial and get in touch with HQ. We were just starting to brew some tea when there was an almighty burst of fire from an RPK which damn nearly hit Rob. An enemy gunner who must have been positioned outside the village had managed to get himself above us in some rocks and put down some effective fire on us. I moved and could just see a black head in the rocks which I could barely get a bead on. I told André to pour fire on the target and the gunner jumped up to run which gave me a shot and I hit him in the ribs, which was the end of him but he gave us a good stonking."

"We collected five dead 'gooks'," says Scheepers, "and I placed the documentation which was a book full of hand-written notes next to the dead man who I considered was the leader. He was the first man I shot coming out the hut."

"Helicopters came in," remembers Watt, "and we were told by one of the men on board it was the Strela group we had engaged and from what I could understand they came from the camp I had attacked previously near Kariba with Bob MacKenzie. In my mind there was little doubt this was an enemy special operations group. ZIPRA troops rarely operated in small groups and credit to them: they were very aggressive. What struck me is the engagement took place directly below the Viscount flight-path and there is no other reason I can think of why they would have been there. I and my men were extracted from the scene soon after, so we did not have much time to investigate further and look for more evidence. I regret that now; if there were missile tubes there we might well have found them but we expected Special Branch to do that.

"It helped me deal with the anger and desire for revenge I felt following what I saw at the first Viscount disaster. We were flown by helicopter back to Karoi and we returned to SAS HQ by road. Immediately upon my return to Kabrit, I reported to Garth Barrett and Grahame Wilson."

"I remember this so clearly," says Scheepers. "I waited outside the office while Darrell went into Garth Barrett's office to report on the operation but also on my performance in the field. Darrell's report would determine my future in the SAS as an officer and I was therefore interested in the outcome of the debrief. I will never forget the feeling when he came outside with a big smile and gave me a pat on the back to signal all was good and we had, in all likelihood, eliminated the most wanted gang in the country. Soon after, I was redeployed so I did not make any further inquiries.

"I think that as things stand on this matter the evidence is certainly in favour of them being the same Strela group involved with the shooting down of the plane. We had reasonable grounds to believe that it was part of the Viscount gang. To deny this would be to ignore all the circumstantial evidence at the time and what happened afterwards. The mood of the country was at its lowest. Why nobody was told about this I fear I may never know but it makes no sense at all. To this day I don't know why our Intelligence Officer did not even file a report. Why he never debriefed us or why Keith Nell was never contacted?"

"The Rhodesian public and politicians would have been thrilled to hear this news but they were never told," says Watt. "I don't know if this was done because I was once again being denied any recognition from the hierarchy or if there was another reason which I don't understand."[2]

"Some months after this I was handed the task of shooting down an aircraft," recalls Scheepers. "Intelligence received confirmed a Danish aircraft was flying recruits from Francistown in Botswana to Dar es Salaam in Tanzania for training and I was told to drop it.

"We were given a SAM-7, taught how to operate it and then deployed into Botswana to shoot down the DC-7. Dave Berry and I went in by vehicle and positioned ourselves alongside the main road north of Francistown leading to Kazungula and Livingstone which placed us under the aircraft's estimated flight path.

"While waiting, we also had the dual task of recording and keeping a log book of all the Botswana Defence Force military movement along the road. We were briefed that under no circumstance were we to engage the Botswanan army as we did not want another front to be opened against Rhodesia from the west.

"While waiting for the DC-7, we started worrying less about the enemy and more about lions. We had been warned of man-eaters in the area but neither Dave nor I took that too seriously. Well, that was a big mistake. The sun was setting when the lions roared but it was not a roar I was familiar with and I said to the men, 'These lions sound like they are hungry.' I could see from the looks on their faces they were in agreement. To give us some early warning I ordered everyone in close and compact and organised a para-cord trip-wire around the perimeter from which we hung water bottles and mugs so there would be a rattle if touched by approaching animals.

"I placed myself securely in the centre of the circle alongside the radio under a bush where I felt reasonably safe. Approximately just after midnight, I was rudely

---

[2] A similar account of this incident has appeared in Keith Nell's book Viscount Down, giving rise to sometimes bitter debate about the veracity of this report. While the truth may never be known as to the actual identity of the slain men, what is certain is weapons, equipment and documents from what was loosely known as a 'strela gang' did come into the hands of Special Branch. Just how and where from is not known to the author.

In an earlier book on the Rhodesian SAS by Barbara Cole, she writes of a contact led by a 'tracker' (who is almost certainly a pseudonym for Darrell Watt) which resulted in the deaths of three members of a group responsible for 'killing the (Viscount) survivors.' The date on which this contact took place is the 24th November based on the flight logbook entry of the helicopter pilot who uplifted Watt and his men after the engagement. It is fair to say the Rhodesian public would have been hugely cheered to have been told simply what was known at that time but word does not appear to have been passed on to the public or to 'ComOps'. Whether this was the fault of SAS HQ or Special Branch is not clear.

awakened by a rush of breath on my face that was seriously rotten. I opened my eyes and saw the face of this big lion smelling my face. It carried a massive mane and looked like a grizzly bear. At the same time James Scorgie on the perimeter tapped on his magazine to alert everyone to approaching danger. The boys were immediately alert and upright in their sleeping bags which upset and alarmed the two lions in the middle of us. They started growling angrily as the boys began frantically tapping their magazines which ended up sounding like a badly rehearsed rock band gone mad with lions doing the vocals. No longer were they double-tapping their magazines to wake each other, but to keep the lions away from them who by this time were racing around in front of us in a panic looking for an exit. The worse thing was that the boys, like good soldiers, sat up in their sleeping bags, creating a human barrier around the lions which made the situation even worse. Pandemonium isn't enough to describe what happened. It was like a circus arena gone mad and for the first time I felt that I would never ever again sleep in the middle of the 'call sign' because the two lions were scrambling around me and jumping over my head in a bid to get out of the circle. Relief came when they eventually leapt over our heads and disappeared. The next morning revealed huge lion tracks just nine inches from my head and none of the mugs had rattled. So much for my early-warning system. I must admit that since then I have never in all my military career experienced such an alert group of men at night as the lions continued to roar in the vicinity in the ensuing days. After the incident we couldn't stop laughing, but it was such nervous laughter of relief that I had to remind the boys we were in an ambush position. After waiting in ambush for a week and the DC-7 failing to arrive, the operation was aborted and we were only too glad to get out of Botswana."

RICHARD STANNARD

In December 1978 Watt's great friend Lieutenant Richard Stannard was back in action on the Russian Front having parachuted in with nineteen men from a Dakota under a full moon. All landed safely.

"My father was a policeman. I was educated at Umtali Boys' High which was close to the Mozambique border and there were great bars there so we used to bunk out of the hostel and go on some serious pub-crawls across the frontier. I kept getting caught and I think the masters got tired of caning me. Eventually the headmaster told me it was better I left. Looking back on those days I feel sorry for the staff there; they tried so hard with me but it was a thankless task.

"I was commissioned and joined the SAS but like a lot of the other guys I went across to the Selous Scouts but found I did not really fit in there. I liked and respected Ron Reid-Daly but did not work well with some of the Scouts and Ron told me it was probably better to go back to the SAS, which I did. Thanks to my old and dear friend Darrell Watt, I was told I could not just come back in and had to do the selection for a second time. This time, thanks to Darrell, it was even harder than the one before and they nearly killed me. This was my first operation after returning to the SAS from the Selous Scouts."

The SAS paratroopers were reacting to intelligence indicating that FRELIMO was about to transport a detachment of ZANLA troops from Maputo to the Rhodesian frontier. After stashing parachutes, they walked for three days towards the target. Finding that the river they were relying on for water was dry, they pressed on and 'cut' spoor of searching FRELIMO patrols.

"Water became a huge problem," remembers Stannard. "I could have called for an air-drop but thought this would invite derision from my peers who were watching me closely after my return from the Scouts. Many were pissed off with me for going in the first place. I sent Willem Ratte to look for water when we heard tree-frogs but he returned with nothing. I just told my guys we would have to tough it out and hope we found water soon."

Arriving close to their destination Stannard and Colour Sergeant Billy Grant went ahead to check and promptly stumbled into over forty ZANLA insurgents whom they did not engage. Returning to the main body, the killer group was positioned with two four-man early-warning sections north and south while Grant laid claymore mines.

"I knew we could not survive much longer without water so just hoped something would happen soon. Then suddenly I heard Dave O'Sullivan on the radio from his stop position and he said the 'gooks' were visual and filing past. It was nerve-wracking because he was counting them as they passed him by and the number just kept getting bigger. I think the 'gooks' were quite relaxed because they believed the area had been cleared by FRELIMO. The road they were on was only twenty metres away. When I heard Dave say eighty I looked at Billy next to me in the killer group and searched his face for guidance. I saw Billy nod, meaning 'Let's hit them.'"

"My heart was pounding so hard I was sure they could hear it," remembers Grant. "I will never forget the moment when I broke from cover and saw the look of sheer terror on the faces of those people as I fired that initial volley and the claymores were detonated. Before they hit the ground the rest of the killer group was attacking."

With half the soldiers armed with RPDs the fire was a solid sheet of lead, followed by grenades. The terrorists crumpled but not without some return fire, and in the initial exchange Corporal 'Mo' Taylor, the popular Englishman, was killed.

Grant remembers, "Some of the 'terrs' sprinted over to the other side of the track where they were afforded some cover. Unfortunately for them their heads were still exposed so Dave O'Sullivan put his sniper training to good use and was bowling them over like at a coconut shy."

"All credit to Billy," says Stannard. "Once the initial attack was over it was Billy who jumped to his feet and shouted to follow him which we did and we ran over the rise to find the enemy cowering in cover, whereupon we got busy again and a lot more of them went down. This was Billy at his aggressive best and close to fifty were dead and blood-trails provided clear evidence a lot of the survivors were leaking. No sooner was the shooting over than we were ripping water bottles off the bodies and guzzling the water. Incredibly, just after the shooting, two FRELIMO suddenly appeared, coming to have a look. We let them get close then Willem Ratte shot them.

"This may have been the most successful rifle ambush of the war. To my everlasting regret I never put Billy up for a medal because he deserved it. The way medals were being awarded it may have been turned down but I'm sorry I didn't try for him. Unfortunately, 'Mo' Taylor never made it; he was a wonderful guy. Just before he was killed he had given some of his water to one of the guys who he felt needed it more than he. That was an act of incredible kindness."

INNOCENTS DIE

Meanwhile the internal war for the hearts and minds of the rural populace continued. News that tribal chiefs were becoming increasingly vociferous in their support of the new political dispensation cheered the new leadership. Their message to the rural populace to reject overtures from the ZANLA propagandists and to support the new coalition government started to gain some traction. In response Mugabe issued a directive to silence the meddlesome leaders.

Following orders, 1978 ended with a senior chief in the Shabani area being stopped on the road by a group of ZANLA. The old man and his entourage were bayoneted and beaten before being burned to death. The terrorists then set fire to his village. Senator Chief Mafala's death only added to a long list of casualties suffered by traditional leaders, but being widely respected by all, his death was a blow to those who sought peace.

To the Rhodesian Special Branch there was another distressing angle. Their information suggested the group responsible had been aided and abetted by none other than the former premier of Southern Rhodesia, Garfield Todd. The message to the people in the rural areas who were unable to defend themselves was once again made abundantly clear: support the struggle or die. The war for the country's soul raged on.

Along the eastern border January 1979 brought little more than tragedy for the rural populace as ZANLA stepped up attacks on civilians. Early in the month, David Mirams, a respected District Commissioner for the Mrewa district, was killed when his Land Rover detonated a landmine. A first-class linguist and expert on African customary law, he had been just promoted to Regional Commissioner and was due to commence duties a week after he was killed. Enormously well-liked by the local Africans, over 3,000 attended his funeral in open defiance of ZANLA commissars who threatened those who showed support for government officials with death.

Despite repeated attacks Mrs Rose Hacking (62) and her husband Bert, eking out a living from a few small cash crops, were hanging on to their farm in the Odzi district when days later she too fell victim to a landmine. Rose, a nurse, had come to Rhodesia from England in happier times as a 'Sunshine Girl,' to join the civil service whereupon she met and married Bert. Grief-stricken, but determined to recover his dead wife's wedding ring, Bert abandoned the search when he stumbled upon her lower jaw.

Shortly thereafter, Pieter Steyn, another elderly Odzi farmer, was murdered and his labour badly beaten. On 9 January Petrus Blignaut, a Shabani farmer, was killed and his wife wounded in a vehicle ambush. Only his sixteen- year-old son's stout-hearted action in returning fire saved the entire family from being killed.

On 12 January the people of Umtali lost one of their favourites sons: Sergeant Clive Cripps of the SAS was killed in action. It was a sad day for the beleaguered townsfolk because the Cripps clan had played a leading role in founding the town and had stood firm in weathering the hardships of life on a new frontier. Through lions, pestilence and loneliness a pioneering family had won itself a place in the sun but at a price and one, it appeared, they had not finished settling.

In Beatrice, Jamie Scott, a fifteen-year-old schoolboy convalescing at home after a fall, found himself in a firefight with a dozen ZANLA terrorists. Hit four times, his rifle temporarily jammed, he went into cover, cleared the weapon and charged, routing the enemy while sustaining another wound in the chest. Lukas Koen, an animal health inspector, was ambushed and killed.

LIGHTS OUT

In late January 1979 a high-level decision was taken to hit central Mozambique's major power supply. This was an act that would outrage FRELIMO and much of the world but the pressures on the Rhodesians were higher than ever. Darrell Watt was given the green light to carry out the task and he immediately set about laying his plans. Orders from high were emphatic: the SAS could do the job but under no circumstances were they to leave any 'fingerprints.' Rhodesia would deny any involvement and insist it was the work of RENAMO rebels.

Getting back into Mozambique unannounced was the first problem. Watt wanted to parachute in but the three RENAMO men accompanying them were not para-trained. Watt's solution was simple, if outrageous: The RENAMO guides would be put in a wooden crate and dropped in as cargo. He was given the thumbs-down by the air force and it was decided they would helicopter in.

The target was the power plant at the Chicamba Real Dam wall, about seventy kilometres into hostile territory. From this point electricity was conveyed to Beira and the port through which much of the material and logistical support for ZANLA was being channelled. It was also an administrative centre for the enemy with personnel from the communist bloc countries a very obvious presence.

The challenge was daunting. Nearby, FRELIMO troops were at battalion strength in the town of Manica. There was a brigade with armour and heavy weapons at Chimoio, while a sophisticated relay station on a hill close to the Beira road provided an efficient state-of-the-art communications network. The raiders were well aware that news of any attack would be transmitted countrywide very rapidly. It was also known that patrols were traversing the target area regularly and a vigorous citizen-oriented information campaign was underway to alert the populace to the possibility of infiltrators from Rhodesia. The local penalties for failure to report suspicious activity were severe.

At the power station itself were two more company-strength FRELIMO units based on either side of the dam wall, equipped with heavy weapons, some of which were positioned to shoot down onto targets in the canyon up which Watt planned to approach the objective. The defenders had strict orders to shoot on sight anyone not immediately identifiable and at night there was a blanket curfew. If it moved it was to be shot.

Flying in at last light the raiders made an uneventful incursion. With painstaking effort to leave as little sign in their wake as possible Watt, his eleven men and the RENAMO operators made their way towards the target from their drop-off point. Moving at night, they watched every step using rivers to walk in wherever possible, and at times, with soft soil underfoot, the men removed boots and walked barefoot. They were pleased with the intermittent rain that helped erase their tracks.

Within striking distance of the objective, the team took stock and studied the target. Watt decided the best course of action would be to simply blow the turbines at the base of the wall and topple as many power lines as they could lay their hands on. He planned to approach under cover of dark leaving lookout parties to cover his back, lay the charges with delayed-time fuses and get out of the area at speed. When the detonations took place he and the rest of the culprits would have long made their escape.

Thereafter, foremost in his mind were his orders. To reinforce the subterfuge, he was unable to return to safety in Rhodesia after completion of the task. Tracks going west would compromise their identity and their origin. He would have to go east, deeper into enemy territory, with all the attendant dangers until deception was complete. Only when he was convinced no case could be made for connecting him and his troops to the sabotage was he to call for uplift.

But on closer inspection of the target, his hopes of a quick fix were dashed. It was not to be as simple as he first thought. The rains had pushed the water level in the dam too high and the water pouring out the floodgates was such they would not be able to access the turbines. Aborting the mission was quickly dismissed. It would be more dangerous and difficult but he would gather his men, all their weaponry and ordnance and bring maximum firepower to bear on the actual power station. "I decided to knock the shit out of the transformers, kill as many of the enemy as possible and then run like hell," remembers Watt.

To assist him in his destructive endeavours he had the use of a RENAMO-supplied 75mm recoilless rifle which would add much to the weight of fire they would lay upon the installation and those who sought to protect it. Medic John Riddick, a late addition to the raiding party, was largely responsible for carrying the weapon: "The 75mm barrel is a sod: too long and heavy for one guy and too short for two. On the way in we had one chap go down with heat exhaustion. One drip later he was back on his feet but I landed up lugging the bloody barrel. At one point I walked into a swamp and disappeared. Darrell dragged me out by the barrel amid much laughter." In charge of the firing of the 75mm was Sammy, a former artillery man and an expert on heavy weapons. With nightfall upon them, Watt issued a final briefing and the saboteurs set off to work. Soon they saw the lights of the garrisons burning brightly on the heights above them and they could hear the distant cacophony coming from the voices of the hundreds of men who sat contentedly within their cantonments blissfully unaware of the danger approaching. Metres away lurked some very dangerous men.

"We managed to get up very close," says Watt. "There were a few guards visible but they were completely unaware. We set up the gun under the power lines, with the intention of hitting the power hose, over 150 metres in the dark, and uphill, about fifteen degrees. I was still unsure exactly as to how to strike but my man on the 75mm insisted he could hit one of the staging valves and we were pretty sure that would set the cat amongst the pigeons. It was dark and it was a long shot. I asked him if he was sure he could hit it and he said he was. I said, 'OK, go for it.'

"He took aim and loosed off a round; it was smack on target, a bull's eye. The moment the first round hit home it was like Guy Fawkes as sparks flew, circuits tripped out and there was a loud screeching sound coming from the turbines. Eight rockets fired and eight hits, it was some sharp shooting. Once the power went out, the gates automatically opened to release the water. We then poured more fire into the place. Small arms with armour-piercing heads and RPG-7 rockets followed. We kept the 75mm going until the heat of the barrel made it unsafe to load and we prepared to evacuate.

"Before leaving we placed a charge on the working parts, destroyed the 75mm and then on our way out we blasted the power lines. There was a slight delay on the power lines because the Shrike detonator failed at first and had to be replaced but the second attempt saw them falling out of the sky. In a minute we had turned the place into a furnace with flames and sparks lighting the sky while the turbines screeched. Then we heard tanks firing at us and knew it was time to get out of there. It was total carnage and we were thrilled with our work but there was no time to savour the moment. We gathered our worldly possessions. Then we ran like bastards."

They needed to. The raiders raced east through the night towards the coast, deeper into hostile territory and the city they had just crippled. The battle for survival had just commenced.

Beira was instantly plunged into total darkness and there was no backup facility. An entire city had been brought to a shuddering halt and the port, the backbone of the local economy, was out of action until further notice. For the FRELIMO leaders, worse was the embarrassment. Recent pronouncements from their hierarchy had suggested that the "Rebel Rhodesians" were all but beaten, news that had been warmly received by most countries with diplomatic representation in the country. Particularly anxious to see the Rhodesians subdued were the Scandinavians who maintained a significant presence in Beira from where they provided strong support to FRELIMO and ZANLA. Finding themselves in the dark did little to boost their confidence in their allies.

Amidst the gloom, the official media initially suggested technical problems as the cause of the blackout but the truth inevitably seeped through the propaganda machine and fury replaced falsehood. The biggest manhunt in the history of the country was launched and thousands of troops and paramilitary were sent into the field and told to stay there until they had captured the perpetrators. Intercepts revealed strident commands emanating from the highest level. Rewards were offered for success and unpleasant consequences for failure. President Machel ordered blood to be drawn and he wanted it soon. The bodies of the attackers were sorely needed to assuage FRELIMO's dented pride.

Years on the Russian Front had left an impression on Watt. He had become respectful of FRELIMO tracking teams and knew how dogged they could be. He also knew he had stirred the proverbial hornets' nest and the enemy were going to throw their all into this particular cause. His initial plan was to devote all energy to speed; careful anti-tracking would have to wait but the raiding party was still loaded down with mines and mortar bombs in addition to their regular food, water and equipment. Each man was carrying close to 100 lbs. Fitness and mental toughness was to be put to the test. Failure would probably prove fatal. The commander warned his men to watch their step; a stumble and a broken ankle or torn ligament could bring about their death.

Fleet of foot and powered by a determination to survive and fight another day, they humped their packs, braced for the long haul and strode into the night as fast as their legs would move them. Virtually non-stop with heads down and shoulders straining, every now and then an upward glance would reveal the twinkling lights of the Southern Cross on their right. Then the stars disappeared behind the clouds and the soldiers could only wonder if a benevolent God had taken an interest in their plight.

He had. In the early hours of the morning the wind in their blackened faces blew stronger and cooler and it was soon followed by lightning bolts lashing the eastern sky to the accompanying sound of booming thunder. It was music to their ears. Then the rain came streaming down and they smiled as they soaked it up. Quickly, little rivulets formed atop the sand, now mud, and the water that flowed took with it the tracks that were their calling card to the enemy. Relief had arrived.

"Without the rain I'm not sure we'd have made it," recalls Watt. "Troops had saturated the area and we knew the local civilians were looking out for us too. There were tanks and other armoured vehicles deployed so if it came to a fight we weren't in with much of a chance. It was pretty eerie hearing them clanking and clunking around us. We walked solidly through the night, virtually without stopping, and when the rain came I changed direction immediately. The following day and night and then all the next day we kept moving as fast as our legs would carry us. It was a race away from almost certain death. Finally, we could go no more and I found a clump of trees close to a bend in a river. If we had to move, we had the option of the river but we could walk no further. Then we burrowed into the thickest cover we could find and hid as best we could in a crevasse."

Sammy remembers the escape. "I think it was one of the hardest forced marches of my career in the SAS. We were still heavy and the rain made our packs heavier. At one point I realised I couldn't keep my pants up anymore. The weight loss was such that they were falling off me. I managed to make a belt out of some bark I stripped off a tree and secured them. I thought if I was going to go down I would rather do so with my bloody pants on. At the end of it we were tattered and torn and so exhausted we could barely think straight."

"The activity around us was frantic," recalls Watt, "and on occasions hundreds of troops passed us by a stone's throw away. We held our breath. The RENAMO chaps were tops. They stayed very calm and promptly followed orders. One mistake then and we were in a great deal of trouble. If the enemy saw us, we would obviously fight but there were not many of us and of course there was the risk of blowing our cover. We could not call for help from Rhodesia because that would give the game away. We were very much alone.

"After four days we were completely out of food and there was still so much activity around us there was no chance of moving. I thought it must subside soon but it didn't. They were utterly determined to find us. Every day the hunger pangs grew worse and unfortunately I'm a big man and like my food.

"I made ten mugs of tea from my last teabag then I ate it. I remembered some survival tips given by Allan Savory and found some grasses that we could eat. Fresh and green but it helped very little in terms of nourishment. Still the search troops kept coming and we were starting to weaken but I was convinced a move would be fatal. I told the troops we just had to lie up and wait.

"A week went by and the boredom was killing. Then the days really started to drag but we knew the alternative might well be death. FRELIMO were desperate to find us, must have known we were close and seemed to be determined to continue the search.

"Two weeks after crawling into our hiding place I knew we had come to the end of our tether. We had to take a chance then and move to an LZ for uplift but there came another problem: the battery for our TR48 radio was stone dead and we had lost our only link with Salisbury. It was a troubling moment but one of the RENAMO chaps came to the rescue. He had worked on a farm nearby and thought he would be able to find it. He would go and find a battery. The next day in came this guy with a smile and a battery he had taken off a tractor. We fired up the radio and talked to home. They said they were coming immediately.

"I think hunger reaches a stage where your stomach forgets what it's for. Two weeks after the attack the helicopters arrived and the crews brought some sandwiches for us but we couldn't get them down. Our stomachs had shrunk and solid food was beyond our ability to digest. None of us could eat a thing. Eventually after a few failed attempts I managed to swallow a piece of bread and then had two slithers of meat and I was full. Normally I could eat half a cow and have room for more. Mozambique was a great spot if you wanted to lose weight."

In February 1979 the Conservative Party produced an election manifesto that delighted the majority of Rhodesians. It affirmed the fact that a Thatcher-led administration would recognise a government formed following the elections planned for April if they were free and fair. Once again it seemed there was hope.

CHAPTER 12

There's a race of men that don't fit in,
A race that can't stay still:
So they break the hearts of kith and kin,
And they roam the world at will.
—ANON

ANOTHER VISCOUNT DOWNED

On the afternoon of 12 February 1979 two bus-loads of casually attired travellers arrived at Kariba airport. In the heavy heat outside two Air Rhodesia Viscounts waited. Shod of their lively livery, now painted a dull matt grey to lessen the chances of a hit from a SAM missile, they served as a reminder of the dangers that lurked in the blue yonder. But among the passengers the mood was one of relaxed confidence. Known to most of them, the pilots were varying their routes from the airfield to confuse the terrorists and climbing quicker to exit the range of most of the known shoulder-fired missiles. They were sure the precautions taken were adequate. Red and green boarding cards were issued arbitrarily by airline staff.

Red cardholders would fly the first aircraft out, green second. One person who drew a green was an off-duty General Peter Walls.

Air Rhodesia Viscount *Umniati* duly took off from Kariba and banked as it climbed. Only minutes later there was an explosion, a Mayday call, a fireball and the old aeroplane tumbled out of the sky. This time the end was mercifully quick for the fifty-four passengers and five crew. There were no survivors. The captain, Jan du Plessis was still mourning the death of his son Leon who had been killed in action only months before at the controls of his 'Lynx' on a raid into Mozambique. In a savage irony, the Boyd family of six was wiped out in its entirety. They were dear friends of Dr MacLaren, the hero of the first Viscount disaster

A Dakota from No 3 Squadron was first on the scene and dropped paratroopers but the follow-up yielded no results. The terrorists had melted back into the local populace.

Joshua Nkomo appeared at a press conference in Ethiopia and gleefully took responsibility. Again the rest of the world was silent. As long as the victims were white the deed was deemed acceptable.

STANNARD BACK TO CHIMOIO

At the same time, less than twenty kilometres north of Chimoio, at Vanduzi, enemy numbers were increasing alarmingly. Effective security measures had made it difficult to reconnoitre and Richard Stannard was tasked with doing a two-man close-in surveillance of the camp.

"Following on from what Darrell and Chris Schulenburg had been doing I was trying to develop the two-man recce concept," recalls Stannard. "While looking at this, Captain Martin Pearse approached me to help him assess a new candidate officer by the name of John 'Jungle' Jordan. We had been at school together but John did very well and I was expelled for consistently bad behaviour! He became a prefect but now the roles were reversed and I was in charge.

"Because 'Jungle' was a TF {Territorial Force} officer he was not well received in the SAS; indeed, there was some hostility. Martin asked me to take him operational and make sure he had a hard time. Martin was pretty doubtful John had what it took to be a badged SAS officer but instructed me to give him a crack.

"I decided to take him on the recce and briefed him on what was going to happen. He was suitably shocked and then another problem occurred to me when considering John was twice my size. I then warned him I would not be able to carry him if he was shot and killed or incapacitated simply because I did not have the physical stature. So I thought I better get our predicament clarified. I explained to him that in the event he went down I would have to burn him and I would do that with a white phosphorus grenade. I told him this was so he would not be captured and if he was dead I would incinerate him to make him unidentifiable. Unsurprisingly I saw 'Jungle's' blue eyes widen considerably on receipt of this news."

In early March six soldiers flew by helicopter to a firm base atop a mountain. Once settled, Stannard and Jordan bade their comrades farewell and set off for the target area, carrying the bare minimum to give them maximum manoeuvrability.

Days after arriving in-theatre, careful to anti-track en route and having moved only at night, the two neared their destination. Creeping in close after nightfall, they saw ZANLA movement and knew they were in the complex. Needing a vantage point nearby, they struggled up a precipitous mountainside in the night. Adding to their problems they encountered swarms of angry bees which stung them repeatedly, but when dawn broke the scene before their eyes delighted them. The camp complex and all the access routes were splayed out below.

"The view was incredible," recalls Jordan. "In daylight the path network was very visible but the bivouacs were well hidden."[57]

The size and complexity of the camp was greater than anticipated and the pair knew they needed more time to watch but water was running low and they looked hopefully to the heavens where dark clouds gathered.

Relaying all the necessary information back to Salisbury via the observation post, the pair waited expectantly for a full ground-air attack on the busy encampment but the word back was disappointing. Resources were tightly stretched and men and equipment were simply unavailable for what was required. An airstrike was all that could be offered. At first light on the morning of 17 March, Canberras swooped. Lying on their backs, blocking their ears with their mouths open to equalise the displacement of air in their lungs that would follow the explosions, they held their breath.

"We felt the earth move when they hit," says Jordan. "Two bombers, two bombs and the vegetation no longer existed. Nothing! It was as if a giant had shaved the face of the earth. Full-grown *mopani* trees had disappeared without trace. The quiet after the noise is what I actually remember more than the actual bang. Nothing: no wind, no birds, absolutely nothing." Then, just as the dust settled, the silence was shattered as a pair of 'Hunters' screamed on to the target. Looking on, Jordan recalls: "Next thing the rockets under the wings ignited, leaving the plane in a cloud of smoke. Our eyes focused on the smoke and we saw this rocket speeding in to the ground. I saw a mangled piece of metal, a huge truck, explode into the air and land several metres away."

The 'Hunters' then struck repeatedly until their ammunition was exhausted. The section leader bade farewell and turned for their base in Gwelo. "We'll have a cold beer for you guys," was the laconic message. "Bloody hell, we were thirsty and hadn't had a meal for days and they would be having both within an hour," remembers Jordan.

Only then did it become clear to the two SAS men how widespread the enemy were and how many more there were than estimated. Following the jets' departure, a 'Lynx' arrived to loiter over the camp, directing helicopter gunships on to targets. Anything that moved was cut down.

But any thoughts of a return home were quickly dashed by the SAS commander in the 'Lynx'. Jordan and Stannard were to be resupplied and ordered to stay and maintain an eye on the complex. With great skill, an Alouette pilot flew his chopper in close and a box with supplies was surreptitiously dropped to ground. There was a welcome surprise. "We now had fresh batteries plus a few ration packs. The best thing of all was the cold beers wrapped in newspaper, fresh bread rolls and some hot food.58

The following morning all was quiet and the only movement was that of the vultures that swooped to gorge on the cadavers. Then the silence was broken by the arrival of a FRELIMO Armoured Personnel Carrier which scoured the area looking at the damage. A report was made but the pair was told to sit tight and watch. The next day more APCs arrived and another signal was sent which brought 'Hunters' quickly overhead. But there was danger below and only a rapid response from the wingman saved the section leader from a heat-seeking missile which was fired at the lead aircraft. Following a shouted warning, the pilot pulled out the dive and climbed to the sun, losing the missile in the process, before the aircraft returned to deal decisively with the armour and the anti-aircraft gunners. All went quiet again. That evening the two men were told to withdraw.

The following afternoon they made their way down the mountain using the same route. Once down, Stannard took a compass bearing and set their line of march. Moving quietly, they were making brisk progress when they came upon a well-worn path and fresh tracks. They froze, then went to their haunches as the world around them exploded. Under a fusillade of machine-gun fire, the two fought back furiously as the trees splintered and clouds of dust enveloped them.

"You can practise as often as you like," says Jordan, "but I challenge anyone to simulate this situation and the feeling that hits you. The desire, want and need to just run like hell is so strong but you have to remain perfectly calm and collected because that is what is going to save your life."[59] Jordan could hear the enemy getting into extended line to prepare for a sweep through their position. The tapping of their rifle magazines was ominous but also helpful in that the two SAS men could gauge the enemy distance.

Jordan felt his leg sting and a warm wetness but paid no attention. He was alive and mobile. "I started praying," he says. "Over and over again I repeated the Lord's prayer. It certainly helped me and gave me direction."[60]

"I saw him get shot," remembers Stannard, "and heard it too as it hit him. There was a break in the firing while they tried to figure out where we were hiding and I radioed a distress signal back to the relay team requesting an immediate hot extraction. Then I think 'Jungle', realising he was wounded, remembered my warning about burning him and took off like the wind. I took off after him but with wounded leg and all I could not catch the poor bugger. He was not running from the 'gooks' but from me! I screamed at him to stop and eventually he did but I was exhausted. When I got to him I told him to relax, that I wouldn't light him up with a phosphorous grenade"

Desperate to escape detection, the two ignored direction and concentrated on finding the rockiest ground underfoot in a bid to reduce their footprint as they hurried away. Jordan's leg pain worsened and he was forced to take stock. Cutting away his trouser leg, he saw two bullet wounds above the knee caked with dirt and drying blood. Dressings were hastily applied and he hobbled on.

Word was then received that choppers would be with them in thirty minutes but the next problem was finding an LZ in the heavily wooded *mopani* forest. As they moved, they heard the voice of the pilot asking them for a radio signal to help him home in on them. Next he was over them but no way could he descend through the tree canopy so a lateral bar was lowered for them to grab. But the weight was too much for the machine and the pilot was forced to get air speed to remain airborne before the men were above the trees. Crashing through the branches, Jordan lost his grip on the bar and was left hanging in a tree. "Had I survived two gunshot wounds in my leg and dodged 'terrs' for seven or eight kilometres only to be left to die or be killed in a tree?" he recalls.

Having stabilised his aircraft, the pilot swung around and returned to the frantic Jordan who, with Herculean strength, launched himself at the undercarriage, managing to grab a wheel. Hanging on for life itself, the chopper lurched then rose and sped to safety. "It was bloody hairy," recalls Stannard, "there were thousands of 'gooks' there and I did think we were history at times but we made it and 'Jungle' did damned well. Happily, he made it in to the SAS."

TWO-MAN RECCE

As the enemy numbers mounted so did a sense of desperation in the ranks of senior Rhodesian security personnel. Watt was ordered to recce and infiltrate a large enemy camp. He knew it would not be easy.

"One of our officers had already tried to get in there but he was quickly discovered and had to run for his life. I knew I would have to take great care and move very slowly if I was to get in to where I needed to be.

"I was with Shane Frawley who had come from Australia. He was wary of me. Earlier, we had been ambushing on the Zambezi and nothing had happened. It was hot and boring when a huge black *shongololo* {Millipede} appeared on the path in front of us and Shane, having never seen one before, was fascinated. He said to me, 'What the fuck is this, sir?'

"I looked at him and knew he was bloody hungry when he asked if he could eat it. I thought we needed some comedy so I said, 'Sure, they're crunchy and juicy.' Then he asked if it was okay to eat them alive and I said, 'Sure, just pick it up, bite its head off then chew.'

"He hesitated but Rich Swan said, 'they're delicious, Shane, eat it quick before it gets away.' That convinced Shane and he grabbed it then bit its head off and stuffed the rest of it into his mouth, chewing like mad. We watched in amazement as this juice started to trickle down his chin, then his face went bright red and the poor *shongololo* exploded out of his mouth with him gagging and swearing before scrambling for his water bottle, gulping it down then collapsing in a heap with his throat on fire.

"On this occasion it took us six days of very careful movement and anti-tracking for Shane and me to sneak right into the middle of their position. It was the most amazing sight: we were completely surrounded by thousands of armed men who knew there was a group of us in the area but did not know where. We lay in thick cover just below one of their anti-aircraft positions. We could hear their chatter which did not stop. Patrols passed regularly just in front of us. The camp was well planned and sensibly spread out so there was no big concentration that could get bombed from the air.

"I decided we had to move if we were to avoid detection and that night Shane and I made for a rocky outcrop and crawled into a cave where I felt more comfortable. We carefully brushed our tracks outside away.

"That morning several people came down to one of the scattered pools in the riverbed to do some laundry and collect water. It was quite clear that they were from the enemy base and thus fair targets but I could see no weapons. I struggled with the dilemma of taking them out or not. I decided I just could not do it and told Shane. He was furious.

"'Damn it, sir, all this and now we're not going to kill any of them. Let's shoot some of the motherfuckers then but let's do something!'

"I told him to calm down and reminded him there were several thousands of them and we were in the middle of their camp. One shot and we would never get out of there alive. But he was persistent 'Let's shoot and run!' When I refused he was very upset.

"'Well, fuck it then. If we're not going to kill any of these cunts I might as well pack my bags and go to Thailand where at least I can get laid!'

"That night we crept out of our position and started the walk out to uplift and home to report what we had seen. Shane Frawley was good as his word: he packed his bags and went to Thailand to enjoy the girls."

BISHOP MUZOREWA WINS POWER

For Ian Smith the end of the line had, in a sense, been reached. By May 1979 it became clear that, in an election closely supervised by the white-led Rhodesian security forces, Bishop Muzorewa had won a poll that drew close to 70% of the electorate in spite of ZIPRA- and ZANLA-inspired intimidation. While David Owen sulked, even the country's harshest critics were forced to compliment the presiding Rhodesian servicemen and women of all races who were probably ushering in their own demise.

Hopes of an end to conflict ran high when on 4 May Mrs Thatcher won the British general election. On the campaign trail she had made it clear that if the election was deemed fair by Lord Boyd, her watchdog on the ground, she would recognise the new black-led administration and the country would be allowed to emerge from the political wilderness. Rhodesians took her at her word. A happy ending to the ongoing tragedy appeared to be at hand but African reaction to her win was immediate. The unelected government of Nigeria promptly threatened British business interests in the country if the new Conservative government softened on recognition. The 'lady not for turning' started to twist in the political wind.

On 31 May Ian Smith finished his last day in office. He and Janet took one last walk through 'Independence,' the house that had been their own for the last fifteen years and which they had grown to love. "We didn't talk, we just felt," Smith recalls. They bade their small staff farewell and left for their new house not far away in the suburb of Belgravia. The next day Bishop Muzorewa was sworn in as Prime Minister of the country that would briefly be known as Zimbabwe-Rhodesia.

COMBAT TRACKING AT SPEED

In April 1979 I was told to take a fighting patrol from A Squadron into the Matibi Tribal Trust Land in the south-east," Watt recalls. "The 'gooks' had established a strong presence there, making it almost a liberated area. The RLI had been in and taken quite a beating. I had good guys with me including Gerry de Lange, Rob Slingsby, Frank Tunney, Wayne Ross-Smith and Mike West. They had good bush skills which was very important and we were very fit and very mobile. Unfortunately, some soldiers believed they could track simply because they had done the tracking course, but it was never that simple. We all had RPDs and carried lots of ammo."

"We were in gunfights virtually every day," recalls Ted. "My nerves were shattered. I got back to our base camp and awoke crawling around looking for my radio. It was physically and mentally exhausting but Darrell was indefatigable; he just kept going. There were some lighter moments. Dave Berry found a python and decided he needed a friend. He went to sleep with it and woke up in the morning covered in bites. He had been rolling on it and it had bitten him. They parted company.

"On another occasion we came upon a 'highway'; about 150 'gooks' walking in file had flattened a thoroughfare coming into the country. There were still only six of us but four of us were carrying RPDs. We caught them and fought a series of running battles. Not sure how many were killed but we were certainly causing the enemy a lot of trouble."

"The success of this operation was based on being able to anti-track and the lessons learned from Jacob and Philemon during my early hunting days were invaluable," says Watt. "I knew exactly how to shake anyone following us when I needed to and to draw them in when I wanted to kill them. The killing ground was very important and had to be visualised on the move well in advance. I always tried to draw them in over hard ground which made tracking tough. They would then have to cross-grain, mingle and circle the area looking for the spoor. I would walk in a buffalo-hook pattern, positioning myself on their flank and then hit them. I knew the key was to keep moving and keep the 'gooks' guessing. At times I deliberately left a trail to lead them into compromising positions. On one occasion I duped them into position and we then hit them on the flank in extended line. This caused quite a stir as the enemy felt they were being attacked in an area they considered their own. They called in reinforcements from Mozambique, some of whom were actually FRELIMO, but we were ready for them and were on their tracks almost as soon as they crossed the border. We simply stayed on their tracks until we caught up with them and killed them. Our bush craft skills helped us anticipate their movements and find them. The 'gooks' did not enjoy it at all.

"This is where this small group of mine did the damage. The enemy thought they were up against a lot of men. We were never more than twelve but were aggressive, extremely fit and possessed shooting skills beyond training. Frank Tunney and Mike Mingay were masters of the machine gun. We were tenacious, enthusiastic and never gave up. This was not the Vietnam scenario of chopper in, quick patrol then chopper out. We ran up to twenty kilometres a day, literally running them out of the area. I was reprimanded for being reckless and told to slow down. But if we were on spoor that was all that mattered. Other troops were moved out of the area because no one knew where we would pop up next. Just how many we killed I don't know but there were a lot of bodies."

"At one stage we were in the middle of an area which we knew was heavily infiltrated," recalls Ted. "Darrell led us up a hill, carefully anti-tracking all the way. At the top he told me to stay put while he and the other four went down to try and flush the enemy. A voice spoke to me; it said get down flat behind a rock and face the other way. Darrell and the others left; I took my pack and lay down. Minutes later there was a loud roar and it was as if I had been hit by a gale as trees shook and the grass around me was flattened. Then the mortars started exploding nearby. I fired back but I knew if Darrell and the others didn't come soon I was going to die. Thankfully they did, and we then counter-attacked which sent them running but Darrell knew they would not go far and we found another OP. Darrell and I sat back to back covering all the approach angles while the others were sent out to flush them again. Then through the binoculars Darrell watched a cow being slaughtered in the distance. He knew this was to provide food for the 'terrs' and we took off. He approached the man who was butchering it and put the heat on him and demanded he tell us where the 'gooks' were. The guy was terrified and led us up a hill. We were barely two metres away when we saw them and those RPDs of ours went mad. They did not know what had hit them; there were bodies sprawled all over the place. We counted sixteen dead but there must have been many more wounded."

By this time, we were virtually out of ammunition and I was hoping we might get an uplift but Darrell was far from finished. He called for a resupply and I think we each took on another 1,000 rounds. Then we set off again.

"Darrell picked another granite hill near a dry riverbed to OP from. On the edge, among the rocks, he spied a bush. Using his *panga*, he cut inside it and cleared a hiding place which he could squeeze into wearing just his shorts and vest. We stayed behind well out of view. Sure enough, from there he spotted about another hundred coming down the edge of the riverbank towards us. I was ordered to contact the Fire Force which was standing by but meantime we got into position to ambush them. The choppers had not arrived by the time they walked into our killing-ground so we hosed them down. They were sitting ducks, running out in the open in the riverbed and there was momentary mayhem before the survivors found cover but then the Fire Force was on them. A 'Lynx' strafed and bombed, sending them running into the stop groups. I'm not sure how many were killed but estimate around forty. Next we heard from some people in Internal Affairs that the villagers were arriving in droves, asking to be taken into the protected villages; clearly they no longer thought it was safe to be associated with the 'terrs' and wanted safety. This was a massive turnaround. In my view Darrell Watt was the best SAS operator of them all. I don't think he got anything like the recognition he deserved."

"The fact that we were consistently successful was because of our bush experiences," recalls Watt. "Our tracking abilities reached a peak after some years when we could almost guarantee that if we were on tracks there definitely was going to be a contact even if it took days and big distances. Remember, the 'gooks'' thoughts were to get into the TTLs and there they felt safe, being looked after by other groups and the *mujibas*. So they would put their heads down and cover great distances day and night to get to those areas. They never considered that we could move faster than them, bearing in mind we were also packing heavy loads.

"We triggered one contact where we simply wore a group down and they could not keep moving. We were fitter and stronger than they were. Exhausted, they were resting and listening to music on a radio when we swept onto them in extended line with the RPDs going like hell. They were completely outgunned and outfought. Some escaped and some were wounded. We stayed on their spoor another fifteen kilometres and hammered them again. We could see them running ahead of us, shouting for help and telling their comrades to get the fuck out of the area. There was panic and we just kept hitting them again and again. All the time the air force was on standby and reacted quickly to our calls so they picked off a lot of 'gooks' running in all directions.

"In one engagement we had over a hundred moving fast in front of us. The Fire Force came in and hit them on the run. 'Horse' Greenhough was wounded by shrapnel from the 'K-Car' in the ensuing battle.

"On another occasion I knew we were close to a group that was tiring. It was midday and very hot. I spotted women carrying food and water and knew it was for the enemy so we grabbed them and ordered them to tell us exactly where the enemy was. The women were terrified. They said they were right here and pointed over a rise nearby. We dropped our packs and attacked immediately. They were completely demoralised and we hit them at almost point-blank range. They just ran. We shot them down but some escaped so we followed them again until we caught them again and shot them.

"Days later I received a signal from a Major van Zyl from the 10th Territorial Battalion (Rhodesia Regiment). The DC's camp and protected village at Matibi had been attacked and they had tracks. I reacted with eleven of my guys and the major joined us with a platoon of his guys.

"On tracks we walked all day through the *mopani* woodland. The 'gooks' knew we were behind them and had their afterburners on. I was impressed with the TF major and his boys: tough guys, they kept going all day and water was short. At times

I was shouting at my guys to keep the pace and keep them tactical. When I saw smoke ahead I knew there was a village coming up and knew they would use that village to warn them that we were close. The TF major asked me what my plan was and I told him we would circle the village in a wide arc and position ourselves well beyond the hut complex. Moving carefully in such small numbers, I knew I could get to where I wanted to be without the 'gooks' knowing.

"I knew it was going to be a big punch-up so I radioed in to request that a Fire Force be prepared for deployment with strike aircraft. Major van Zyl asked me how I could make the call without having actually seen the 'gooks'. I said I knew they were there and Captain MacKenzie would listen to me. Cocky Benecke was flying the 'Lynx' and he told the FAF {forward airfield} commander that it was me on the ground and if I said there were 'gooks' there then there were 'gooks'. Bob [MacKenzie] agreed. The officers at the JOC wanted a physical sighting before ordering a deployment but they were persuaded. Troops were quickly deployed by chopper but dropped far enough away so as not to alert the enemy. Cocky's 'Lynx' was airborne but also out of earshot. I checked for tracks beyond where I thought the enemy were positioned and found none. Then I knew for certain that they were between where I stood and the village.

"I fanned my blokes out into extended line and we moved slowly back to the village. Soon I saw movement ahead and gave the Fire Force commander the signal to strike. The RLI paratroopers jumped precisely where the tracks came in and the stop groups on the flanks were perfectly placed.

"On hearing the choppers, the 'gooks' stampeded but right onto us so we were able to nail them as they ran towards us. I could just hear someone shouting 'Fuck me . . . Fuck me' as these guys boiled out of the bush and ran into us. 'gooks' were dropping all around us. Those that broke away were shot by the Fire Force.

"At the end of it the major said, 'How the hell you figured all that out I'll never know. I've never seen anything like it in my life.' "We killed all of them, close to forty, and carried on with these ops for a few more weeks, by the end of which we had pretty much cleared most of the 'gooks' out of the area."

"We in the air force got used to Darrell's marathon tracking efforts at high pace," remembers Benecke. "I did a number of contacts with Darrell over the years and there was always action. He was a tracker of unbelievable note."

"Not everyone liked to work with Darrell," recalls Ted. "He had muscle rolling over his knees. He would pull his pack on and then there was no stopping him. We were carrying packs weighing over forty kilograms and we would end up staggering after him. His stamina was incredible and his tracking ability was absolutely amazing. I carried the TR48 radio when I was with him. That, in addition to water, food, spare batteries, sleeping gear and 700 rounds of ammo, was quite a load. For radio communications we used Morse code except when under fire.

"There was another time where we were on tracks and moving fast for two days. Six of us and seventy of them. The enemy had established themselves very well and we were tasked to dislodge them. We had been shot at so often that we were very jittery. At one point we stopped. Darrell was looking down at the tracks and then I saw black heads ahead. Darrell put up his hand to stop me but it was too late and I opened up. Darrell led us charging forward into heavy fire and the 'terrs' ran into a rocky outcrop. Darrell and I got behind a log, lying on our backs and I called for air support which came about twenty minutes later. We killed a few but I was left behind to man the radio when the others ran forward."

"We were running on blood spoor," remembers Johan Bezuidenhout. "Darrell told us to go around the *kopje* {small hill} to cut them off but Rob Slingsby didn't listen. He went straight up and they were waiting there."

"I think Rob may have become complacent in a way," says Ted. "He had been shot at so many times he thought he could get away with it but not this time. The bullet hit him square between the eyes."

"I told him not to do it," says Watt, "and unfortunately he did not listen. It was on the eleventh of April and the last year of the war. He was the only man under my command I lost through the entire war; still one man too many."

"I know that Rob died in a team that he loved and respected, not that anyone wants to die, but dying in your team made a difference," says Mike West.

"Back at barracks after I was commissioned I never felt comfortable in the officer's tearoom for the daily 10h00 teas," says Watt. "I wasn't well liked there and they struggled to say anything positive about our recent successes. The officers there said they had been covering our movements in the southeast from the operations room and had never seen 'call signs' moving at such speed, but my great troops received no praise at all. They would never identify us to 'ComOps'; the reports would just say 'SAS operations.'

"Later I heard Bob MacKenzie spoke quietly to Gerry de Lange and congratulated him on what we had achieved. He told him that all the 'gooks' in the sector were on the run and 'ComOps' had sent their congratulations. Reports received told of the people in the area having been shocked by the activities of an unknown 'call sign' that had reversed the enemy dominance in the area."

"I know for a fact that Darrell Watt in particular got the tough, shitty jobs that the glamour boys did not want," says a former SAS officer. "He spent way more time in the bush than most soldiers, let alone officers. As a junior officer I did not get along well with all the SAS officers. I missed the RLI where the atmosphere was very much more friendly and everyone was focused on killing the 'gooks'."

"All I asked of my superiors was for a small medal for Rob Slingsby as a measure of respect and something for his family but it was turned down," remembers Watt. "I'll never forgive them for that; he deserved it a lot more than other people who were decorated. Medals are always a big problem in any army but I did wonder about what it took to get one. On one of the few occasions when I was non-operational following my wounding, I was tasked with standing in as Squadron adjutant. Whiling away the time I scratched in the drawers for something to read and discovered a clip of medal citations. Among them was one awarding me a Silver Cross. Others were for Captains MacKenzie and Willis. They received theirs but I was overlooked. Looking back, I feel sorry for some of the chaps who served with me. I put some of them up for medals but nothing happened and I think that was because they were my guys. No matter what we did we were not considered good enough. A sort of 'Devils Guard,' I suppose."

"Darrell was not popular with the senior officers," remembers former soldier Brian Murphy. "But I don't think there's a single man who served in the Rhodesian SAS who believes he got the recognition he deserved."

By the end of June hopes for recognition of the new Muzorewa government were fading and Foreign Secretary Peter Carrington was having his political way with Mrs Thatcher. The aristocratic former Guards officer revealed his contempt for her when he described her as a 'fucking stupid, petite, bourgeois woman.' On Rhodesia, he was firmly against her honouring her campaign undertaking. Convinced the white Rhodesians still held too much power, and anxious to see them properly punished for their vainglorious unilateral declaration of independence, he pushed firmly for a return to the bargaining table.

At the same time, Lord Carver, along with other figures in the British political hierarchy and the press, were making it clear that Nigeria, amongst others, would extract an economic price if principle was allowed to override the pragmatism that went with conforming to the dictates of Africa's dictators. To make it clear that they meant business, General Olesegun Obasanjo ordered the seizure of BP's assets in Nigeria. The Americans, with Andrew Young assiduously courting the Nigerian dictatorship, were also dancing to the tune beating out of Abuja. Distancing himself further from the Muzorewa government, Carter somehow decided the new constitution was the work of "white" people. Although his premise was wide of the mark, the fact that it was 'white' was sufficient cause for him to denounce it.

When, out of the blue, the Rhodesian CIO broke a CIA spy ring exposing sensitive links that ran from Rhodesia through several African countries, alarm bells rang at the highest level in Washington. Salisbury received word that the US administration would move to lift sanctions and recognise the Muzorewa government in return for their agents. A naïve Muzorewa took the Americans at their word and the spies were released. The Carter administration promptly denied knowledge of any deal and it was back to deadlock.

MORE FARMERS MURDERED

For the farmers there was no respite. In late June the Rhodesian farming community mourned the death of one of their stoutest of heart. A Second World War veteran captured at Tobruk, Ben Stander, a tough Afrikaner, returned to Rhodesia after the war and carved a small ranch out of hostile country in the south-east Lowveld. Aptly named 'Battlefield Ranch,' he took on lion, leopard, drought and disease and built up one of the finest Brahman herds in the country. First ambushed in 1976, he escaped injury but his wife Gerda was shot through the legs. Soon after this incident one of Stander's nephews lost both legs in action against terrorists while another was killed in early 1978 in an ambush on a neighbouring farm. In August 1978 Ben and his son Adrian were ambushed again. Adrian was killed outright. Ben, despite a severe chest wound, survived. Having then moved his wife to safety in Salisbury, he returned to the ranch to press on but on the 20 June 1979 his fight to protect his property came to an end when he and a friend were ambushed and killed.

In the Midlands Denis and Marita Hofmeyr were ambushed on their way to collect their children from school. Denis survived but Marita died on arrival at a friend's farm.

Outside Marandellas terrorists attacked a lonely farmhouse, killing eighty-one-year old James Jeffreys. The next day Tom Hartley, an elderly farmer, having abandoned one farm to be closer to the capital, was murdered. When Abraham Botha (60), his wife Susanna (50) and two grandchildren arrived back at their farm near Gwelo they were attacked by terrorists hiding nearby. Susanna returned fire but was hit and went down. Abraham, crippled without his artificial leg attached, struggled to shield the children and managed to crawl into the house with the baby where the two survived. The little boy, two years old and frantic with fear, ran haphazardly before being shot down alongside his dying grandmother.

THE 'IRON LADY' FOLDS

In a rare break from protocol the Queen entered the political arena. President Kaunda had warned Her Majesty of a possible rift in the Commonwealth if Mrs Thatcher went ahead with her commitment to recognise Muzorewa. This threat gained the Queen's full attention and, urged on by the Foreign Office, she brought the full weight of Royalty to bear on her prime minister. Many in Rhodesia believed the Sovereign was a silent Rhodesian supporter; they were proved wrong.

Adding weight was Australia's Prime Minister Malcolm Fraser who was in bellicose form as the African leaders cheered his stand against the new democracy in Salisbury. Australia, he made clear, shared the continental desire to see Mugabe in power.

The Nigerians bluntly reiterated that their commercial ties to the UK would be affected if Britain did not tow the African line, and luminaries in the British ruling establishment such as Lord Carver made no apologies about bending principle to economic expediency. Britain, he insisted, should and would oblige the Nigerians.

The pressure worked; the iron in the lady residing at 10 Downing Street turned to straw. On 6 August, Mrs Thatcher formally reneged on her promise to recognise the winner of the April elections.

A new all-party conference, under the chairmanship of Peter Carrington, would be convened at Lancaster House and all options were on the table. For the soldiers there would be no relief. Some of the biggest battles of the war awaited them.

CHAPTER 13

Tonight we mourn our dead. Those brothers
Who still lie; wrapped in camo shrouds
Beneath Rhodesian soil.
—CHAS LOTTER

CHOPPER DOWN

By 1979 intelligence services estimated over 10,000 ZANLA were operating from inside Mozambique. Rhodesian commanders looked with alarm at the reports coming in about the massive build-up of war matériel in Maputo and noted the growing concentration of enemy troops in the town of Mapai. With Rhodesia still ostracised by the rest of the world, Samora Machel had decided to help Mugabe deliver a knock-out blow and committed a thousand FRELIMO troops to Mugabe's forces when they took up a strongly defended position in Mapai under FRELIMO command. The recent infiltration into Rhodesia of unprecedented numbers of FRELIMO troops alongside ZANLA had already sent a strong signal to Rhodesian Intelligence that the Mozambicans were going for the jugular. When the CIO reported that FRELIMO infiltration into the country was to be boosted and ZANLA and FRELIMO were to be comprehensively integrated into a single unitary force the alarm bells rang loud. The Rhodesians had to react and they had to do so fast. What was now clear was that the enemy was dangerously repositioned only forty kilometres from the border, and thanks to Soviet military expertise they were well dug in and well-defended. An aerial photograph of the area revealed five separate camps and defences bristling with well positioned anti-aircraft guns. Clearly the enemy was going to stand and fight and another battle loomed.

As a result, an ambitious plan, codenamed 'Operation Uric', was drawn up; it would be the biggest offensive of the war. The aim: to demolish the five main bridges in Gaza Province and cutting the supply line to the enemy from Maputo. In the process, of great importance, the road and rail bridges over the Aldeia da

Barragem agricultural scheme were to be destroyed along with the irrigation canal which would trigger a ruinous flood that would disrupt the communications infrastructure and cause considerable damage to the economy. Demolitions complete, the force would then attack and destroy the heavily defended staging base in Mapai through which some 50% of all insurgents passed en route to Rhodesia. If Mapai could be overcome it was expected the enemy would have to relocate further south, increasing the distance they would have to travel through inhospitable country before entering Rhodesia. Thereafter, an intensive campaign involving ambushing, mining and aerial attacks would be mounted to frustrate the movement of infiltrators.

The operation would comprise a large invading force of 360 drawn from the SAS, RLI and the Corps of Engineers, 350 kilometres into Mozambique and a little over a hundred kilometres from the country's capital. The Rhodesian Air Force was told to make every aircraft at its disposal available. These included eight 'Hunters', six Canberras, six 'Lynxes' and twenty-eight helicopters. News that South Africa would assist with helicopters, attack jets and manpower came as an enormous relief. P.W. Botha, it was reported, was incensed by news that the British government was yet again moving the goal-posts on the Rhodesian dispute and made it known that he took the growing threat so close to his country's borders very seriously. Accordingly, he gave the nod to his commanders to help eliminate it.

Looking at the Mapai defences it was clear to the planners that taking it was sure to be no pushover. Ideally, a conventional force using artillery, armoured cars and tanks would be deployed but attacks in the past had shown how effective lightly armed Rhodesian troops were against seemingly insurmountable opposition. Time and again their skilful musketry, discipline and reckless aggression had won the day. The hierarchy, looking to scale down the force levels as much as possible, gambled on a repeat performance. The air force would launch pre-emptive strikes against targets Barragem, Maxaila and Mapai in a bid to do the softening up, while the soldiers would do the killing at close range.

Prior to the main attack 200 troops with fuel and supplies were positioned at the designated administrative base east of Mapai. Thought to be an island within a swamp which would provide some natural protection, it was discovered to be dry.

"We were told to prepare for a serious scrap but the start of this operation was a pleasure for me. We were positioned in beautiful game country," recalls Watt, "flat, open grassland studded with magnificent palms, there were quite a lot of wildebeest in the area. We flew in in a wave of ten helicopters and the place was deserted except for an old Shangaan hunter who sat at his fire with his cooking pot. Dressed in animal skins, armed with bow, arrows and a spear, he had one of those strong faces that told a long story and I was fascinated by him. The commotion around him did not faze him at all. I asked him what he was cooking and he offered me some wildebeest tail. In a calabash he had some of the local beer. He was quite happy with his lot. As far as he was concerned, we could get on with our war and he would get on with his life. I envied him."

Meanwhile back in Rhodesia there was anxiety as low cloud and low visibility kept the air force grounded and delayed the main attack. With troops already deployed in enemy territory at 'Oscar Bravo' Administrative Base near the village of Chigubo, and reports that FRELIMO were searching for an enemy presence, the advance-party there was dangerously exposed but vigilant.

Finally, on the morning of 5 September, the weather cleared and four Hawker-Hunters in formation streaked down the Limpopo Valley at low level, and under sustained anti-aircraft fire successfully blasted the bridges at Barragem before forty-eight helicopter-borne SAS troops deployed, neutralising the protective batteries, while commandeering some of the 23mm cannons for their own use.

At the same time that the 'Hunters' struck, a FRELIMO platoon stumbled upon the Oscar Bravo admin base but an RLI troop under the command of Major Peter Farndell had been watching them and was quickly into the fray with devastating effect. Out of the twenty-five that approached all but one were killed.

Amid furious exchanges of fire, the bridge-demolition teams went into action, mining the bridges at Chicacatem, Folgares and Canicado and it was not long before they took casualties. To the rescue flew Flight Lieutenant Dick Paxton. Summoned to 'casevac' Corporal 'Amy' Amos and take him to the relative safety of the helicopter holding area six minutes away, he knew it was not going to be easy. Nearing the stricken soldier, he received a radio warning from Colonel Garth Barrett telling him that the bridge was 'live' and to avoid flying too close. Paxton altered course and spotted a smoke flare ahead, signalling his LZ. Noticing troops below, he hovered momentarily before spotting a soldier ahead waving him forward. Lifting the aircraft to air-taxi in the direction indicated, he never knew what hit him. An RPG-7 rocket smashed into his gearbox, sending the rotors flying and the aircraft crashing to the ground. Unconscious, his helmet lacerated by shrapnel, his gunner Alex Wesson dead, Paxton sat slumped over the controls of the burning machine until Sergeant Mike Smith, fresh from clearing an enemy building, came sprinting to his rescue. Unlatching the pilot's harness, Smith pulled Paxton to cover and relative safety.

Minutes later, with some alarm, the SAS men noticed Paxton recover consciousness and in a state of dazed aggression produce a snub-nosed .38 revolver from his flight-suit while struggling to his feet and loudly proclaiming his determination to continue the fight. Believing the wounded pilot might become a liability, the soldiers distracted Paxton, removed the revolver, quickly emptied the chambers rendering it harmless then returned it to him.

At the same time as charges were laid on the strategically important Barragem Bridge an RLI section under Captain Joe du Plooy took the town itself while inflicting maximum damage and capturing a Bulgarian water technician.

Meanwhile, South Africans from D Squadron SAS took care of the bridge at Maximchopes. Using mainly *pentolite* in boxes stuck to structures with 'super-glue,' and with Captain Charlie Small in overall command, the tasks were completed soon after midday and with the exception of the road bridge at Barragem all the targets were demolished. Bridges down, all troops and aircraft returned to the administrative base to await the big assault in the morning.

"I was at the administrative base," remembers Andrew Standish-White, "when Captain Wilson appeared and told me to accompany him in the morning as his radio operator on the assault on Mapai itself. I braced myself for trouble."

The morning of 6 September got off to a thunderous start with 'Hunters' and Canberras pounding the enemy defensive lines with Alpha and Golf bombs in a furious bid to break down the enemy defences and destroy morale. The first strike destroyed a command and control centre, an armoury and the facility housing the Soviet advisers along with other accommodation. This was followed by another destroying a fuel dump, radar station and anti-aircraft battery, but regrettably for the Rhodesians the enemy was far from beaten. With 37mm and 23mm guns generously deployed, the air force was also under pressure.

"Going in in the morning was spectacular," remembers Standish-White. "Fourteen Pumas line abreast as the jets pounded the position, we were charged up and itching for action."

Flying in the third Puma in line was Watt. Knowing the territory and the array of anti-aircraft weapons ranged against them, he was nervous. Standing behind the pilots so he could see out the open door, he noticed with some alarm that they were following the road. "I knew they had antiaircraft guns near the road and shouted to the pilot to fly away from it. He jinked left but then I just heard this massive explosion as the Puma behind us was hit by a rocket. All fourteen of our soldiers and the three South African Air Force guys were killed."[61]

"I remember seeing the Puma go down in a plume of thick black smoke and thought to myself, 'What a way to start an assault,'" remembers Scheepers. "But while in the assault line I saw the 'gooks' in trees watching us as we drew near to the sandalwood belt of trees. Behind that was a cleared belt of land before the trenches and I saw them slither down the trees like snakes. I couldn't do a thing as the momentum of the assault had begun."

"I was in command of an assault group," remembers Watt, "and remember seeing André and Frank Tunney jump into those trenches and I thought to myself they'll be lucky if they don't get killed. It was bad on the ground, we were outgunned and I could see tanks coming towards us while artillery pounded us."

"Miraculously I got into the trenches first and cleared about a hundred metres in front of the rest of the troops behind me who were pinned down," says Scheepers. "To the enemy's credit they did stand and fight because they kept on shooting at my head over the parapets and I had to use percussion grenades around each bend in the trench. Eventually I ran out of these."

Standish-White recalls: "Hitting the ground and skirmishing forward into their trench lines, we all knew immediately that we were dealing with a different sort of adversary. The incoming fire, including 122mm rockets and mortars, was accurate and incredibly heavy. With all the other explosions the noise was absolutely deafening. Captain Wilson took us forward but progress in the extreme heat and slogging through soft sand underfoot was slow. The enemy this time was not going to be rattled and we were battling to make any real headway. The Canberras were trying to help us but there were so many anti-aircraft positions pumping away at them they had to bomb from high altitude. The ground was shaking, I felt like I was on Omaha Beach during the D-Day landings. Over the radio I obviously heard the reports coming into Captain Wilson and they were bleak. There seemed to be no end to the trench lines and we got bogged down.

"At one point in the fighting I managed to crawl behind a large anthill with Trooper Gordon le Fèvre alongside me and quickly realised nowhere was safe. We looked wide-eyed at one another as the incoming fire literally chewed the hill away above us. Without armour and heavy-calibre support weapons the Rhodesians were in trouble against a well dug-in enemy that was prepared to stand and fight."

"We were light on the ground against tanks and heavy artillery," remembers Watt. "We were getting hammered but managed to clear the first line of trenches but there were a lot of lines left and it looked like we were going to take heavy losses. The problem was that we cleared some of the trench lines but then the enemy seemed to reappear where we had cleared. Some of these troops were aggressive and brave."

General Walls was in the command Dakota and a decision had to be made. He knew his forces but it looked like the costs in men and matériel were going to be unacceptably high. He made the decision to call it off. For the first time it looked like the Rhodesians had failed to take an objective.

"Obviously we did not know it at the time," says General John Hickman, "but later I discovered the British knew about our plans for Mapai through electronic interceptions. The British SAS in Botswana were not there merely to guard the BBC propaganda radio station. They are well known for their high degree of efficiency and versatility. Need I say more?"

For Watt however, the extraction phase was to be as harrowing as the entry. "Before leaving the target I, along with Mike West, was ordered to place a homing device up a tree which would serve as a directional beacon for another big airstrike. We had to run two kilometres then climb this tree while having the shit shot out of us, then position it and wait until I got the signal indicating a pilot had locked onto it then down the tree and run like fuck to the waiting Puma. Buccaneers from the SAAF came in first and I've never felt ground shake like it did then. We dived into the sand and the earth rocked and shook. Then we ran again and I scrambled into the helicopter but no sooner were we airborne than I saw choppers scattering. At little over a hundred feet, hearing the ground fire, I knew the mobiles were onto us again but it was almost too late when bullets smashed the Perspex in the cockpit and the senior pilot slumped forward having taken a hit through his helmet in the head. I saw blood on his forehead and assumed he was dead. The whole aircraft lurched then fell from the sky and I thought we were also dead before the co-pilot got a grip as we crashed into trees and pulled us slowly upwards. At the same time a 'Lynx' and a 'Hunter' ripped into the gunners below, giving us some covering fire while we limped forward. We started to gain speed when the windscreen collapsed in on the faces of the pilots and we took another death-dive. The injured pilot then came round from his concussion. The bullet that hit him must have missed killing him by a millimetre. When the helicopter landed I could barely believe I'd survived. I went on my knees, stuck my face in the sand and kissed the ground."

On receipt of instructions from General Walls, RLI Major Pat Armstrong in an orbiting 'Lynx' relayed the order to withdraw and weary troops commenced the eight-kilometre hike to the pick-up areas, while six Canberras dropped the final bomb loads. Little did they or anyone else on the Rhodesian side know how decisive this action was.

Richard Wood writes: "A defector from Malvernia a few weeks later would reveal that the FPLM {FRELIMO troops} in the trench network were prepared to stay and fight it out until the Canberra airstrike. They then pulled out en masse from the trenches and ran to a pre-arranged RV {rendezvous'} and did not return until two days later."

In the biggest battle of the war it appears the Rhodesians had snatched defeat from the jaws of victory. "What puzzles me to this day," says Watt, "is why we did not use the tanks we had luckily acquired. They were Russian T-54s which were being shipped to Uganda when the boat carrying them was intercepted by the South African Navy and seized. The South Africans gave them to us and our crews were trained and ready to go. Mapai was a conventional battle and we needed conventional weapons. The tanks would have won the day. We had great soldiers but in this situation we were badly outgunned and outnumbered."

'YANKEE SECTION'

In early September 1979, Ian Smith arrived in London as part of the Muzorewa delegation to join the conference to be chaired by Peter Carrington. With him were General Walls and Smith's long-time lieutenant, finance Minister David Smith. Chief Justice Hector Macdonald arrived soon afterwards. Smith's hackles were soon up. He did not trust Carrington and could quickly see British diplomacy in action at its duplicitous best. "I'd been dealing with dishonest British politicians since 1963 when 'Rab' Butler lied to us about granting us our independence. I could see right through Carrington and I think he knew it."

But Carrington was unfazed. With Anthony Duff, Robin Renwick and John Gilmour primed to pounce, he set about prying Smith's coterie away from the former prime minister. The first, according to Ian Smith, to do a political summersault was Macdonald, who went from sceptic to ardent Carrington supporter in the time it took him to accompany Carrington on a drive to the airport. David Smith succumbed to Carrington's wily entreaties soon after but the big prize, Walls, remained chary. The British went to work on him.

While Smith was kept at a distance, Walls was accorded special status. Renwick recalls, "I took him out to lunch, dinner, everything you can think of."

Meanwhile, a crack team of Rhodesian signals interceptors known as 'Yankee Section' were squirreled away in Coghlan Buildings in Salisbury and listening closely. Vigilance and luck paid off. A telex intercept unveiled the British code and an intelligence bonanza arrived. The sleuths discovered that at the end of every plenary session a summary of the proceeding was compiled and signed off by Carrington. The contents were then transmitted to the British High Commission in Dar es Salaam, whereupon it was hand-delivered to President Nyerere by the High Commissioner himself. After perusing the details, the Tanzanian president then added his comments before it was re-encoded and transmitted back to the Tanzanian High Commission in London for forwarding to Mugabe. It was this last transmission which the Rhodesian code-breakers successfully intercepted and in some cases managed to deliver in clear within twenty minutes of receiving the intercept. The contents of these intercepts were passed to the Rhodesian Communications Centre in London within twenty minutes of transcription, making it virtually certain that Walls and Flower were both fully informed of the treachery afoot.

The thrust of the message to Nyerere from Carrington was starkly clear; "Keep your man [Mugabe] talking and all will be his." He was merely playing out a pantomime for the benefit of the rest of the audience.

Smith was not privy to this intelligence but his instincts told him all he needed to know. Dismayed, disappointed and abandoned by his own people, he decided to return to Salisbury. But before leaving, the former premier confronted Carrington and bluntly accused him of plotting the formation of a new government which would be headed by Robert Mugabe. Carrington blustered, insisted such a scenario was anathema to him and re iterated it was his intention to see a government of national unity installed, combining Smith, Nkomo and Muzorewa. Smith was utterly unconvinced and passed on his sentiments to Walls who listened but reserved his judgement.

'OPERATION BUMPER'

With the approaching prospect of peace talks in London, 'ComOps' decided to up the pressure on Samora Machel with the initiation of 'Operation Bumper' early in September which would involve the deployment of troops to establish a semi-permanent presence in Mozambique to bolster RENAMO.

Much to his surprise, the Squadron Administration Officer, Lieutenant Charlie Buchan, was given command of the northern vanguard where, as one of twelve men, he joined Matsangaissa and 300 rebels. What the SAS needed in the area was somewhere close to the action, where they could hide, which was defensible and which the redoubtable André Matsangaissa and his small band of warriors were familiar with.

They decided on Gorongosa Mountain. Dominating the landscape of central Mozambique, it was well watered and covered in a thick green blanket of lush tropical forest, offering sanctuary to myriad species of strikingly colourful birds. The abundance of wildlife around them was to prove a lively relief to many of the SAS men who were to spend time there.

Below, to the south lay the wild plains of the Pungwe River system which was home to elephant, buffalo, lion, leopard and hyena. A landscape of weaving watercourses, oxbow lakes, swamps and plains, it was studded with towering palms and flat-top acacias. Bygone years had seen the early Portuguese settlers try to develop the area for agriculture but they had failed miserably. Most had died of fever and other nefarious diseases, some at the hands of hostile natives, and others in the jaws of the great predators that threatened from land and water. Soon the survivors got the message and left, and the Gorongosa reverted to its previous owners. To the north of the mountains was the Zambezi wending its way slowly towards the delta and the end of its long journey from the Congo to the sea. To the east the littoral was an endless labyrinth of mangroves broken intermittently by muddy, crocodile-infested creeks; and beyond, the blue sea of the Indian Ocean.

Of great importance to the planners, the top of the mountain flattened out into a small plateau offering an LZ to helicopters and altitude made the position eminently defensible. Attacking enemy troops would have a long climb through tough terrain if they chose to try and take the mountain redoubt. Buchan and his men, along with their new allies, set up a few small tents and made themselves as comfortable as possible. From their mountain perch they were ready to pounce and soon they would do so with devastating effectiveness.

While Buchan would open the account in the north, Darrell Watt was earmarked to play a major role in the south where the SAS would join 300 rebels under the command of Luke Muhlangu on Sitatonga Mountain within sight of the Chimanimani Mountains close to the Revue River. Muhlangu was an imposing, charismatic man who had risen quickly through the ranks having only defected to RENAMO earlier in the year. He and Watt clicked immediately and a very potent partnership was born. From here they would strike south to the Save River and east to the Inchope–Maputo road. This rebel force would grow rapidly to number over a 1,000 by the end of the year.

"My orders were quite simple," remembers Watt. "Central Mozambique had been correctly identified as providing fertile ground for fomenting resistance against FRELIMO and I was to go and stir up as much trouble as possible. We were lucky in that FRELIMO had become very unpopular. We wanted to add to their problems and establish our own liberated zones in enemy territory."

The Gorongosa initiative was almost instantly effective as RENAMO, with the SAS, soon had FRELIMO reeling with camps and garrisons attacked repeatedly.

MONTE XILUVO

Soon after the command decision had been made to have SAS troops permanently positioned in Mozambique, additional high-priority targets were selected. For Watt and his comrades there was to be no break from war.

Watt remembers: "We had arrived back at Chipinda Pools from the Mapai attack and we were all bloody tired. We had not been on the ground back in Rhodesia for an hour when I received orders from Colonel Barrett to prepare to return to Mozambique with André Scheepers to attack the communications station at Monte Xiluvo deep into central Mozambique. I was surprised; the events of the last few days had taken a lot out of all of us and I felt we all needed some rest.

Colonel Barrett told me I was to tell André to get his men ready for immediate uplift to Grand Reef air base outside Umtali. There André and I were to plan the attack.

"I went to André whom I greatly admired and gave him the news. He was having a shower. He listened then told me in a soft but firm voice to tell Colonel Barrett that he would go when he was ready and he was not ready at that particular time. I was quite taken aback and reminded him that he was refusing a direct order but he was very reluctant to move, insisting he would do the job 'in his own time.'"

"By this time I had had it," says Scheepers. "My hair was falling out and the slightest noise sounded like an explosion. My nerves were shot and I felt I could not operate any longer at the level required. I felt I was becoming a liability but I did not get much empathy. Willem Ratte spoke to me and with a wry look on his face suggested someone on our side was trying to get me killed. It looked to me like my seniors were spending a lot of time back at Kabrit writing their medal citations while the rest of us were being sent to die. I spoke to Rob Johnstone who was one of the few senior officers I felt comfortable with and told him I was losing confidence in our own people. Adding to my fears I had become convinced someone close to us was leaking information because the enemy always seemed prepared for us. And making it all worse, news from the political arena seemed to suggest we were going to be handing over the country anyway, and I began to wonder if all our efforts were going to count for anything."

"Eventually I talked André round," says Watt, "and we flew to Grand Reef to begin planning the attack. Once he had re-committed himself, André was back to his old self and totally focused on the task."

With Watt overseeing the operation from Rhodesia, Scheepers led a twelve-man SAS team with some RENAMO support and was inserted into the country by helicopter on 12 September 1979. Their target, a sophisticated signals centre providing the nexus for all FRELIMO transmissions countrywide, was heavily defended. With the Mozambique security forces already reeling from sustained attacks, this raid was designed to add fuel to already raging fires by demolishing their state-of-the-art means of communication. The fall-back system the enemy would have to revert to would be less advanced and easier for the Rhodesians to monitor.

Thanks to their RENAMO counterparts who were familiar with the terrain and enjoyed a friendly relationship with the local populace, the two-day walk-in was uneventful. Following a long and arduous climb up the mountain, Scheepers left his men and did a solo recce of the target.

Four 23mm guns were identified along with a strong detachment of FRELIMO defenders. Also in the back of the ground commander's mind was the knowledge that heavy armour including tanks was ready to react from the nearby base at Dondo on the main Beira road.

At the gate he found a sleeping sentry in the guardhouse and quietly fiddled the gate before using bolt-cutters to cut the chain securing the opening. The chain dropped with a clang, causing the sentry to stir and Scheepers looked on anxiously, his silenced .22 pistol pointed at the man's head. When the guard resumed his slumber Scheepers opened the gate slightly and returned to his troops.

"Right next to the gate was a seven-man section of FRELIMO sleeping in their sleeping bags on either side of the road in. After I collected all the men we managed to walk right past them without disturbing anyone. It was a very daunting manoeuvre and to this day I think our stealth was amazing; it was a daring move but it worked. Once inside I then took stock of all their bunkers and positions then took the bolt-cutters and cut escape holes in the fence."

Confident that their disguises under cover of the night would suffice, Scheepers told Berry which one of the 23mm guns would pose a threat to them on their line of flight and tasked him and his section to destroy it before exiting. That done, he then made his way to the central radar room, the nerve centre of the facility.

"It was a protected by a huge, heavy door," recalls Scheepers. "I used a 'knock-knock' explosive to blow it down and then threw a large bunker bomb inside."

The blast was followed immediately by the roar of guns, rockets and explosives. A slumbering enemy was cut no slack as fast-fleeing figures were shot down by the raiders. In the return fire Scheepers was shot in the wrist and Frank Tunney in the foot. In no time flames flickered, brightening the night.

Ten minutes later the lieutenant, mindful of the need to escape with enough hours of darkness, gave the order to end the mayhem and led his men down the mountain, leaving behind blazing buildings, mangled equipment and soldiers dead, wounded and terrified.

Struggling downwards through heavy thickets, the attackers were cheered by a farewell explosion that lit up the sky. Moving at maximum pace, Scheepers raced for the main Beira road, determined to cross it before first light.

"I made this call because Frank's foot wound was a factor I had to consider and we only had a few more hours of darkness and I wanted to get across the road before light," remembers Scheepers. "I knew about their capacity to rapidly deploy reinforcements from our intelligence briefing and they were considerable."

Hitting the road, the commander decided to do what he was taught not to do and follow it. It was a gamble and it did not pay off.

Waiting in ambush was a well-armed and -organised FRELIMO platoon which opened fire at close range, scattering the saboteurs in all directions. Running to the right of the road Berry jumped into a dry riverbed where he found some of his men already in defensive posture. Relieved to see his signaller was safe and still in possession of the TR48 radio, he then turned his attention to the whereabouts of the rest of the party. Shouting into the radio in a vain effort to make himself heard over the sound of heavy machine-gun fire, he was distressed to hear no response from his commander. Unbeknown to him the rest were trapped on the other side of the road, taking fire from the FRELIMO patrol and the surviving defenders at the radio station.

"I was pinned down for approximately twenty minutes," remembers Scheepers. "Some relief only came when the armoured vehicles took hits from the men higher up behind me and shifted their arc of fire. When eventually we crossed the road we were confronted by a FRELIMO mobile column. The FRELIMO commander cried out 'Holta' to me when he saw us approaching. I was in front and saw the 12.7mm mounted on the front truck. Dave Berry, my beloved colour sergeant, did the right thing by leaving because I couldn't move; honestly I prayed because I thought I was going to die. Later as I crossed the road I saw a T-34 tank heading towards us. We ran for our lives for approximately 700 metres. The tank driver turned off the road and chased us. The mechanical noise of the tank crashing over the small trees was a sound that I will never forget."

"The RENAMO guys were amazingly brave," remembers Bas Jolliffe. "An armoured vehicle, a BTR-60 I think, was putting us under heavy fire from the road junction and these little RENAMO guys went straight at it with only their small arms. We shouted at them to stop, sure they would be killed, but they went at that vehicle and put them to flight."

Adding to the confusion, but unbeknown to the rest, a lonely trio consisting of two SAS and one RENAMO man found themselves separated from the two main groups. Taking control of their situation, they wasted no time in striking out in a bid to distance themselves from the crime scene which they knew was soon certain to draw angry reinforcements.

Harbouring the same sentiments Dave Berry led his men away from the mountain under fire, crossing the main road without incident, but their nerves tightened to the clanking sound of approaching tanks. Tiredness notwithstanding, their pace quickened as the sergeant set course for the predetermined 'crash rendezvous' from which they hoped they would be airlifted back to friendly soil. Having passed uneventfully through a line of kraals, Berry made radio contact with Darrell Watt and summarised the events before explaining, as best he could, the current situation on the ground. With a pair of Hawker-Hunters on standby, Watt immediately boarded a 'Lynx' and flew over the border.

With Watt somewhere overhead, Berry was thrilled to hear Scheepers's voice on the air as he communicated with his boss above. More good news followed when the two ground commanders deduced they were barely two kilometres apart but that was tempered when a closer inspection revealed they were three men short. No one wanted to leave anyone behind but there was no way of knowing if they were dead or alive.

Nerves jangled when Berry and his men heard the sound of tanks and transports closing on them but Watt responded quickly by calling the 'Hunters' in. With typical efficiency the men in blue struck quickly and effectively, putting the FRELIMO to flight. The threat reduced, choppers arrived, loaded the troops and staggered into the air under heavy loads and by nightfall all but three were home safe.

Despite being relative newcomers, the two SAS men left in theatre kept calm and pondered their plight. The odds were heavily stacked: an angry army was swarming over the countryside, they were tired, low on water and ammunition and had no radio. Wits, stamina and presence of mind were all they had to work with.

Moving away from the road, their pace quickened when they heard tanks, which turned into a sprint for their lives when one of the armoured behemoths appeared to be rolling straight onto them. Massive relief followed when the machine suddenly veered away and followed a different track. The men drew breath and kept moving. Barely stopping, they walked through the night and were thrilled to arrive at a river in the early hours of the morning. Thirst slaked, water bottles recharged, they weighed their options. They could head north aiming for the SAS base on Gorongosa Mountain or they could turn west and face a long hike back to Rhodesia.

A feeling of general gloom was suddenly shattered by the sound of a helicopter. Uncertain of its provenance, wary eyes searched the skies and concern turned to elation when they saw a 'Bell' {Bell UH-1 Iroquois ('Huey'). Rhodesian Air Force nomenclature was 'Cheetah'} helicopter painted in friendly colours. Smoke and phosphorus were hurled with abandon but with a sense of dismay they watched as it flew away and was lost in the distance. Surveying their position and surrounds, spirits dropped again when they saw FRELIMO sweep lines on either side of them. If help was not soon in coming their future was grim. Frustration turned to fury when another helicopter flew over without seeing them but excitement returned when a chopper went to ground to refuel and the three fugitives raced for it with all possible speed. Thorn and thick bush slowed them but they hurled themselves forward in desperation; however, utter despair was visited upon them as they heard turbines winding up then saw their salvation lift and disappear into the blue yonder. It looked very much like they were doomed—the Blues were off their game. Behind them smoke from the grenades billowed aloft—not only were they forsaken but they had also notified all who would find and kill them of their whereabouts. Tired and close to despair they found a bushy copse and lay low and still.

In the early afternoon a pair of 'Lynxes' appeared and bereft of grenades, the soldiers signalled frantically with their heliograph but again to no avail, so they quickly lit a fire but again they were not noticed. Utter despair came with the sound of the aircraft fading into the distance. Hours later a 'Lynx' returned and the heliograph was flashed while flames were fanned but still no help arrived.

Chopper pilot Terry McCormick was on standby back in Rhodesia at Grand Reef airfield. He and his gunner Mark Jackson had already pulled off some hairy 'hot-extractions' to rescue beleaguered SAS soldiers and they were ready to do it again.

"We heard that a couple of SAS guys were on the run in Mozambique but did not have much more information when I received a call to get airborne and was given a rough area across the border to cover but it was all quite vague. I was soon in contact with a 'Lynx' pilot who was heading the search. I could tell immediately from his voice that he was high and on oxygen for fear of heat-seeking missiles and did not blame him for being cautious. Unfortunately, we, being in a chopper, did not have that luxury so we just hoped like hell we did not get shot down. There was plenty of enemy activity below so I knew we would be needing some luck getting in and out safely.

"Next thing I heard the 'Lynx' pilot saying he had spotted smoke from a fire and he was wondering if it might be the guys we were looking for. The chatter was about why they would light a fire when on the run and trying to avoid detection by the enemy. Well the answer was pretty clear to me; they probably had no option because they had no other means of attracting our attention and were playing the only card they had left in their deck. I told Mark to get ready and headed for the smoke. Sure enough I saw these poor blokes running like hell and waving madly at us. I dropped fast and circled them to let them know I had them visual but enemy troops were firing and closing in fast. Looking out the cockpit I searched frantically for a suitable clearing to put the chopper down but it was too densely wooded so I circled, weighing the options when I saw them clambering up a tree and realised it was our only chance.

"I hovered above but close was not close enough. They were at the top of the tree and I could see the desperation on their faces as they tried to reach out for the skids but we were still just a stretch too high for them to get a grip. I knew there was only one way and went in lower to the point the skids were buried in the branches and just prayed we did not get snagged when I felt the guys launching themselves on the skids and then held the hover while Mark pulled them aboard. As they collapsed on the floor I swung us up and around and we raced home to safety. It was worth it. They bought me a few beers that night and Bob Jones still owes me a few more!" The operation was over. The radio facility had been destroyed and all the attackers were safe but this was an army that ran on a shoe-string and Jones-Davies had lost a section of his rocket launcher in his frantic scramble to safety. This was noted and he was charged with dereliction and faced a spell in dreaded Detention Barracks in Bulawayo when Scheepers intervened and insisted on the charges being withdrawn.

Days later an SAS team hit Beira with the help of the South African Navy and sank the vessels in the port approaches. Further attacks on the city itself were aborted but the sinking of the dredgers caused considerable problems as siltation levels rose, making maritime movement around the harbour problematic. Leaflets were spread by the raiders, sending a bogus signal indicating the sabotage had been conducted by RENAMO.

SCHEEPERS BACK IN THE FRAY

By late August reports indicated a renewed ZANLA build-up of men and matériel in a heavily wooded area of Mozambique east of the Chimanimani Mountains but the exact location was unclear.

"If 'monte' refers to a mountain, then this is certainly an accurate depiction that this operation had on my life," recalls Scheepers. "A 'mountain' challenge indeed, to me personally and to my professionalism.

"This operation took place on the 30 Sept 1979. The 'New Chimoio Circle' as it became known, was located about 50 km north east of Umtali. It consisted of a huge complex of camps (at least five) spread over an area of approximately 60 square kilometres. Dominating this terrain was a huge granite hill we called Monte Cassino. We were ordered to locate the camp and try and capture some of the ZANLA hierarchy alive by ambushing them in their vehicles. The complex was situated on the east side of the Chimoio/Tete road. Intelligence garnered by Winston Hart informed us that the 'New Chimoio' housed approximately 2,000 ZANLA fighters and that senior Soviet officers were present in the camp. This, I found a very exciting challenge."

With the regular SAS snipers otherwise disposed, a decision was made to call in a sharp-shooter from the reserves.

"I had been attached to the SAS for some time working under Captain Rob Johnstone," remembers Mike. "I was summoned to 'ComOps' and informed the country needed a major propaganda coup and the SAS wanted to capture ZANLA commander Josiah Tongogara and bring him back to Rhodesia. My role was to be part of an ambush party and to use a silenced pistol to shoot out the tyres of the Toyota Land Cruiser in which he was known to travel, so that he could be apprehended and spirited out of Mozambique. All other members of the enemy were to be dispatched but Tongogara was to be captured. I was a little apprehensive about my ability to shoot out the tyres with a silenced pistol for technical and other reasons and explained my reservations but was urged to simply do the best I could.

"I was subsequently taken to a RENAMO training base near Rusape where I met up with Danny Hartman and the four RENAMO personnel who would accompany and guide us on the mission. They had seen Tongogara on numerous occasions and described his routine, the road he used to travel between camps and gave us more detail on how to recognise the vehicle he used which they told us was coloured beige."

Scheepers; "Eleven SAS operators were assigned to me for this task, including the 4 MNR operators. Rob Johnstone, 'A Squadron' OC, a very fine commander was in command. To his credit one of the first tactical decisions he made was to set up a radio relay station 90 miles (145km) from the target to help facilitate our communications because of the considerable distances involved and the fact that we did not operate with the most modern signal equipment. This later became a life-saving decision that he made. The relay team was made up of 'wounded warriors' consisting of Bruce Langely, Henni Pretorius, Barry 'Pegleg' Deacon and Rob Hepple.

"We were told that the base was well planned, organised and defended and that they were digging in for a fight. Following final orders, we flew by helicopter from Grand Reef late afternoon. The walk-in was about fifty kilometres and took us two days. There was plenty of civilian and enemy movement in the area. On the second night I noticed that we were stepping over trenches. Having an interest in geology, I assumed that these were prospecting trenches and was the work of prospectors looking for either tin, nickel or copper. I prided myself in being a potential geologist."

"I was doing the tracking," recalls Bas Jolliffe, "and I got a big fright when I saw the tracks. There were hundreds of them walking on both sides of the road. We heard voices and listened. The RENAMO guys told us they were talking about helicopters so they knew we were stalking them. We crossed trenches in the dark and then decided to rest on a hilltop until the morning. Little did we know it then but we had actually positioned ourselves on a hill in the middle of the complex that they were using on occasion as an observation point."

"Next morning," recalls Scheepers, "the area was flooded with ZANLA prodding the road for landmines and sweep lines searching the bush. Quite logically I suspected that we must be near to the camp but I didn't know I was actually in the camp so I decided to go and do a recce with one of the RENAMO blokes leaving Dave Berry and Bas Jolliffe in charge. The grass was fairly tall and the bush relatively lush so visibility was poor. We had only walked about 4 km and passed under the Cabora Bassa power lines, when I noticed huge spoor made by at least 50-70 people. This got my close attention. Next minute we bumped into a few noisy civilians.

Even though I was camouflaged black in vegetable dye, I decided to go down to ground and sent the MNR chap forward to ask them where the camp was. I told him to tell them we were slightly lost. I watched cautiously to make sure that there weren't any suspicious signs of compromise coming from him. After about 10 minutes the MNR soldier came back to me to inform me that the camp was in the direction where we have just come from! The spoor, we were informed, was from soldiers going to a nearby 'beer-hall' for drinks.

"We immediately made our way back to our position only to confirm that we were actually in the middle of the 'New Chimoio' hence the reason for all the ZANLA activity and vehicle movement. It was soon after this that I heard the startling news from Dave Berry that a ten man ZANLA clearance patrol was walking straight towards one of our early warning positions.

"I remember telling Dave to let them come close up (5-7 meters) and then to take them out. I enquired what weapons they were carrying and how they were carrying them. This quickly helped me to ascertain the level of their alertness and hence the immediate threat level. David successfully carried out my orders in typically efficient fashion.

Bas Jolliffe recalls: "Chunkie Chesterman and Roger were the two guys in the early warning with their RPDs and they opened up as Dave Berry, I and Richard (one of the RENAMO men) moved towards them. They dropped three on the spot and others were hit. One had a FN which I gave to Richard and then we checked the bodies. The survivors fled down the hill."

"We were on the run in minutes as mortars came raining down on us," remembers Mike. "Their mortar men must have been able to see us because the bombs followed us as we raced down the side of the hill. We now knew thousands of the enemy were alerted and after us. I was terrified and certain I would soon be dead. Our only radio contact was with the relay team on the mountain in Rhodesia. They were passing information on our situation to Rob Johnstone. On reaching the flat land after our descent, we ran west with me believing our only slim chance of survival lay in a helicopter 'hot extraction' which Scheepers was surely organising. Breathless, we reached a stream and stopped and I waited to hear André tell us to prepare for uplift and merciful rescue but this was not to be. Very calmly and with astonishingly cool delivery he ordered us to charge our water bottles while we had the chance and prepare to fight. I could scarcely believe my ears!"

"André was very calm," says Bas Jolliffe. "We still had a job to do and he was not about to abort the mission. He wanted to draw more of them into our fire so we could kill and snatch someone, preferably a Russian or a top ZANLA man."

"Once we reached the road next to the main boom gate to the camp, I told the men to set up an ambush including several anti-tank claymores," remembers Scheepers. "I also positioned Dave in the front with the RPG to smack the vehicles."

"My heart went out to young David," remembers Mike. "Barely out of school, he was positioned some considerable distance away from us all alone with a rocket-launcher. I had to marvel at what amazing young men this country had produced."

"As I expected, it wasn't long before the hierarchy decided to evacuate the camp," says Scheepers. "I think they thought we were on the run at this stage. There was quite a commotion as they came driving out in two white Land Cruisers with bodyguards running on either side of the vehicle, rifles held on the high. They did not get far.

"We initiated and Dave was bang on target with his rocket and one truck exploded. We then raked the vehicles with intense machine-gun fire. They had no chance and soon both vehicles were blazing. Dave Berry and Dave ran up to see if anyone was alive who we could grab to take home but it was an inferno and there were no survivors in the cars, just charred bodies everywhere and quite a few Europeans among them, but we managed to catch a straggler. We then made a hasty retreat back west where we came from, anti-tracking at speed in extended line as I had been taught by the master himself; Darrell Watt.

"We covered about 1500 meters, which in itself was a very tiring exercise, and then I called in the choppers for immediate uplift. Next minute Sgt. Jolliffe informed me that women trackers were heading towards us and that they were running on our spoor. Their reaction time amazed me because we had just stopped for about 15 minutes to clear a DZ for the choppers and they were on to us. Sgt Jolliffe was a very able and reliable operator and so I instructed him and Dave Berry to deal with the ZANLA women trackers. Once again they competently engaged the enemy while I was trying to organize uplift on the radio. I would not have survived without these fine men.

"On the flanks of the ZANLA advance line was two Goryunov medium machine guns putting down sustained heavy fire while two-inch mortars rained down upon our position. The percussion from the exploding bombs dazed me slightly and I had to work on maintaining my focus and judgement. A heavy firefight ensued close by and the men on initiation managed to kill six of the enemy. It was a little surreal; the trees around me turned white as the bark was stripped off them from the incoming fire.

"I hastily gave the order for us to withdraw further. In fact, not so much a 'withdrawal'; I recall shouting above the din telling the men to run for their lives. Dave Berry was always very eager to let me know when he thought it was best that I should 'pull out' and he was in full agreement! He said I tended to be a bit thick-skinned in this area. This was an amazing race to see as we all frantically sprinted for our lives while trying to return fire on the run. The men need no encouragement to proceed at speed! Surprisingly Dave Berry, quite a chunky man, passed me with his radio handset dragging several meters behind him and I thought I was pretty quick! Mike, our sharp-shooter, older than the rest of us, also passed me like an Olympic runner. I had to chuckle because earlier he had complained about the heavy weight of his pack during the anti-tracking exercise. No one cared about the whereabouts of the prisoner at this stage so he managed to escape.

"This was the most frightened I have ever been in my entire life," says Mike. "I was next to Chunkie Chesterman on the left flank. I was sure I was about to die but determined to make the most of my last stand and kill as many people as I could prior to departure. Initially I heard André shouting but misheard him and did not understand that he was telling us to pull back until it was almost too late. Suddenly I realised the others had gone and I had to run like the wind to catch up. When I did there was much laughter which I took exception to because I could not see what was so funny about perishing in Mozambique! The joke was on me because the speed with which I had caught up with them proved to them that my earlier moans about the weight of my pack were nonsense."

"The fire was so heavy the chopper pilots were reluctant to land," recalls Jolliffe, "and Captain Johnstone in a 'Lynx' was having the shit shot out of him but he made it clear to the pilots that nobody was going home until he had recovered his men on the ground. There were at least 200 ZANLA running us down when the 'Lynx' dropped a bomb which got their attention. We then let some more claymores go and there was a lull which gave the choppers an opening and they landed."

"I remember getting airborne on the first chopper," says Mike. "I looked below as we gained altitude and saw the six we had left behind flattened by the down-draft from the rotors. They were almost surrounded by hundreds of enemy shooting at them and I thought little of their chances. Amazingly, the next chopper rescued them and they all survived."

"Back at Kabrit it was confirmed by our intelligence people that we had killed five senior Soviet officers which was later confirmed in a newspaper report," says Scheepers.

"This operation for me was a very successful reconnaissance and yet also extremely stressful. In one day we had 3 major contacts with overwhelming enemy numbers, consisting of approximately 2000 ZANLA, and that in their own backyard. My nerves were tested to the limit. I think what saved the day in the end was Rob Johnston's excellent command and commitment to his men. But also my men; the very best any officer could ask for. Right on the brink of dying they never yielded. But one lesson was learned; never again would I wear my geologist's hat and confuse enemy trenches with prospecting pits!

"Later, John Gardner from Selous Scouts, another fine operator whom I knew, was deployed back into the area, to do a close recce of the New Chimoio but he had to be 'hot extracted'. The area was like a hornet's nest that had been upset."

CHAPTER 14

Less passionate the long war throws
It's burning thorn about all men,
Caught in one grief, we share one wound,
And cry one dialect of pain.
—*LAURIE LEE*

THE RUSSIANS ARE COMING

Back in Salisbury there was increasing alarm when a capture brought first-hand news of a Soviet-orchestrated invasion plan that would see conventional forces attack Rhodesia from bases in Zambia in a three-pronged offensive through Kariba, Chirundu and the Victoria Falls. It was clear that drastic action was required. Once in the country, with support of forces already in situ, the Soviet-backed army would take over the airports at Wankie, Kariba and Victoria Falls, then move on Salisbury and claim military victory. To oversee the plan, the Soviets appointed Vladimir Buchihev, a hard man from the KGB, along with twelve advisers, to help Nkomo and his lieutenants get the job done. As tanks and heavy weapons poured into Zambia, news came in that at least 4,000 of the ZIPRA troops standing by to enter Rhodesia were trained in conventional warfare.

An SAS section was deployed to destroy bridges on the Great East Road, the main arterial link into Lusaka from eastern Zambia and Malawi. Rhodesian Intelligence now indicated 30,000 troops spread out in hidden camps running south to the Zambezi and east to the Luangwa. The plan was to rupture their supply lines and force them to rely on a local populace which was already hostile to the foreign fighters.

Ten days later, having completed their reconnaissance, they waited on the arrival of a twelve-man contingent from Support Commando of the RLI.

Barry Gribben recalls the flight in to Zambia aboard the 'Bell 205s': "Traffic was fairly busy with trucks, cars and buses passing only a hundred feet below us. We

219

were hanging out the doors, feet on skids, looking down and the people in the cars were looking up in amazement, smiling and waving to us so we grinned and waved back too." On landing, "the SAS guys were happy to see us, glad to have some extra firepower and a team of RLI donkeys to help carry a few tons of explosives across the countryside."[62]

But there was little time for pleasantries and orders were given with second-in-command Dave Berry looking on. The RLI would take one of the bridges and the SAS the other. Once both groups were in position with charges laid, a signal would be passed and a time set for simultaneous demolition after which the two parties would do a quick damage assessment, move to a predetermined position to rendezvous and then move to a point which would be determined by the SAS.

Traversing rugged terrain, climbing mountainous country, the men struggled with the boxes of explosives which cut into their hands but they pressed on and made their respective objectives. After a brief respite they were happy to discharge their cargo under the cover of night and lay the charges. All in place, confirmation was radioed through and the two groups took their leave, turning to watch the fireballs and feel the thump of the blasts. "The whole valley around us was lit up like the noonday sun," writes Gribben. "Someone said, 'Fuck me, there goes the neighbourhood. They're gonna hear this one all the way to Lusaka.'"[63]

As dawn broke the SAS signaller was listening in to Salisbury. The men were told that the bangs had indeed been heard in Lusaka and signals intercepted revealed instructions had gone out to the Zambian Army and Air Force to use all possible means to hunt down the culprits. An army battalion was already en route to the area to find them and kill them. No sooner had they heard the news than Zambian helicopters soared overhead and dropped troops at the bridges. "For the first time on the mission I had one of those moments wondering if we would actually make it out of there," writes Gribben.

But Berry was calm and confident. Anticipating his pursuers' actions, he made their LUP {lying-up-point} obvious then booby-trapped it. Then he told the men to prepare for a thirty-kilometre walk to a mountainous area where he was sure they could keep watch over the approaches and best defend themselves. The men walked through the entire night, staggering into their new position in the early hours of the following day. There they rested but not for long. Sure he had shaken the Zambian

Army; Berry was not finished; he gave instructions that they would be returning immediately to the road to look for targets to ambush.

Arriving back on the highway after dark, Berry split the men again into two groups and quickly led his section back to the road to look for something to hit. Positioning himself at the top of a rise, he soon saw what he wanted to see: a convoy of enemy vehicles. Gribben and the RLI were watching.

"There was nothing we could do but watch the show. The SAS guys were armed with nine RPDs, plus two RPG-7s and one FN that belonged to Dave Berry. We were perhaps 300 to 500 metres behind them, sitting in a natural amphitheatre among the trees. Below us we watched the headlights of an enemy truck as it slowly wound its way up the road. There was a gradient and he was down into the lower gears making the climb. Over the radio we heard, 'Take him out.' Half a second later there was a sharp flash-boom as the first RPG went off; half a heartbeat later the second RPG fired and struck instantaneously with a huge flash-double-boom, and all the machine guns opened up on the vehicle. Streams of red and green tracers poured down at point-blank range into its dark bulk, absolutely hosing it from end to end; the air ripped with the outrageous popcorn-stuttering from the guns as their roars overlapped like waves of hailstones on a tin roof. Another RPG went home in the middle of it all with an enormous flash-boom-boom lighting up the attackers . . . then suddenly it was all over. In the utter silence that followed someone said; 'Fuck me, that was wild!"[64]

Wasting no time, the SAS linked up with the RLI troops and set off at pace heading south, leaving bodies and a burning wreck in his wake. "If they were pissed off about the bridges they would be mad as hornets now,"[65] recalls Gribben.

Walking through the cool of the night the exhausted men made it to the top of a mountain where they crashed to the ground and rested. But not for long when the silence was broken by the boom of fast-flying jets and the men were suddenly transfixed by the sight of two Jastreb fighters turning towards them and diving out of the blue. Not knowing if they had been seen they lay still, weapons ready, but well aware they would have little chance against the firepower on the aircraft that raced towards them. Anxiously expecting the worst, they were motionless as the first then the second roared over them so close that the soldiers could see the pilots under white helmets looking out their canopies for signs of the Rhodesians. Repeated passes followed and the troops realised their position was somehow compromised.

Belatedly the fighters roared away and Berry quickly gave the signal to abandon the position and led his men down the mountain and into thick cover while he pondered his next move. They moved again but the day was constantly broken by the sight and sound of all types of aircraft overhead. It seemed the entire Zambian Air Force had been scrambled. Making the situation even more fraught, the raiders stumbled upon a remote village and there was instant consternation. "The children had never seen Europeans before," recalls Roger. "They were terrified and their shouts brought people out their huts to see us hurrying past."

But Berry and his officer commanding wanted more. Knowing their pursuers expected them to run south to the border, they bided their time for a few days then ordered the men to turn and head north again. They were going back to the highway to do more damage.

Arriving back at the road, Berry went forward to reconnoitre. He watched and waited but disappointment set in. Word had obviously spread that the road was too dangerous and traffic was light. Hoping for a break, they waited the whole of the next day but bar a dump-truck carrying a repair crew, nothing moved. While they were frustrated it appeared they had achieved their task and shut down a main arterial route.

Awaiting further instructions, the raiders went on a two-day hike back into the mountains of the Zambezi Valley escarpment, enjoying the sights and sounds of elephant, lion and buffalo as they marched. "I always used to think to myself," remembers one of the men, "that I hope peace comes soon and I can come back to these places as a visitor with my wife and family. Such beautiful scenery and so much game in places, I felt it was such a pity we were only there because we were fighting a war."

But such reveries were soon broken. Resting in cover atop a hill the silence was again broken by aircraft; this time the solid thud-thud of the blades of a large helicopter. Hoping in vain that it signalled the arrival of friendly forces coming to take them home, there was shock when the bulbous body of a Zambian Air Force helicopter gunship clattered into view. Pointing ominously downward out the side was a cannon and all braced for big trouble as Berry gave the order to "Take cover and hold fire." Nervously they watched the chopper circle and search, anxiously waiting on the order to fire.

"We knew we would cause a big problem politically if we shot it down so we had to lay low and hold fire but if we'd been seen we were going to drop it," remembers one.

Bordering on panic, one of the RLI men wielding a rocket-launcher was pleading for permission to fire. Hearing his pleas, he was pained to hear one of his men say, "You fire that thing, you fucking Dutchman, and I'll shoot you myself!"

Eventually the helicopter left and the SAS men were on the march again. At midday they stopped to rest. The men were tired; they had been constantly on the move and under pressure for over a week. A signaller rigged his TR48 and an instruction was received for them to prepare for extraction. The RLI men were not so lucky; they were to stay.

A LEADER DIES

At the peak of his power and with his movement in full sail, RENAMO suffered a huge loss with the death of André Matsangaissa on 17 October 1979. The facts surrounding the circumstances of his death have proved confusing but Stephen Emerson explains as follows:

"For defensive reasons, a 90-man RENAMO company was positioned at the bottom of the [Gorongosa] mountain in the M'sucossa area. Just to the south lay the fortified FPLM garrison at Gorongosa town. The roughly 400-man FPLM garrison was a particular target of RENAMO attention; roads were mined, raids on outlying outposts launched and the threat of ambushes ever present. Apparently in response to this harassment FRELIMO launched a retaliatory operation against RENAMO positions north of Gorongosa in mid-October. Despite the guerrillas putting up strong initial resistance they began to run low on ammunition and the attacking FPLM force was able to gain the upper hand and overrun the RENAMO position. Upon hearing of the deteriorating situation Commander André grabbed about a dozen men from the main camp and all the ammunition they could carry and charged down the line from the mountain with a SAS 'call sign' in pursuit to rally his beleaguered forces, according to a former RENAMO guerrilla fighter. The Matsangaissa-led counter-attack was successful in recapturing the old RENAMO position and routing the weary FPLM troops. After pursuing the fleeing enemy to the outskirts of Gorongosa town itself, André paused to consider his next move when he and a group of his men were attacked by fresh FPLM troops. André was shot and killed with a bullet to his head. The SAS team called for a RhAF 'casevac' mission, but it was too late and the resulting fighting too intense to recover the body."[66]

There was an immediate response from the 'Funny Farm' in Rhodesia from whence Afonso Dhlakhama was dispatched by helicopter to take over command. Dhlakhama had big boots to fill and lacking his predecessor's charisma and combat record, he struggled to establish himself. To settle his edgy troops Lieutenant Richard Stannard led a team in to help him consolidate his position on the mountain. A semblance of a conventional cantonment took shape while Stannard and his men drilled new recruits into soldierly shape and offered tactical advice to the commanders. All the while a full-blown political-action campaign was on the go whipping up popular support for the overthrow of the Machel regime.

Confident his RENAMO allies were pumped and ready, Stannard started to lead highly successful raids into the lowlands below and these brought a bounty of captured weapons, ordnance and equipment.

"This was a really exciting period for us," remembers Bas Jolliffe. "The RENAMO guys were so keen but they lacked expertise. Afonso was very keen to go on the offensive and they had rough ideas of what they wanted to do but needed us to help with planning. We used to sit together in Dhlakhama's little thatched office on the mountain and cover the details with him.

The women were also very involved. They carried the ammo boxes when we went on our raids and they were brave and tough. In the middle of some big battles they would come running into the fire with the boxes on their heads. Some tough people. One poor chap had his foot blown clean off. He bandaged it up and walked a long walk home on the stump without any complaint."

Morale soared and the SAS men were the toast of the territory. Soon FRELIMO defectors, getting wind of the view they were on the losing side, started to arrive and offer their services. There was no doubt that the tactical tide was again turning in favour of the Rhodesians.

LIFE WITH LUKE

"Towards the end of 1979," Watt remembers, "six of us parachuted back into Mozambique. We landed at a place close to the main Maputo road and I was amazed to see how many resistance fighters were there waiting for us; close to a thousand.

We had created massive momentum and word had spread through the populace of a force that could topple FRELIMO and there was overwhelming local support. Many were disaffected FRELIMO troops; others were just young men sick and tired of living under a Marxist dictatorship, who sensed the time was right to join what increasingly looked like a winning side."

Roger remembers. "At the briefing before going to Mozambique we were told about this guy Luke and how he had been trained at the Officers' Academy outside Moscow. He was a senior officer in the FRELIMO and then got pissed off and did a total 180-degree turn and joined the resistance. We were told he was very intelligent and very ruthless. Hearing he was bright and literate, I thought I'd take him a present. My grandfather had left me a leather-bound Complete Works of Shakespeare which, being a lance-jack in the SAS and having only scraped a few 'O Levels' together, I could not make head or tail of. I thought they might be more use to him so I ended up jumping into central Mozambique loaded down with William Shakespeare.

"I landed but my parachute caught the trees some 150 feet above the ground, leaving me swinging in the branches. I jettisoned my pack with my books inside and then swung to the trunk of the tree and slowly worked my way down using vines and branches to get to the ground. I remember thinking what a beautiful setting. With a river running right through the camp, luxuriant foliage and plants and trees I'd never seen before, it was an earthly paradise or close to it. The birdlife was exceptional and there was always the soothing sound of them singing. It was difficult to believe there were close to a thousand fighters hiding in there. From the air you would never have known it.

"When I later presented the books to Luke he was very surprised and very grateful and took an instant liking to me. I was allocated two batmen to fetch and carry for me for the duration of our stay. For a bloke with one stripe on his arm this was quite a big step up the ladder. Over the months ahead Luke would often come to me to tell me how much he enjoyed Shakespeare and that he treasured the books immensely. If my grandfather was looking down at us I wondered what he thought of where his books had ended up."

For Watt in his position of 'southern' command and coming from an all-white unit he was a little apprehensive about the fighting qualities of his new friend Luke and the men under his supervision, but excited nonetheless at the prospects. It was also a pleasant surprise to see that the ranks of the resistance had swelled dramatically beyond what he expected as word had travelled of an organised opposition to FRELIMO. And with the numbers, enthusiasm and confidence had soared.

Wanting to firm up their presence, Watt's men and their new allies went to work with a flourish and trenches and bunkers were soon in place. Orders were given for camp defence and proper operational procedures explained. In a short space of time a rag-tag collection of tribesmen had mutated and a small but willing army was beginning to take shape.

But he knew the support of the local populace was essential and wanted to have the resistance establish their credentials with the local people before lashing out at the enemy. Mao's dictum was clear in his mind: the insurgent is like the fish; the people are the sea. Once local support was established, he would switch to a more aggressive role and take his fledgling army onto the offensive.

Extensive patrols were sent out into the populated areas between the Revue and Save rivers which was to be their operational zone. Much of the movement was at night and the larger RENAMO groups were invariably accompanied by a small SAS delegation which stayed out of the public eye. The Rhodesians would approach the villages with their allies then hide and wait while the RENAMO officers went in to enlighten the locals as to what their goals were and encourage their support. Rebels and civilians alike were thrilled with what they heard. Indeed, the response was so overwhelming that the SAS men found themselves positively swamped with aspiring recruits and well beyond their means of supply. As a result, many had to be put on hold while efforts were made to boost organisational capacity. But what was clear was little persuasion was needed: the people were feeling the pain of life under Machel and they wanted him and his Marxist party out as soon as possible.

For Watt and his men, apart from all the other departures from their normal operational lives, the provision of batmen was an unexpected bonus: young recruits who were to have as their first objective the comfort and welfare of the SAS men they served. For the first time the Rhodesians found they had a little personal support network which carried their packs, made their beds and cooked their food. War had never been quite like this before. "The batmen were terrific little guys," Watt remembers. "Tough little chaps, willing, enthusiastic and always smiling. A real joy to have around and work with."

While the SAS had no way of being sure where it would all end up, they knew what they were busy doing was adding the small but vital ingredients that all armies need to be effective: of paramount importance, leadership and organisational skills. What was not lost on them was they had just tapped into an extremely rich seam of soldierly talent that needed only to be trained, armed and led and an amorphous collection of men would quickly take on a dangerous complexion.

Feeling they were ready to go on the offensive, Luke and Watt put their heads together to plan their moves. Two men, one white, one black, from hugely disparate backgrounds who shared no common language, country, culture or ideology, were quickly united by the common bond that comes so easily to fighting soldiers with a common enemy. Together they were destined to take the war in Mozambique to a new level.

Roger recalls the events. "The first big camp attack was agreed on by both Luke and Darrell and it was decided that 600 RENAMO men would attack from two sides of the camp in a fire and movement format. We would then position on the other side where the escapees would have to flee across an open riverbed.

"We positioned ourselves up on a high riverbank to pick the enemy off as and when they tried to run through the dry riverbed below. For a while we had excellent kills but then the 'gooks' got wise and took up a holding position opposite us. We were chuffed as we had a real punch-up on our hands. Unfortunately, they couldn't stay there long because Luke brought his troops in behind them and they had to run for it again, straight into our fire. It was easy pickings for us.

"After the attack the MNR were victorious and thrilled with their victory, however, they had used up virtually all their ammunition, some 32,000 rounds in one camp attack. It sounded like a world war. Later I questioned some of the jubilant fighters and they told me that the more noise they made the more the enemy ran. We radioed back to Salisbury for a resupply which was dropped two days later by parachute.

"There were several times when tensions ran high following attacks where we took casualties. We were pushing them hard so some held us responsible for the losses suffered. As a precaution we would bunk up for the night separately then move quietly at around 22h00 to another location. We slept back to back in case any dissidents within their ranks wanted revenge for their comrades who'd been killed.

"We ranged through the area for over six weeks. Spread out in single file, it was a line stretching over three kilometres. Darrell positioned some of our guys out front as scouts and the rest at the back. I was at the back and it looked like ants on the march. Some strange things happened. One time during a break, when everyone would find a shady place to rest for a while, there was gunfire which created panic amongst the troops. I went to investigate and it turned out that where a group of them had sat down to rest they had sat down on a log that turned out to be a huge python. They shat themselves and immediately let off several magazines of ammo into the poor snake.

"On another occasion I heard a ruckus and went to investigate. A group of them had chopped down a tree and were busy killing a 'galago' {Bushbaby} with sticks. Pissed off, I stepped in to protect the animal and pulled them off but I was too late. The mother was dead with two terrified babies clinging to her. I warned them away and took the two little ones. The RENAMO boys were not happy with me taking part of their supper but I made it clear I'd kill anyone who touched them and strutted off with my two babies. For the next five weeks they lived under my cap or inside my shirt. At first I fed them with grasshoppers which I told my batmen to find but then when they grew and settled down they would go off at night, hunt for insects on their own then return to me in the early hours of the morning and off we'd go to war together. They saw quite a lot of action with me. When the shooting started they would grip me tight and hang on for all they were worth. When it was all over I'd see their little heads come out of my shirt from behind my webbing. With huge brown eyes they would look at me to see if it was safe then relax. Wonderful companions, they never complained. When I returned to Rhodesia I gave them to Gwen Watt, Darrell's wife.

"The RENAMO were a hard bunch. With such a long line of soldiers, some sick with malaria and other ailments, some wounded and with not much in the way of medical care, individuals would literally fall by the wayside while on the march. Unable to help themselves the others would stop only long enough to loot the casualty of everything of value then leave him to die naked. A completely different mentality. I found it heart-breaking walking at the end of the line seeing these men lying there, eyes wide open, pleading for help but there was nothing we could do. We just had to continue our march and leave them there.

"Most evenings we would stop at a kraal for the night and Luke's troops would help themselves to their livestock; goats mainly and any fruit on their trees. If their officers deemed anyone in the village to be an informer he was executed immediately. Then the fighters used to have their way with the women from the village. I used to think to myself 'all's fair in love and war' and these were our allies but they were still savages. On occasion one of my batmen was sent to ask if I wanted to participate. I would refuse, so invariably I was sent a plate of roasted goat meat as a consolation.

"Because I could speak some Shona I got to know a few of the fighters very well. Some had once worked in Umtali as houseboys and cooks and talked fondly of their former white 'madams' and 'bosses.' Others had worked on farms in the eastern districts of Rhodesia before they were recruited. All seemed genuinely fond of the white people they had known in Rhodesia."

Another SAS man with Watt was Jerry Engelbrecht. The son of an itinerant, alcoholic father, he had experienced an unstable boyhood during which he went to ten different schools before joining the army. "It was actually in the SAS that I first found security and a sense of direction. My SAS years taught me about more than being a soldier. The RENAMO deployment was a truly memorable experience. We all became close friends with Luke. As a gift he presented a bolt-action 98K Mauser rifle to each SAS member. This was partly because Darrell had been fondly admiring one, turning it over and over and testing its cocking mechanism. We discovered quite a few Mausers were brought home by allied servicemen at the end of the Second World War, rechambered to 7.62mm and used for hunting purposes. The rifle was noted for its reliability, great accuracy and an effective range of up to 500 metres. The precision workmanship that went into each and every weapon made them a desirable collector's item. Quite how these RENAMO chaps acquired them remained a mystery to us."

"We were only about twenty kilometres from the sea," Watt remembers, "when Luke and I got together to go through our future plans. We were going to go with a handful of RENAMO and blow the bridge across the Buzi River. Then we were going to destroy the next one and keep going until we cut Beira off from the rest of the country. It was going to be a big embarrassment to the Mozambique government and RENAMO would accept responsibility so there were no Rhodesian fingerprints. This was vital because at Lancaster House an assurance had been given that no

Rhodesian troops were in Mozambique. Once we were finished with those bridges the Mozambique authorities and the enemy support network would have had very big logistical problems. As Mozambique's second largest city, once in our hands, I felt sure we could go on and win the war in the east by proxy."

"As a first stop en route to blowing the bridge Darrell decided to take about fifty RENAMO and six of us to attack an enemy position in the river that RENAMO had told us about," remembers Engelbrecht. "The island was home to FRELIMO and ZANLA and was along our route so Darrell wanted to hit it. He selected a small RENAMO group to carry the heavy plastic mortar boxes packed with dynamite for dropping the bridge, and rationed the remaining RENAMO to about fifty rounds each. The plan was for the RENAMO to attack the island while we, the SAS, would direct the operation from the banks of the river. There was no way we were keen to be caught in the crossfire of a highly excitable bunch with only very rudimentary training. It was not the most clandestine operation, as the line of RENAMO kept breaking ranks and ADs were not uncommon.

"Reaching the island, which was about 250 metres long with the river split on each side, we had a good look at it. The island was very dense, but the bank on our side was pretty clear and we had a good view of its entire length. We could see no movement. We set up a command point behind an anthill about fifty metres from the river. The SAS men took up positions to best observe the proceedings, each having his weapon at ready as well as the Mauser from Luke. We were all hoping for an opportunity to put the Mausers to the test.

"After some final instructions Darrell sent the RENAMO in. They were very excited and quite difficult to contain, and it was obvious that they would not follow any structure. They simply crossed the river en masse and disappeared into the thick growth. At first nothing happened, then the roar of gunfire was deafening as the island erupted. We heard some loud thumps, and the 'tack-tack-tack' of a Goryunov machine gun. This went on for a period, while ZANLA recruits broke away into the river, coming directly towards us. It was the opportunity we had been waiting for and we began firing on them with our Mausers. The Mausers needed quick zeroing and adjustments but soon we started picking ZANLA off nicely.

"Eventually all gunfire ceased and an extremely excited group of RENAMO returned from their excursion to give wild stories of success and destruction, most of which we were a little circumspect about. A quick check revealed that most of their ammo was spent. Darrell ordered them back to camp, save for the bridge-blowing contingent. FRELIMO dropped a few misdirected mortars but we got the impression they had had enough. Darrell then saw an opportunity to ambush. Sending Luke and his men ahead with two of our guys, Darrell set the ambush up and true to form twelve ZANLA approached looking disinterested, probably thinking we were long gone. It was their last walkabout."

"I can honestly say," Watt recalls, "that after twelve years in the SAS my time with the RENAMO was some of the most rewarding and enjoyable of all that time. Never did I feel so relaxed and confident. I realised then that we had erred in not having black men in the Squadron. Some of them were outstanding and no doubt they would have served with distinction in the best of military outfits.

"It was quite incredible but we became so organised I used to spend much of the day lying in my hammock listening to a music station on short-wave coming out of South Africa. I was so happy there I actually told Colonel Barrett that we did not need to be relieved.

"Once all our plans were in place we had excellent early-warning systems. The RENAMO blokes were very sharp and missed nothing. FRELIMO sent armoured brigades in a couple of times to nail us. Early-warning sentries would pick them up well in advance and out would go our RENAMO sections to harass them. While they distracted them we went and planted mines on the enemy routes in and out and we blew the shit out of them. They just couldn't get close to us. It was great having the enemy come to us rather than us having to chase them which is what I'd done most of the time I'd been a soldier. On a couple of occasions when the columns looked too big I called in the air force who sent in 'Hunter' strikes. FRELIMO deployed BTR-152 armoured trucks and vehicles carrying 122mm rocket launchers which they used against us but with only little effect. It was a little like watching a game. I used to go to the top of the hill to direct the aircraft onto the targets, watch the battle then go back to my hammock and listen to the music while my cook prepared my next meal. It was like a bloody holiday camp at times.

"One of the funniest incidents during this time was the arrival of reinforcements consisting of Sergeant Major 'Koos' Loots and eleven other operators. They were sent in to see what we were doing. I heard the Dakota coming and I lay on my hammock watching them jumping out the aircraft. The next moment I saw one of the poor blokes coming in hanging from a parachute in a tree. Eventually he cut himself free and hit the ground in a puff of dust.

"The sergeant-major walked up to me, mad as hell 'What the fuck do you think you're doing?' he said. I could see he was seriously pissed off but he had to be careful, I was a senior rank.

"'Relax,' I said, 'sergeant-major, just calm down and I'll explain!'

"'But what the fuck are you doing with that?' He pointed to the radio, he was shaking with anger. 'What the fuck are you doing listening to this music? Turn it down, for fuck's sake!'

"'I'm enjoying it,' I said. I think they thought I had gone completely ape. I was living in a hut, maps on the wall, pots full of food, music blaring, and 'Koos', being a good warrant officer, immediately started shouting at the 'troopies': the place looked more like a holiday camp than an army camp. 'Koos' said our whole situation was not acceptable. I told him to just calm down; everything was quite fine here and explained why we were secure. It took 'Koos' a few days but then he understood this was different and he relaxed.

"My sidekick I called 'Mongoose' because he was ever-alert, always on the move looking and checking; he knew everything; an ex-FRELIMO officer, he was a wonderful guy. He kept me posted on everything I needed to know. His local knowledge was exceptional. He did full reports on all the FRELIMO bases for me so I knew everything in advance. I had never had such good intelligence. Before doing anything 'Mongoose' would go into the enemy camp with informers and check it out carefully before reporting back to me. As soon as I was happy I told Luke to prepare his men for an attack. I would then draw up a battle plan for him and he would act according to that plan. I would get on to a hill with a Dragunov and fire bursts occasionally while supervising. All the section commanders had radios so I could maintain overall control. In the middle of the fighting 'Mongoose' would appear with my tea. From these attacks we became almost self-sufficient in weapons, ammunition, food and general supplies. HQ kept asking me how the hell we were surviving without resupply but we were living like kings.

"One place we attacked had an airfield and a hospital. Then the informers arrived to tell us there was an aircraft there. We attacked immediately and captured the place. We told the medical staff they would not be harmed and asked them to carry on what they were doing which they were happy to do. We left a RENAMO section there and carried on. I sent a message to Salisbury to tell them to send a pilot and technicians to collect the plane. I was not there when they came but I believe they did so. All the time we were closing down the ZANLA infiltration routes, and given a little more time, I think we would have broken the back of ZANLA there and won the war in Mozambique."

A MYSTERY DEATH AT LANCASTER HOUSE

But back in London at Lancaster House, talks chairman Peter Carrington was at his most cunning best. As negotiations dragged on the British diplomats, past-masters in the art of political seduction, continued to soothe, flatter and cajole the man they desperately needed to control: General Walls. Without him and the Rhodesian security forces reined in, all their hard wrought political plans would come to nought.

While Ian Smith had been disinvited, Walls was accorded VIP status including outriders, plush accommodation and tickets to rugby at Twickenham. It did the trick. Walls, much to Smith's dismay, duly softened. "Clever people at the Foreign Office," Smith conceded ruefully, "the British plan worked and they had no real problem with Walls after his time with the Queen Mother." Smith's observations were later confirmed by Ian Gilmour. "Yes," he admitted with a chuckle, "we were up to our old Foreign Office tricks. That's how negotiations succeed . . . his visit there [to Balmoral to meet the Queen Mother] affected him greatly."

When Smith had dismissed outright as a lie Carrington's categorical assurance that Mugabe would not form the new government, Walls still held his counsel. Becoming increasingly withdrawn, it did not escape the attention of some of his colleagues that the general had suddenly dispensed with his staff officer and taken to dealing with the British on his own.

"Walls, like most generals, quite correctly relied on junior officers to do all his staff work for him," recalls an officer who worked with him. "Not having a personal staff officer at his side was certainly seen as very unusual. Suddenly, there he was typing out telexes with one finger, something he had never been seen to do before but clearly, for reasons known only to him, he wanted to work on his own at this stage. Whether he had something to hide we'll probably never know. Eventually General Barnard in Salisbury decided to send him a staff officer with or without a request from Commander 'ComOps.'"

Smith's fear that treachery of the worst kind was afoot peaked with the sudden death in early October of constitutional lawyer John Giles. It has subsequently become clear that all the rooms at Lancaster House were bugged and filmed by British Intelligence and the eavesdroppers would have heard the lawyer's strident criticism of the proffered constitution and his outspoken clarity on Carrington's shenanigans. Giles, like Ian Smith, had read the situation correctly: Carrington had cunningly compartmentalised the delegations and was telling each in private exactly what they wanted to hear. Ian Smith was bitterly blunt. "I have never believed Giles's death was suicide and never will. I am certain he was eliminated. Carrington is the most evil man I've ever met."[67]

Despite an official verdict reporting the death as a suicide, having leaped from his balcony, there is considerable doubt about this to this day and Andre Scheepers' recollections in this regard are revealing.

"I was a world away and with much else on my mind," he recalls. "We only had a vague idea of what was going on in London but BOSS {South Africa's Bureau of State Security} obviously had their sources there because their Special Forces Commander General Loots was very well informed on developments there. A most impressive, very polished man, he was always beautifully dressed and he really cared about us in Rhodesia. I think his links to Israeli intelligence were a factor but he knew there was a leak somewhere in the Rhodesian special forces hierarchy and it troubled him greatly. It was he who contacted me. I received a message from the general to say that a lawyer representing the Rhodesian Government had been killed at the Lancaster House conference. He was very angry and went on to explain that they knew who had done it and wanted to retaliate. He asked me if I would be prepared to go to London and kill the men who had done this. From what I gathered the lawyer had been killed with a syringe which caused an embolism leading to heart failure. It sounded interesting and challenging and I considered this carefully. General Loots told me they liked the quiet way I operated and they thought I would be ideal for the job. But I doubted this. I was a bush-soldier who had become skilled in operating in a bush environment in Africa against a particular type of adversary. This did not equip me well for the task of urban assassin and a relatively sophisticated enemy on home turf. London, to me, was a very strange and faraway place. I felt I would be like a fish out of water and resisted General Loots in his bid to persuade me to take the job. Looking back, I think I did the right thing."

When Walls, now warming warily to the British view, asked Carrington for the assurances he had given regarding Mugabe and the election outcome to be given to him in writing, Carrington suddenly equivocated. He explained that such a document in the hands of the Patriotic Front would torpedo the talks. Instead, the wily foreign secretary pulled an ace out the pack and offered another sop: Walls was whisked off to see Mrs Thatcher herself.

Charming but deceptive, she concurred with Carrington. Using blunt language, she vouched for the assurances her foreign secretary had given, soothed the soldier's fears and assured him her door was open to him in the event subsequent developments were not to his liking. According to Walls, she went on to assure him that she too was opposed to terrorism and was as opposed to Mugabe coming to power as he was. Sadly, in the light of subsequent events, and dismissive of Smith's warnings, this was good enough for Walls. Smith could only look on in dismay as his top general finally turned his back on his former prime minister and walked into the British camp. "One of my great regrets," said Smith, "is that I didn't insist on the job of military supremo going to Air Marshal McLaren rather than Walls."

The next step in the plot was for Carrington to cajole Muzorewa into surrendering power. He did this with the assistance of both Ken Flower and Walls by assuring the Bishop that this was only a temporary means to an end that would see him back in the power in the very near future. The fact that both Walls and Flower were party to this fiction, in light of the fact that they were receiving regular intelligence from the 'Yankee Section' signals interceptors in Salisbury informing them of Carrington's shenanigans, provided clear proof that they had in effect swapped sides. A lone voice in the wilderness was that of Ian Smith but he was ignored.

For the fighting soldiers at home their most senior commander was buckling. Unbeknown to them, the war they had risked so much to win was being decided by men in suits in luxuriant surrounds where courage and fortitude played second fiddle to lies and deception.

CHAPTER 15

We had packed. We waited
In the cathedral hush.
Eight men sat. Some read Some drank.
All Unconsciously part
Of a ritual for the dead,
For those about to join them.
—CHAS LOTTER

BUST THE BRIDGES

While the politicians bickered, operational commanders looked at the allowable options. On the table was a plan to sweep through southern Mozambique and destroy the remaining communication infrastructure, but this was shelved when news filtered through from Zambia. It appeared Nkomo and his high command were panicking. There was political movement at Lancaster House and a ceasefire suddenly seemed possible. Before that materialised Nkomo and his generals understood the urgent need to rush troops and equipment into Rhodesia to grab territory that would otherwise be seized by ZANLA. It appears another frustration for Nkomo's men was the delay in the formation of a Soviet-supplied air force which had not materialised due to the failure of the pilots to complete their training. An offer of Cuban aviators was rejected by the ZIPRA high command. Notwithstanding this deficit, the order was given to move forces south and move fast.

"ZIPRA suddenly became a big threat," remembers an officer. "Nkomo had held his forces back but with the possibility of political change they decided on a full-scale conventional assault through Kariba and Victoria Falls which would involve armour, thousands of men and possible air support. It was clear we had to destroy the bridges as a matter of urgency and 'Operation Dice' was launched.

Reconnaissance teams were sent in immediately to prepare for the demolition teams. On 16 November it all started to roll."

"Before 'Operation Dice' kicked off we agreed on an inter-squadron competition for the operation—six crates of beer for the squadron that did the most damage and killed the most 'gooks'—so there was a lot of excitement amongst the troops and much enthusiasm about getting stuck in to the enemy," recalls Roger.

The morning the operation commenced four 'Bell' helicopters left Kariba and flew into southern Zambia. Two 'call signs', each armed with 20mm cannons were positioned on overlooking hills to provide protection while three groups below set about the task of demolishing three separate bridges.

When the Zambian army intervened later with light armour and trucks loaded with troops the 20mm cannons went into action along with a barrage of mortars. While holding up civilian traffic to avoid any unnecessary casualties, the demolition teams completed their tasks and the bridges were destroyed almost exactly as planned.

However, the extraction phase was hindered for one team when mechanical problems meant that one of the 'Bells' was unavailable for the uplift. The men in the mountains with the 20mm cannons were told to 'hold the fort' and keep fighting until another aircraft arrived.

It was clear their task was far from over when reinforcements appeared, but with some of the enemy vehicles below on fire and bodies strewn along the roadside, the scene that greeted the new arrivals was a daunting one. The observing SAS men were pleased to note fear seemed to paralyse the arriving Zambian soldiers who sat tight until whipped into action by a furious officer, but their contribution to the proceedings was minimal. By the end of the day a chopper was airborne and the troops safely recovered. The operation had got off to a fine start.

Days later, following the speedy destruction of the Kaleya bridge, the SAS men were surprised to see that their antics had drawn a large crowd of fascinated onlookers. Knowing they had a long wait before the helicopters returned and not wanting to sit in the limelight too long, they hijacked a vehicle and drove themselves some distance south, well away from the excitement. From there they were safely uplifted to Kariba.

Searching for a suitable road and rail combination, Captain Bob MacKenzie decided on a target ninety kilometres outside the capital. Troops on the ground immediately took incoming fire and a 'Lynx' was called upon to strafe the enemy position while the teams went to work. Under sustained fire they bustled around the bridges while civilian traffic piled up at both ends. Drivers and passengers were calmed by the SAS men tasked with protecting the demolition crew but when the bridges went up in smoke it was very clear to the motorists that they would have to alter their travel plans. The demolition was a complete success and with helicopters waiting nearby, the raiders were back in Kariba in time to re-equip and re-engage in the afternoon.

Still to be dealt with was the bridge closest to Lusaka that straddled the road south. It would constitute a vital crossing for enemy troops heading to Rhodesia and it had to go, but with a Zambian army camp almost at the bridge itself, it was also the best defended.

Thirty men were dispatched for the task. Six would demolish the bridge, the rest, split into four 'call signs', would be deployed in defensive roles on both sides of the road and on the surrounding hills. Arriving on the scene the infiltration went off without a hitch and when Nick Breytenbach went to work on the Zambian army with his 20mm cannon there was more panic than fight as sirens wailed and troops ran for cover.

In the midst of the semi-controlled mayhem, despite repeated orders to halt, a civilian-driven vehicle tried to break through a roadblock and was fired upon. The driver, a Swiss national, died despite feverish efforts by an SAS medic to save him.

"Dumping of one of the southern bridges was tasked to a section that included Dave Berry, Roger and me and we had some RLI guys along with us," remembers Jerry Engelbrecht. "We were also told to set up an ambush for known white Toyota Land Cruisers regularly using the route; intelligence revealed they were transporting high-ranking ZIPRA officials.

"We were dropped late in the afternoon by two choppers and then proceeded on foot. It was getting dark rapidly; sound carries at night and dogs in nearby villages sensed our presence and barked incessantly. Darrell was concerned we would be compromised, so he quickly arranged us in a defensive circle for the night in the hope the dogs would settle down too.

"At first light we sought a suitable ambush position to press on with the mission. The difficulty was that the vegetation was sparse and thin, and the dogs resumed yapping, so we quickly settled on a rocky outcrop near the tar road, where the men could lie up, hide and wait for the Land Cruisers to show. The two teams were expectantly on high alert with weapons at the ready. By midday there was still no sign of them, and Darrell advised headquarters who instructed us to proceed and drop the bridge and ambush any responding enemy. We needed no further encouragement, and the packs of heavy charges were manhandled across the broken ground to the bridge. By late afternoon the charges were fixed, and the bridge was dropped in an eruption of dust and debris."

"The bridge blown, Darrell said he wanted to fuck them up some more and win the beer prize," remembers Roger. "So we walked for about three hours during the night to an ambush position. It was a long hike over a range of mountains in wild, unpopulated country which dropped down into a valley. We were following game-trails and elephant paths and we were surprised to walk into a settlement in the middle of nowhere. The natives there looked at us in horror then fled, leaving the children behind to fend for themselves. It was like nothing I had seen before. Their dwellings were in the trees and their only clothing was loin-cloths. I am certain they had never seen white people before. The children were terrified but we calmed them down and gave them boiled sweets and sugar from our rations. Their faces lit up and they then warmed to us. Eventually the parents returned but they were very wary and by the way they stared at us I know they had never seen Europeans before. They were the most primitive people I have ever seen.

"Eventually we got to a point on a road where we decided to ambush. We were told we might be here for a few days. It was bloody hot and I thought I wouldn't last too long in that heat. I was feeling pretty miserable because everything was so quiet and I did not think anything was going to happen when all of a sudden a Scania truck appeared, loaded with enemy troops. Our position was perfect: we were on an incline so the vehicle was climbing slowly. Darrell looked and said, 'Okay Rog, this is the one, let's hit it!'

"They came into the killing zone and had no chance. We had nine RPDs and a rocket launcher aimed at them. We fired and the earth shook Most died in their seats; of roughly thirty, maybe one or two escaped. Then we ran like hell. That night we climbed back into the mountains and reached the top in the morning. The Zambians were mad at us and Galeb strike jets and choppers arrived overhead looking for us but we hid among the trees. We then called for uplift but we had to clear a landing zone of trees so we machine-gunned the trunks to fell them. Then the choppers came and we went back to Kariba with a 'Hunter' escort. We won the beer and had a hell of a celebration."

When the dust settled and the news of the attacks reached Lusaka the Zambian press went berserk, calling for immediate international action to save the country from total destruction. But in Salisbury their howls fell on deaf ears. No sooner were the district bridges down than two raiding parties closed in on the capital and blew two more just outside the city at the same time as the big terror base at CGT-2 was again attacked by the air force. This left the country, the Commonwealth and much of the world in an uproar. Between the SAS and the RLI they had successfully dumped ten bridges and the ZIPRA invasion plan was in tatters.

Militarily the operation had been a complete success; the SAS had in a sense done what it had long clamoured to do, and had brought the country to its knees. For Kaunda the idea of continuing the war held less appeal than ever. For Nkomo, his invasion plans a shambles, his hosts beleaguered, the pressure to settle politically intensified.

The politicians had asked the soldiers to provide the pressure that would give them the leverage. The SAS had done their duty. The ball was in the political court. All the soldiers could do was hope that their hierarchy would demonstrate the same skill and courage under a different kind of fire. Unfortunately, that was not to be.

With negotiations continuing and General Walls folding slowly under British pressure, Darrell Watt resumed his covert campaign in central Mozambique.

A BIG SURPRISE

"We were told little about the talks at Lancaster House but just that we should stay where we were in Mozambique for the time being," remembers Watt. "We heard some sort of ceasefire was close to agreement and Mugabe, along with a guarantee from President Machel, had told Carrington that no further infiltrations into Rhodesia would be allowed by ZANLA. We were told Mugabe had been reluctant to agree to this and was insisting on a military victory but Machel was starting to worry about the war threatening his own hold on power. We continued our operations and expanded our area of dominance through harassing attacks, ambushing and mining."

With generally not more than twenty-four SAS men working with RENAMO, the SAS had all but crippled central Mozambique and pretty much paralysed the economy. Using all their resources, FRELIMO had been unable to stop the insurgents and suffered heavy casualties in the process.

"Then one day an amazing thing happened. I was just taking it easy, waiting for orders from Salisbury when Luke came to see me. 'Come,' he said to me quietly, 'we've got something to show you.' Then he cautioned me; 'You are not to treat them badly or talk to them harshly.' I nodded my agreement, picked up my webbing and weapon and asked him how far we were going. He said it was not far so I grabbed some water and off we went.

"The RENAMO chaps had recently been busy with axes and cleared a space the size of a football field preparatory to my arrival so there was a large clearing. I could scarcely believe my eyes when I came out of the trees and saw what was before me. They were lined up with their weapons in rows with packs behind them, about seventy ZANLA men and some women. They were sitting very quietly and I had to get a grip of myself. This was incredible. I was completely blackened as we always were then and I reached for my water bottle and a handkerchief. I poured some water on it and wiped the black camouflage cream off my face. Suddenly where there had been a black face now there was a white one. I could hear them gasping and I could see lots of eyes that had doubled in size. Then they looked at one another and there was much nervous shuffling around.

"Luke asked me to explain. I said, 'I'm an officer of the Rhodesian Army and I am in command of this area.' They just looked on in a mixture of fear and disbelief. There was complete silence as I suppose they came to terms with the fact that anything now was possible. I said I wanted their commander to stand and come forward. There was a lull then he stood and walked slowly towards me. I looked at him carefully.

"When he got to me I stopped him and he saluted. I saluted him back then I asked him to tell me his name. I explained I wanted his full name, not his nom de guerre. He told me immediately and I introduced myself formally then held out my hand to shake his and so we met. I looked again and liked the look of the guy.

"I said to him, Commander, I think you can see that the circumstances you and your men find yourselves in are unfavourable to you. He looked at my blokes and the RENAMO chaps and nodded his head quite vigorously in agreement. I told him he was breaching the ceasefire agreement his leader had entered into in London. He agreed that was the case but that he was following orders. I said I understood and that I had a proposition for him. He asked me what it was.

"I looked him in the eyes and said it was quite simple. 'We want you and your men to join us in the fight against Mugabe.' Incredibly he seemed not to hesitate. He replied that he and the men under his command would do so. It was almost unbelievable but we had just captured seventy ZANLA without even an argument, let alone a fight. I saluted him and asked him to inform his men of his decision whereupon he walked away to explain what he'd decided. I looked on a little warily but there appeared to be no dissension from the ranks at all, in fact there seemed to be quite a bit of excitement.

"When he came back to me I explained to him that we in the Rhodesian Army were not fighting for Ian Smith or white rule because Bishop Muzorewa, a black man, not Ian Smith was now the prime minister. I told him that we loved our country and simply wanted peace, justice and an end to terror. I told him he was now on the right side and he seemed genuinely in agreement. I told him he was to prepare to leave immediately for the border town of Chipinga where he would be met by our support troops and taken to a Special Forces Camp where he and his men would be well cared for.

"Moving closer, I checked their weapons and was pleased to see they had removed the magazines and cleared them. One of the RENAMO guys then came to me and said: 'Captain, you may do anything you want with these people but you must not kill them.' I liked that in a strange way. Not often one sees compassion in African wars. I was happy to tell him that they would be well cared for.

"Then I looked at Roger England and told him and two other guys to escort them the sixty kilometres back to Rhodesia. Two days later he arrived and handed them over. It was after this incident that I knew, given a little more time, we could win the war."[68]

In his memoirs, bearing in mind his loyalties were at best divided, Ken Flower's lament seems to confirm that Watt and his men were on a roll to victory. "Subsequently the RENAMO seemed to go from strength to strength and I wondered if we had created a monster that was now beyond our control."

TIME TO SAY GOODBYE

But the finger of fate was pointing in another direction and Watt's hopes of continuing the campaign would soon be dashed. A signal was received at SAS HQ to immediately halt all hostilities.

"It was a huge disappointment," recalls Watt. "We were looking forward to blowing the bridge and morale was very high. We were on a roll and wanted to finish the job. All I was told was that something had happened at Lancaster House and we were to make plans to get out of there immediately. Helicopters would be coming to collect us the following day. I was very upset but there was little I could do. I had my orders and had to follow them.

"In the morning I went to explain the news to Luke. He was pretty shocked because it came so out the blue and I could see he had no idea what to do. Our two units had become almost one and we had forged a fantastic fighting alliance. It was a symbiotic relationship; we needed one another to survive and here I was telling him we were going home and ditching them probably for good. The sad looks on the RENAMO commanders' faces told the story and I felt desperately sorry for them. Soon word spread and all 750 knew what had happened and there was a lot of unhappiness. Then the tension rose and you could have cut the atmosphere with a knife. If it turned ugly we were in big trouble: twelve of us and 750 of them.

"Luke went on his radio to talk to Dhlakhama who was on the Gorongosa Mountain. I waited, then he came over to me and looked me in the eyes and said we were to hand over our weapons to him immediately. I felt the temperature rising and at first was a little at a loss as to what to do but knew I had to keep calm at all costs. If any panic set in it could have turned into a bloodbath.

"I spoke to him quietly but confidently, 'Luke,' I said, 'we are all soldiers and we have fought hard and well together. As you know we all have senior officers from whom we must take and obey orders. As fighting soldiers who have not been defeated,' I explained, 'I and my men will hand our weapons to no one. Our weapons are our right and ours to keep. We will not be disarmed under any circumstances.' He did not like what he heard and said his orders were clear: to disarm us immediately.

"When I saw he meant it I knew I had to move fast if we were to survive this. I went to my guys and told them to get ready: we were in with a chance of the fight of our lives. I told them to put claymores up all around our position. Then I got on the radio and said I needed Sunray immediately. I told HQ—unsure if I spoke to Wilson or Barrett—in clear what was happening and said we needed air support immediately. I told them we could be attacked at any moment. Their question was, 'What do you suggest we do?' I said get the Canberras up here and bomb them. I will go and tell Luke he is about to get bombed. They agreed immediately and Wilson came himself in the one Canberra. I remember them coming; one was low the other was at high altitude. I said to Luke, 'Listen, they're coming. If you touch us, we're all going to die under the same hail of bombs so it's your choice now.' He looked at me and said okay just as one of the aircraft flew over us.

"Asked what to do next, I said, 'Send in the choppers to uplift us and the RENAMO commanders.' I told Luke that I would do what I could to help them and we organised to move them back to a safe defensive position east of the town of Chipinga. Two SAAF Hercules transports arrived which we helped unpack. I helped their commanders set themselves up. New mortars arrived and I helped them position them. They had enough to keep them going for a few months when it was time to say goodbye.

"I said, 'Luke, I am sorry, but I have to go now. My war is over for me but yours continues and I wish you the best.' I said, 'When you have won I am coming back to see you and you must help me get a game ranch and an island.' He said that would be no problem. He saluted me and said goodbye.

"Only later I discovered that the RENAMO commander Afonso Dhlakhama had ordered Luke to capture and hold us but Luke ignored the instruction. We heard he was assassinated later but this was never confirmed. I think he may have become a threat to Dhlakhama as a result of our successes. Luke's area of dominance, as a result of our joint effort, had become far larger than that covered by the Gorongosa contingent. Then helicopters came to collect us. It was a very sad moment in my time as a soldier. I watched Luke move away with his men into an uncertain future. After all we had achieved it was hard to have it end this way but that is war, I suppose. I remain convinced that if we had been allowed to blow that bridge we would have taken Beira—complete control of central Mozambique—and turned the tide absolutely in our favour. But we had fought our last battle. The war for Rhodesia was effectively over."

With a heavy feeling in his heart Rhodesia's veteran of countless encounters with the enemy was going home. He had been on the first of the SAS's forays into

Mozambique, now he was returning from its last. He and those with whom he served had given their all in the defence of their country but events had passed from their hands.

"Darrell Watt was the complete fighting soldier," says Roger. "Absolutely fearless, incredibly tough, he was always in control of the situation on the ground and he had an uncanny knack for survival. I had the most exciting days of my life with him. He commanded the respect of all who fought with him."

"The war ended too soon for us," says Mike West. "At that point I felt we were unstoppable. That team of guys we had at the end was the best group of fighting fuckers I ever served with and I felt nobody could beat us. A fucking shame it ended when it did."

"Towards the end I did a lot of thinking about the war, wondering what we had done right, what we had done wrong and our chances of winning it," says Watt. "The size of the forces ranged against us was daunting but I always thought we could win by an aggressive strategy, hitting the enemy in their bases. Once they were in our country we were in trouble.

"I was determined not to lose anyone under my command but that did not happen. The fact that I only lost one of my men considering what I went through is, I suppose, an achievement, but still one too many. We all came to know each other very well but I tried to avoid getting too emotionally close to anyone for fear that I would lose them.

"I was lucky to have had with me some great soldiers; young and fearless, I don't believe there was any order in battle they would have refused. There were times when I felt they were too aggressive and the only person who could stop them getting hurt or killed was me. Unlike the Squadron commanders who could pick who they wanted to operate with, I had to take what I was given but I have no complaints."

CEASEFIRE

On 12 December, with important issues still outstanding, Peter Carrington took a gamble and dispatched Lord Christopher Soames to Salisbury to take up the post of Governor of what was once again technically the colony of Southern Rhodesia. Soon a critical sticking point arose, with Mugabe demanding the addition of another assembly point right in the centre of the country. Walls had made it known that he had conceded all he was going to concede and reacted with outrage when approached for the concession by a governor who, Walls noted, came to the meeting less than sober. But despite a blustering denunciation of the British request and some bad language, the general relented again.

On 15 December, a day after a senior member of the ZANU (PF) delegation had categorically rejected the British call for a ceasefire, Mugabe was forced into a corner by an exasperated Samora Machel. The Rhodesian raids and RENAMO activity had taken their toll and the Mozambican leader was throwing in the towel. Either Mugabe agreed to the British terms for a ceasefire or he was told he could look for another country from which to run his war. Mugabe, well aware he had no option, promptly agreed and a cessation of hostilities was agreed to. But that was only for show. While Rhodesian cross-border raids were immediately halted, Mugabe's men continued the murderous mayhem within the country. Their orders: to spread the certain word that anything less than a Mugabe victory in an election would result in further war and ruthless retribution. It was quite simply a message of vote Mugabe or die. A formal ceasefire was announced and the withdrawal of Rhodesian troops to their bases began. In terms of the agreement all ZANLA and ZIPRA combatants were to congregate in predetermined assembly points scattered throughout the country, however it soon became evident that most of the guerrilla forces would remain outside the designated zones. In their stead they sent young collaborators to make up the numbers. When reports of rampant intimidation by gangs loyal to Mugabe reached Walls, he complained to Lord Soames who fobbed him off and no official action was taken. The SAS became restless.

Just to let the whites know it was business as usual despite the ceasefire, attacks on them were stepped up. Kobus Odendaal, an elderly Selous farmer, was ambushed and killed and in the Lowveld Max Stockhill died in a landmine blast. On the eastern border Don Harvey-Brown, a sixty-six-year-old caretaker on the Courtauld Estate near Umtali was killed, while nearby, Ivor Tapping, headmaster of a school for black children, was murdered in front of his pupils. On 26 December Basil Beverley, aged seventy-one and a Lowveld icon who had devoted his life to the area, was killed.

Days before the end of the year news arrived of the untimely death of ZANLA military chief Josiah Tongogara. The cause was given as a car accident but it was well known that the ZANLA commander's moderate views on a future Zimbabwe were not playing well with the radical mainstream led by Mugabe who was wary of his charismatic general. Tongogara had on at least one occasion made it known in public that he and Peter Walls could sort the problem out alone and could do so without the politicians. Having grown up on the Smith family farm in Selukwe, he told the world during the peace talks in London how kind Ian Smith's mother had been to him as a boy. Spotting Smith at the opening of the Lancaster House deliberations during an informal gathering to help the different delegations get acquainted with one another, Tongogara broke the ice by striding over to the former prime minister, introducing himself and then explaining to Smith in blunt terms how he foresaw no future for Zimbabwe without Smith and the whites. His brash pronouncement jarred with Mugabe whose disapproval was noted.

Back in Rhodesia frontline commanders fretted but their anxiety was somewhat allayed by unofficial word that whatever happened Mugabe would not be allowed to assume power and, if necessary, military force would be used to achieve this. "Unit commanders throughout the Rhodesian security forces were assured that Mugabe could never come to power," writes Jerry Engelbrecht. "This was relayed to us at Kabrit Barracks by the CO. Afterward Darrell said, 'What bullshit! If it were true he would not be on Rhodesian soil in the first place.' He could never know just how accurate he would be."

Despite uncertainty, the SAS and others were instructed to piece together a drastic response in the event that the political solution went awry.

The modalities fell into two operations, Hectic and Quartz. Hectic, with Watt in a command role, comprised the planned elimination of selected enemy personnel in Salisbury and Bulawayo including Robert Mugabe, Simon Muzenda and Rex Nhongo. Quartz involved the destruction of enemy targets which in the main constituted select assembly points. In on the act were elements of the South African Defence Force under Colonel Jan Breytenbach which were tasked with the two large assembly points close to their border.

"It was a big switch for us being back in Rhodesia in an undercover role," remembers Watt. "We had to get the bush out of our brains and look like city-slickers. Some of them just couldn't pull off the identity change and it was obvious."

"Plans, preparations and training for the pseudo operations were coordinated by Darrell," recalls Jerry. "The usual camouflage uniforms were traded in for civilian clothing, and the operators were relocated from Kabrit Barracks to flats and houses at various locations around Salisbury."

Military vehicles were replaced with civilian 'Kombis' {VW station wagons} purchased in South Africa from a special slush fund. Rehearsals were thorough for setting roadblocks, house-clearing drills, battle preparations, intelligence gathering, drive-pasts and laying clandestine ambushes on roadsides. Every possible contingency was practised. Members exchanged automatic rifles and machine guns for semi-automatic Star and Browning 9mm handguns.

The SAS was split into three for the purposes of future operations: A Squadron was tasked with killing Mugabe at home in Mount Pleasant; B Squadron was to deal with his deputy Simon Muzenda at his new home on Enterprise Road as well as eliminating about a hundred ZANLA officers at a nearby arts centre; C Squadron was to attack a University of Rhodesia facility accommodating about 200 officers along with senior commanders Rex Nhongo, Dumiso Dabengwa and Lookout Masuku. Depending on the state of the political play, Masuku and Dabengwa—both ZIPRA commanders— along with their men were possibly going to be offered an 'out' and taken into custody rather than being killed.

"Everybody was very pumped for action," remembers Watt. "The targets we had been chasing for so long were now very close and we badly wanted to nail them. Unfortunately, we would only find out later but the Brits knew too much at this stage."

Adding to the Rhodesian challenges it was confirmed that British SAS operatives were masquerading as election monitors. To help them identify their opposite numbers in Rhodesia they brought with them at least one former member of the Rhodesian SAS then residing in the UK. Quickly identified by a Rhodesian SAS officer, the individual was confronted and told quietly but firmly that it would be 'extremely unhealthy' for him to continue his subterfuge and no more was seen of him. Furious with their erstwhile brothers-in-arms for joining with the enemy, another officer conspired to lure his 'tail' into the shadows where his troops lurked with baseball bats. "We were going to beat the shit out of them but they were wise to us and we couldn't get them into the alleys where we wanted them. Lucky for them. They made sure they didn't go back to Hereford with some large lumps on their heads."

"We did a quick course with Special Branch," remembers Watt. "It was a very good course on surveillance and I had a good team with me. We worked out which Brits were following us; some were Brit SAS I think. I tried to get them to follow me out of Salisbury. I had two of my chaps with RPDs in the back seat and we were going to blow them away but they would not follow us in the dark. Lucky for them.

"If we were being tailed on foot we simply walked into the park and they would not follow us in there so it was quite easy to shake them. We were watching them and the 'gooks' and they were watching us watching the 'gooks'. On top of that Mac McGuinness's guys were also watching us. On one occasion we had a high-speed chase and managed to lose Mac's people out at Cranborne near the RLI barracks. It was a strange time; nobody was sure who was on what side anymore."

"Many weeks were spent in detailed surveillance and reconnaissance," says Engelbrecht. "As a result several roadblocks were hastily set up and 'terr' leaders captured and bundled into the waiting Kombis. They were handed on to Intelligence. One evening Darrell and three SAS operatives in their civilian Kombi gave chase to a known terrorist civilian vehicle and its single occupant down the Borrowdale Road, waving pistols at him to try and pull him over. However, the terrorist thought better than to stop so Darrell raced ahead and set up a hasty roadblock. The terrorist realised he could not outrun the pistol-wielding stop group and was reluctantly hauled off for further interrogation."

With Patriotic Front intimidation rampant throughout, a tense standoff hung over the country. While a largely ineffective Commonwealth Monitoring Force was thinly deployed countrywide, Walls fumed as reports poured in of ceasefire violations throughout the country. His pleas, as well as those of a similarly aggrieved Joshua Nkomo to Governor Soames, to disqualify ZANU (PF) fell on deaf ears. "This isn't Puddleton on the Marsh," explained the portly representative of the Crown in a display of flippant racism which left white Rhodesians wondering why they were being pilloried for similar alleged crimes. "This is Africa and they behave differently . . . they think nothing of sticking tent-poles up each other's what-nots and doing, filthy, beastly things to each other."

The ball was back in Walls's court, and his juniors were waiting with anxiously for him to give them the order to strike. Operations Hectic and Quartz were in place; all they needed was the word but nothing happened.

Ominously, on 27 January, Mugabe made a triumphant return to Salisbury and soon thereafter met with Jim Buckley, the governor's private secretary. At this meeting Buckley was assured that, notwithstanding the supposedly binding electoral regulations attendant on the Lancaster House agreement, Mugabe had his armed guerrillas in place outside the assembly points and imbedded in enough constituencies to guarantee him victory.

Another meeting with the Governor was hastily arranged and Mugabe went to Government House to meet Soames himself. The ZANU leader was in combative mood and expecting trouble but need not have worried. What he was about to hear was pure music to his ears. With Duff in attendance Mugabe was told that the British government expected him to win and secondly, while they knew his forces were intimidating the populace, the Governor would forfeit his right to annul the election as long as the violations were not so brazen as to become embarrassing. Meanwhile the Governor and his staff would continue the deception, designed to keep the Rhodesian forces on a leash, by persisting with the lie that Britain would not accept a Mugabe government, while nurturing the falsehood that their real plan was a coalition government coalescing around either Nkomo or Muzorewa with significant white representation including Ian Smith.

Duff later explained to David Dimbleby that the big confidence trick had to be carefully played out to the final conclusion. ". . . in a way we were playing a confidence trick on the white population . . . representing to them that the level of intimidation was not so much as to distort the results." But, he explained in an admixture of piety and pompous patronising, that he and his team were only being dishonest because they knew so much better what was good for the white Rhodesians than they, the white Rhodesians, did themselves.

On 1 February, at Gokomere Mission near Fort Victoria, two black priests were hauled before a kangaroo court, accused of being 'sell-outs' and summarily sentenced to death. They were tied down and beaten to death over a period of some hours. No one will ever know the exact figure but they were the latest of some 20,000 black civilians to die in this way at the hands of ZANU (PF) terrorists in the course of the conflict. No outrage however, was enough to attract the attention of the British supervisors. The course to ZANU (PF) power, decided on by Carrington and endorsed by Thatcher, would not be deviated from.

MORE ATTEMPTS TO KILL MUGABE

With intimidation in the countryside now so severe, a meeting was called on 4 February and the service chiefs from 'ComOps' went to see Soames. In a stormy meeting they demanded the British government adhere to what was agreed and at the very least delay the election while intimidation was brought under control. Soames blustered and temporised and the meeting achieved little. It was becoming increasingly clear to the Rhodesian commanders that this was a no-rules-barred affair; the enemy was being given licence to run amok and they needed to respond quickly.

Secret orders were issued to the SAS to kill Mugabe. An explosive device was placed beneath a culvert on a road near a stadium in Fort Victoria but detonated too late, missing the speeding convoy.

In another attempt a black Selous Scout got press accreditation masquerading as a journalist for 'Drum' magazine. An explosive device was fitted to a microphone designed to blow up in his face but Mugabe abruptly cancelled his attendance.

Waiting on board a flight to Bulawayo an air hostess whose husband had been killed in the war was waiting to poison him. He walked up the steps and just as he was about to enter the aircraft there was a call and he stopped. Moments later he turned, descended the steps and walked away.

Another failed attempt took place when explosives were hidden at the intersection of Jameson and Prince Edward avenues where operators waited, pending detonation on the passing of Mugabe's convoy. This too was compromised.

On 24 February General Walls and Ken Flower visited Maputo for high-level talks with FRELIMO civilian and military officials, including the future president and then Foreign Minister Joaquim Chissano and army commander Sebastio Mabote. Both Flower and Walls were somewhat surprised by a sense of paranoia regarding RENAMO. Giving the lie to official Mozambican information policy which routinely dismissed the movement as 'bandits,' Chissano reportedly "talked intensely of the Resistance [RENAMO] and our alleged support for it"[69] and went on to demand an assurance that it would be disbanded in return for forcing Mugabe to make peace.

When General Walls assured the Mozambican leadership that he would undertake not to allow the SAS to continue their operations with RENAMO, Chissano was relieved but sceptical. When Walls convinced him he could do it and would do it. Chissano was reportedly thrilled. He was quick to offer a critical quid pro quo in return: Mozambique would no longer provide sanctuary for ZANLA offensive action. For Mugabe, there would no longer be sanctuary in Mozambique.

RENAMO "brought the Mozambique Army to its knees," writes Wilfrid Mhanda. He adds that "Machel applied inordinate pressure on Mugabe to accept less than favourable British proposals . . . This he did on account of the pressure the Rhodesians were in turn applying on him through RENAMO's military operations."[70]

History now strongly suggests that Darrell Watt and a handful of his fellow SAS men, along with their RENAMO allies, constituted the biggest threat to power thus faced by the FRELIMO government. But the trump card they handed their political and military masters was dropped from the pack. On their return to Salisbury, Walls and Flower met with Ian Smith, Air Marshal McLaren and P.K. van der Byl. Walls talked glowingly of his meeting with the FRELIMO leaders and indicated he was reluctant to be party to any action which might upset them. When Smith pressed Walls for his views on what action to take if the election went to Mugabe, Walls was vague.

By this time, even the British monitors were reporting to Soames that the intimidation was at an unacceptable level but there was no response from him or Walls. Considering the height of the stakes, the level of tension and the tempting targets in play, it is a credit to the discipline that prevailed in the Rhodesian armed forces that no one lost control.

One shot could have set the whole country on fire and Watt had his finger tight on that trigger. "We were tasked to watch Mugabe who was staying at a house on Quorn Avenue, in Mount Pleasant," says Jerry Engelbrecht. "Darrell hand-picked two team members and they spent several nights hiding along the roadside, in a bushy patch behind a telephone exchange, using infra-red binoculars to monitor his comings and goings. On one occasion Mugabe showed himself, briefly exiting a car and exchanging a few words with his cadres. He was exposed and Darrell had him firmly in his sights but he was, at that point, under strict instruction to observe only. Being the professional soldier he was, he followed orders. That one shot would have changed everything."

Days before the election results were announced an SAS section made ready to shoot down a jet bringing Mugabe and his entourage of twenty-eight people into Salisbury. They would do this with a heat-seeking missile but the soldiers were unhappy about killing an innocent flight crew and the plan was aborted.

WALLS WOBBLES THEN FOLDS

On 27 February 1980 voting commenced amid an atmosphere where tensions were strained to breaking point. With the early election results signalling a Mugabe victory, the pressure on Walls from his subordinates to give them the order to attack reached breaking point. Shunning the boldness demanded by them, Walls decided to play his trump card and reach out to Mrs Thatcher who had promised him her ear in the event the circumstances demanded it. He sent a message pleading with her to appreciate events were running out of control, also to understand that her own representatives on the ground in Rhodesia were in agreement that ZANU (PF) had been, and remained in persistent and flagrant breach of all the Lancaster House agreements. But the general was about to pay for his naivety and his refusal to heed Smith's earlier warnings at Lancaster House that he was being duped. With Mrs Thatcher not even deigning to respond directly as promised, Walls received a dismissive response through a Downing Street intermediary that the Prime Minister did not consider the situation in Rhodesia sufficiently serious to warrant her intervention. The general had served his purpose in her view, now he could go hang.

On 2 March a meeting convened at Ian Smith's home in Belgravia. Present were van der Byl, McLaren, Walls, Flower, Sandy MacLean and Frank Mussell. The news coming in was anything but encouraging but the assessment was that a coalition government could still be formed that would prevent Mugabe taking power. Smith was by this time deeply sceptical that a political solution was still available considering the scale of the electoral abuses, and asked Walls bluntly what he planned to do in the event Mugabe won a majority of seats. Walls equivocated. Pressed by Smith he answered, "In the final event we will not allow Mugabe to win."[71]

But that was far from the truth. To the dismay of the men who had served under him with such distinction, Walls ignored Smith's entreaties to call Governor Soames's bluff and insist that the election results be annulled on the basis of massive irregularities. Instead he answered the call from his erstwhile enemy and went to meet Mugabe. In a short conversation with Mugabe who was at his charming best, the soon-to-be Prime Minister explained to Walls that Marxism and Christianity were not in conflict and that the two former enemies actually shared much in common. Walls, quickly persuaded, promptly accepted Mugabe's offer to serve as his first head of the army, saluted and left. Having been played like a drum by the

British, it was now Mugabe's turn to have his way. "I talked to him and gave him the impression I had faith in him," recalls Mugabe. Asked by Mugabe why he had tried to kill him, Walls somewhat incredibly denied the charge. "I never trusted Walls," says Mugabe, "we decided to bide our time, then get rid of him."

THE ORDER THAT NEVER CAME

"The day before the election results were announced we were convinced something would happen but it didn't. Every day we expected the order to attack but it never came," recalls Watt. "There was a sense of disbelief when we heard the news. The blokes just couldn't believe it was all over and Mugabe was taking over the country," recalls Watt.

"Darrell looked so sad and I felt for him," Engelbrecht reflects. "I think he felt bad for us, that he had let us down. He kept glancing at each of us, not saying anything as if to say sorry. Nobody said a word. It was the end as we all now knew. And it felt like the end of our little world. That was Darrell; he loved his men and cared deeply about us."

"My happiest and most adventurous years in the SAS was when I joined A Squadron and landed up with Darrell as my boss," recalls Mike West. "He was my fucking hero and I'd have died for him any time. Darrell was a fighting machine and all those who served under his command became like him, invincible and unstoppable. Every operator that went into combat with Darrell had harrowing and near-death experiences and there were many hair-raising incidents out there, but believe it or not, knowing you were going into combat with the best in the business made it so much easier; in actual fact many of us looked forward to going back into the bush and action with Darrell as we all knew the shit was going to hit the fan, but that he would out-think and out-manoeuvre whatever they could throw at us and if we had to gap it because the odds were insurmountable, who better to be with than Darrell. His commands were clear and his entire stick functioned like a well-oiled machine. He was extremely calm under pressure and could out-think the enemy even when the odds were stacked against him and his fighters. He was a born leader and could get his men to do the impossible and always had a good chuckle after the battle was won as he saw the funny side of many a contact. And if it was quiet he would go and look for trouble and normally he found it. He kept us committed and positive and this came from dedication and combat experience.

"Darrell belonged in the bush, not on time-wasting parade grounds with spit and polish, but in combat with blood, guts and gore and a stick of don't-give-a-fuck operators who would follow him to the end of the earth and to their graves if they had to. He would have needed back support for the weight of all the medals he should have received for outstanding bravery in the face of the enemy.

"A forgotten hero but remembered by us few who served with him and are alive today with wives and children because of one unselfish, remarkable man. We were crazy about this calm, relentless bush-fighter who loved his job and his country; when you look at the evil in the modern world I know we need more people like him. The war is over for us but I, Sergeant Mike West of the C Squadron Rhodesian SAS, want to thank you for your outstanding leadership and devotion to duty and to us, your soldiers; for leading us into battle with the ferocity of a grizzly bear and being a dear friend when we were back in Civvy Street. I know I speak for one and all when I say you are always in our thoughts."

A FAREWELL TO ARMS

Soon Garth Barrett was approached by General Walls and offered the opportunity of taking the SAS to South Africa. This split the regiment with some deciding to go but others, led by Grahame Wilson, deciding to stay. Amidst the prevailing gloom and while there was nothing to celebrate, there were some final flourishes as messes were drunk dry, sorrows were briefly drowned and memorabilia was salvaged for posterity.

"Rich Stannard and I went a little mad. We were frustrated, angry and I suppose sad. We went on a drinking binge. One day we were getting pissed in the officers' mess when Colonel Barrett came with some visiting English colonel and the colonel's wife.

"We had always suspected that Gilbert the barman was a spy and we decided to hold a quick trial and convict him of treason. Once we decided he was guilty we sentenced him to death by hanging. Gilbert took it all in the spirit of the moment and was happy to play along with us for a laugh. I had him on my shoulders while standing on the bar and Rich tied some Para cord to the ceiling. Blokes were shouting at us to be merciful because with Gilbert gone there would be nobody to supply the booze. Old Gilbert was yodelling nicely when the Colonel walked in with this snotty Brit and his wife. They got a hell of a fright when they saw us two about to hang the barman and Barrett gave us hell. We commuted the sentence and Gilbert went back to serving drinks."

Making their frustrations further known, Watt and Stannard returned from the city with ZANU (PF) election posters and fixed them to the walls of the same mess before a visit by General Walls. An angry adjutant admonished the pair, reminding them it was unacceptable to insult the commander of the Rhodesian Army in this way but the two were unrepentant, refusing to attend a lunch in honour of the country's military supremo. If the general had been in any doubt of the depth of the anger felt by some of his senior fighting men, it had been rudely dispelled.

Also behaving badly across the way at New Sarum air-base was Chris 'Green Leader' Dixon. Having received an invitation from Governor Soames to a garden party he tore it up in disgust and trashed it. Later, when the governor's secretary called air force HQ to confirm the attendees, Dixon's non-reply was raised. An undertaking was made to enquire and the matter was passed to an army general to seek clarity. When asked on the phone if he would be attending Dixon replied in no uncertain terms to the effect that he certainly would not be there. The general then explained to the obdurate bomber pilot that he owed the governor the courtesy of a reply but was told he 'owed the governor fuck all'. Summoned immediately to appear before the general he was given a direct order to respond to the invitation and refused. His parting words on leaving the angry general was 'the difference between you and me sir, is I have identified the enemy and you haven't.'

Charged with insubordination and refusing a direct order, one of the country's bravest 'men in blue' ended the war defiantly but ingloriously. "An order was given instructing all personnel not to communicate with me so I was effectively 'sent to Coventry'. Told to stay in my office; do nothing and say nothing. I think they were worried I might stir some of the other blokes up if I had a chance and they were right!"

Scheepers, meanwhile, was pondering his options. "Towards the end of the war I had a personal interview with General Loots in Pretoria," recalls Scheepers. "By this time I was becoming more embroiled with offers from South African Intelligence, with them looking to how I could be used by them in an espionage role. I was also approached by British SAS and offered an immediate rank of captain with no conditions but I declined. Colonel Barrett was furious with me when he discovered I had been in touch with General Loots. As a result, I was confined to barracks for security reasons. This did not make much sense to me. General Loots was on our side right until the end. It was the people reporting to the British who were with the enemy but the whole process was now beyond our control. The war was over for us.

"Overall, I see myself as a poor soldier, always scared to die. The medals I was put up for really belonged to the men who served with me. Most of the supposedly brave acts I performed were out of pure fear and adrenaline. I never fought for racial domination. I fought against a force that I thought would destroy the country I loved. Sadly, we soldiers were not allowed to complete our task and I have been proved right. Zimbabwe is a ruined country. This is the truth from my heart."

"There was a lot of drinking going on," says Watt. "I ended up in town in a pub with 'Karate' Carruthers-Smith from the Squadron. He was very angry and wanted to fight. A small guy, he tried to take on the biggest bloke in the bar but I grabbed him and calmed him down. He finished his beer and then held out his hand to say goodbye to me. He said, 'Goodbye Darrell, thanks for being a great friend. I'm going now and I'll not see you again.' Then he walked out, leaving me wondering what he meant. He went home, put a grenade under his pillow and blew his head off.

"We were soldiers," says Watt, "and that is all there is to it. We could not fight every battle but when we were given a job to do we did it to the best of our abilities, believing our cause was just. We forget the young boys that came to us as new soldiers and how we brought them to battle and placed them in terrifying situations. We too were scared but had to try not to show it. I always remembered how frightened I had been in my first encounters. From beginning to end I longed for a happy end to the war but when it finally came it could not really have happened on a lower note. After all I had been through, I felt very empty and confused. We had won the battles and lost the war.

"I stayed on for a while with Grahame Wilson after the war finished," says Watt, "but told him I would not wear a uniform. When trouble flared outside Bulawayo with ZIPRA attacking, Grahame told me he was getting the SAS ready to engage but I told him to count me out and I'm pleased we did not get involved. I left the country with my family and little more than what I could carry. I had no idea what I would do next. For us there were no thanks and no support. We just had to dry our eyes and move on."

No disbandment order came from Army HQ but the majority of the SAS resigned from the army with effect from 3 December 1980. The regimental silver was sent to Hereford in the UK and funds in the regimental fund were disbursed to next of kin who had died in the war. Those left congregated for one last jump and then disbanded at Kabrit Barracks on the 13 December 1980. A short address by Grahame Wilson followed:

"We will leave here not only in sorrow but filled with pride, dignity and honour in ourselves and in 1SAS. We have much to be grateful for.

"I am eternally grateful to those men who served with the unit before we did; to those amongst us who have lost loved ones; to those who were wounded; to those friends and there are many of them, who have stood by us; to those wives and families who stood behind us; to those who have fought with such courage beside us, and especially to those who gave their lives for Rhodesia and the unit.

"We have not let them down and we will not forget them.

"I know that in the years to come we can, with the greatest pride say, 'I served with the Rhodesian SAS.'

"May God bless you and thank God we did our duty."

APPENDIX A

The Unilateral Declaration of Independence

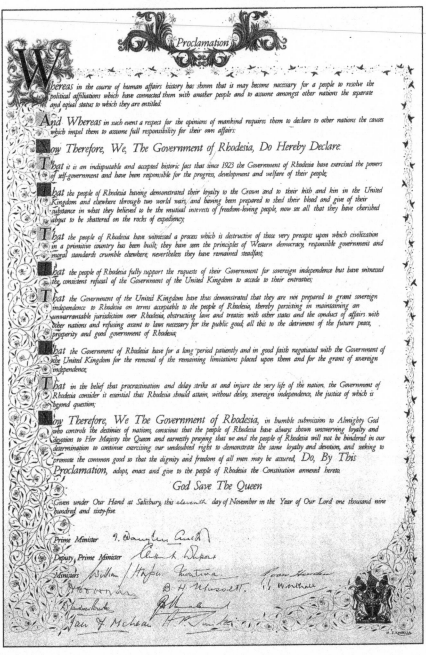

Proclamation

Whereas in the course of human affairs history has shown that it may become necessary for a people to resolve the political affiliations which have connected them with another people and to assume amongst other nations the separate and equal status to which they are entitled:

And Whereas in such event a respect for the opinions of mankind requires them to declare to other nations the causes which impel them to assume full responsibility for their own affairs:

Now Therefore, We, The Government of Rhodesia, Do Hereby Declare:

That it is an indisputable and accepted historic fact that since 1923 the Government of Rhodesia have exercised the powers of self-government and have been responsible for the progress, development and welfare of their people;

That the people of Rhodesia having demonstrated their loyalty to the Crown and to their kith and kin in the United Kingdom and elsewhere through two world wars, and having been prepared to shed their blood and give of their substance in what they believed to be the mutual interests of freedom-loving people, now see all that they have cherished about to be shattered on the rocks of expediency;

That the people of Rhodesia have witnessed a process which is destructive of those very precepts upon which civilization in a primitive country has been built; they have seen the principles of Western democracy, responsible government and moral standards crumble elsewhere; nevertheless they have remained steadfast;

That the people of Rhodesia fully support the requests of their Government for sovereign independence but have witnessed the consistent refusal of the Government of the United Kingdom to accede to their entreaties;

That the Government of the United Kingdom have thus demonstrated that they are not prepared to grant sovereign independence to Rhodesia on terms acceptable to the people of Rhodesia, thereby persisting in maintaining an unwarrantable jurisdiction over Rhodesia, obstructing laws and treaties with other states and the conduct of affairs with other nations and refusing assent to laws necessary for the public good, all this to the detriment of the future peace, prosperity and good government of Rhodesia;

That the Government of Rhodesia have for a long period patiently and in good faith negotiated with the Government of the United Kingdom for the removal of the remaining limitations placed upon them and for the grant of sovereign independence;

That in the belief that procrastination and delay strike at and injure the very life of the nation, the Government of Rhodesia consider it essential that Rhodesia should attain, without delay, sovereign independence, the justice of which is beyond question;

Now Therefore, We The Government of Rhodesia, in humble submission to Almighty God who controls the destinies of nations, conscious that the people of Rhodesia have always shown unswerving loyalty and devotion to Her Majesty the Queen and earnestly praying that we and the people of Rhodesia will not be hindered in our determination to continue exercising our undoubted right to demonstrate the same loyalty and devotion, and seeking to promote the common good so that the dignity and freedom of all men may be assured, **Do, By This Proclamation,** adopt, enact and give to the people of Rhodesia the Constitution annexed hereto.

God Save The Queen

Given under Our Hand at Salisbury, this eleventh day of November in the Year of Our Lord one thousand nine hundred and sixty-five

Prime Minister

Deputy Prime Minister

Ministers

APPENDIX B

SAS Roll of Honour

MALAYA

SGT. O. H. ERNST	13 JUNE 1951
CPL J.B. DAVIES	25 JUNE 1951
CPL V.E. VISAGIE	23 APRIL 1952

RHODESIAN WAR

WO2 R. BOUCH	12 OCTOBER 1966
C/SGT J. WRIGHT	12 OCTOBER 1966
C/SGT M. P. CAHILL	12 OCTOBER 1966
TPR M. MULLIN	26 MARCH 1968
SGT F. L. WILMOT	19 JANUARY 1973
TPR J. MENDES	22 AUGUST 1973
SGT A. RABIE	16 SEPTEMBER 1973
TPR M. J. MORRIS	31 JANUARY 1974
TPR N. WILLIS	14 FEBRUARY 1974
L/CPL K. R. SMITH	8 JUNE 1974
TPR J. WALSH	3 SEPTEMBER 1974
TPR W. R. WALTON	14 MARCH 1975
CPL K. STORIE	2 SEPTEMBER 1975
TPR E. LOTRINGER	31 OCTOBER 1976
LT B. BURRELL	16 DECEMBER 1976
TPR E. VAN STADEN	16 DECEMBER 1976
L/CPL G. J. NEL	22 DECEMBER 1976
TPR S. D. SEYMOUR	22 DECEMBER 1976
CAPT. R. WARRAKER	12 JANUARY 1977
SGT A. CHAIT	24 MARCH 1977

APPENDIX B

TPR F. J. NEL	23 NOVEMBER 1977
SGT R. L. BIEDERMAN	6 DECEMBER 1977
TPR C. M. MEDDOWSTAYLOR	20 JANUARY 1978
LT N. J. THERON	20 JANUARY 1978
TPR C. T. VERMAAK	20 JANUARY 1978
L/CPL A. W. LYNCH	6 SEPTEMBER 1978
L/CPL S. DONNELLY	21 SEPTEMBER 1978
L/CPL J. D. COLLETT	19 OCTOBER 1978
L/CPL M. TAYLOR	17 DECEMBER 1978
SGT C. CRIPPS	11 JANUARY 1979
L/CPL N. BARBER	7 JANUARY 1979
TPR G. MACMILLAN	7 FEBRUARY 1979
CPL R. J. SLINGSBY	11 APRIL 1979
TPR S. HARTLEY	6 JUNE 1979
TPR R. HICKMAN	7 JUNE 1979
CAPT M. F. PEARSE	26 JUNE 1979
TPR G. MAGUIRE	1 AUGUST 1979
L/CPL D. MCLAURIN	19 OCTOBER 1979

ENDNOTES

1 A.P. DiPerna, A Right to be Proud, Books of Rhodesia, 1978.

2 It is noteworthy that from the time of the formation of the British South Africa Police until 1963, this excellent force did not kill a single person in the course of exercising their duties. Through the war years patrolmen and women carried out the bulk of their duties unarmed.

3 Tribal Trust Lands were designated areas of the country where European settlement was forbidden and set aside specifically for native settlement where chiefs governed with limited autonomy and government was represented by a District Commissioner.

4 Mnangagwa was later arrested. Convicted and sentenced to death for sabotage, his sentence was reduced to one of imprisonment when it was proved he was a juvenile offender.

5 Tongogara's parents were employed by Prime Minister Ian Smith's father and Tongogara knew Smith as a boy.

6 Stirling would later pay close attention to the looming crisis in Rhodesia as a founder member of the Capricorn Society which lobbied for greater black political involvement in Britain's African colonies.

7 Coventry would make his last combat jump with the Zimbabwe Parachute Regiment when he went into action against RENAMO rebels in support of Mozambican government forces. He did so with a pipe and walking stick.

8 The Spectator, 7 November 2009.

9 Christopher Andrew, The Defence of the Realm, Penguin, 2009.

10 Carl Watts, Killing Kith and Kin: The Viability of British Military Intervention in Rhodesia, 1964–5, Twentieth Century Brit Hist (2005) 16 (4): 382–415.

11 Ken Connor, Ghost Force: The Secret History of the SAS, Orion, 1998.

12 PRO PREM 13/1116, see Sir Burke Trend to Wilson, 10 February 1966: "We must not forget that during our recent secret meeting with Flower he told us that the senior members of the Armed Forces were perhaps more 'reliable' than we had hitherto supposed . . ."

13 Considered by some to be a sub-tribe, these reclusive and primitive people lived in remote reaches of the Zambezi Valley where they avoided human contact. Some members of the tribe suffer from a genetic deformity known as ectrodactyly, resulting in the absence of three middle toes. This unusual condition made them remarkably adept at scaling trees.

14 At this point, the main source of armed resistance was out of Zambia, primarily from the movement known as ZAPU (Zimbabwe African People's Union) whose military wing would later become ZIPRA (Zimbabwe People's Revolutionary Army) while the other faction, ZANU (Zimbabwe African National Union), would eventually coalesce under the leadership of Robert Mugabe, with its military wing ZANLA (Zimbabwe African National Liberation Army) that would later move its HQ to Mozambique.

15 Al Tourle was one of the country's finest marksmen. He later died of his wounds after a lion snatched him away from a campfire while on patrol near the Zambezi River.

16 Plumtree alumni include former Rhodesian Air Force Commander 'Raf' Bentley, army commander General John Hickman and Armed Forces Supremo General Peter Walls. Also Wing Commander Chris Dixon of 'Green Leader' fame, Major Grahame Wilson who emerged as the country's most highly decorated soldier, Colonel Jeremy Strong who would command the Selous Scouts and Colonel Charlie Aust who was the last commander of the Rhodesian Light Infantry.

17 The last Rhodesian to win the Sword of Honour at Sandhurst before the Rhodesians were deemed personae non grata.

18 Alexandre Binda, The Saints: The Rhodesian Light Infantry, 30° South Publishers, 2007.

19 P.J.H. Petter-Bowyer, Winds of Destruction: The Autobiography of a Rhodesian Combat Pilot, 30° South Publishers, 2006.

20 Binda.

21 Ian Smith, The Great Betrayal, Blake Publishing, 1997.

22 Forced to resign as leader of the Liberal Party in 1976, Thorpe was charged in 1978 with conspiracy to murder Norman Scott, his former lover, but was acquitted.

23 The original Mbuya (Grandmother) Nehanda fomented the 1896 Mashona Rebellion and was hanged.

24 Later known as General Solomon Mujuru he became Army Commander in Zimbabwe and one of the most powerful men in the country before he died mysteriously in a fire at his Bindura home in 2011.

25 Robey went on to work for the South African security services and later gave evidence to the Truth and Reconciliation Commission in connection with the deaths of anti-apartheid activists.

26 Hawkesworth was walked to Tanzania where he was held before being released a year later following representations from the British government.

27 Loyal or 'turned' black troops who infiltrated enemy ranks or masqueraded as insurgents in order to act as spies. The genesis of the Selous Scouts was in the BSAP Special Branch, but at this time, under Major Ron Reid-Daly, it was being transformed into a military unit with a Special Branch contingent on permanent attachment.

28 South African Minister of Foreign Affairs from 1977.

29 A Cornishman and son of a pastor, Flower joined the Rhodesian police (BSAP) in 1937 then saw wartime service in Somalia and Ethiopia before returning to Rhodesia in 1948. He was instrumental in setting up the Central Intelligence Organisation (CIO) in 1963. He would go on to play a pivotal and controversial role in the war that followed.

30 Tongogara would go on to command ZANLA and play an influential role in both the military and political arenas.

31 Wilfrid Mhanda, Dzino: Memories of a Freedom Fighter, Weaver Press, 2011.

32 Smith would work for SA intelligence after Zimbabwe became independent and later be sentenced to death for his hand in the bombing of an ANC safe-house in Bulawayo that killed one man. His sentence was commuted to life imprisonment and he was released in 2006 after serving nineteen years.

33 South Africa was very involved in running Mozambique's harbours and railways and a significant amount of South African rolling stock was in the country. It was reported that Pretoria registered strong protests with the Rhodesian government because the attacks were deemed detrimental to their interests.

34 Some years after the war ended Emmerson Mnangagwa, then minister of state security, revealed in an interview that barmen at the SAS barracks had indeed been passing information to ZANLA operatives.

35 Peter Stiff, Selous Scouts: Top Secret War, Galago, 1982.

36 Situated in the Park Lane Hotel, the restaurant was well patronised by members of the armed forces. Ironically, it was owned by John and Aelda Callinicos, the latter the aunt of Richard (later Lord) Acton, husband of Judith Todd. She and her father, former Southern Rhodesian Prime Minister Sir Garfield Todd, were vehemently opposed to the Smith government and both Acton and his sister, Mary Ann Sheehy, worked for Robert Mugabe's first Minister of Justice, Simba Mubako. In the post-independence period, former security force members were no longer welcome at the Park Lane where, Todd claims, "they had been known to threaten people and in some cases, had even taken to exposing themselves."

37 Beryl Salt, A Pride of Eagles, Covos Day, 2001.

38 A Rhodesian invention, these percussion bombs contained amatol. On detonation the casing burst into more than 80,000 fragments that were lethal at sixty metres, with an accompanying stun effect over another sixty metres. A 'Hunter' could carry two Golf bombs.

39 Also a Rhodesian invention, these 'bouncing bombs' were designed to hit the surface before rebounding and detonating approximately three metres above the ground, causing extensive horizontal damage.

40 Binda.

41 Appointed Vice-President of Zimbabwe in 2004.

42 It was later discovered this vehicle had been stolen from Elim Mission in the Vumba.

43 Quoted from Steve Kesby , 'Pride of Eagles'.

44 David Dimbleby, 3-part documentary series, 1999.

45 Further evidence appears in Bhebhe's and Ranger's book, Society in Zimbabwe's Liberation War: "In 1978 an official in the Foreign Office called Patrick Laver told Griffiths (former head of Elim mission who was absent on the night of the killings) that Robert Mugabe had 'unofficially' apologised for the [Elim] massacre. Mugabe further stated that he had called the platoon commander responsible back for disciplining but the guerrilla in question had refused to return.

46 David Caute. 'Under the Skin'.

47 Peter Stiff.

48 Jonathan Pittaway, Special Air Service: The Men Speak, Dandy Agencies, 2009, p. 308.

49 Keith Nell, Viscount Down, 2010.

50 Max Hastings, Going to the Wars, Pan, 2001

51 The plaque in the Anglican Cathedral commemorating the victims has been removed on orders from Bishop Kunonga, the Anglican Bishop of Harare. An outspoken supporter of Robert Mugabe's, he has been actively involved in human rights violations.

52 Ken Flower, Serving Secretly, John Murray (Publishers) Ltd. 1987.

53 Salt.

54 David Dimbleby.

55 Ibid

56 Gutu passed information on the location of the ZIPRA logistics base in Lusaka and the whereabouts of a prison containing captured Rhodesian servicemen and dissenters from the revolutionary cause. The jail was soon attacked by Selous Scouts and the inmates freed.

57 Pittaway.

58 Ibid.

59 Ibid.

60 Ibid.

61 One of those killed was rugby fullback Leroy Duberley who had been a late withdrawal from the Rhodesian team that had travelled to Durban to play Natal. His death was announced at the game and the crowd stood for a minute's silence.

62 Binda

63 Ibid.

64 Ibid.

65 Ibid.

66 Stephen A. Emerson, The Battle for Mozambique, 30 Degrees South, 2013.

67 Carrington delivered an ultimatum to the delegations putting a strict time limit on acceptance of his proposals. Giles had spotted the flaws in the constitution and made them known. On Tuesday, 4 October, the day the Rhodesian delegation was

set to meet and decide, Giles went missing and was later found dead. Ken Flower went from shadow ringmaster to take Giles's seat at the negotiating table. Giles had been shopping for his children the previous day and spoke to his wife on the morning of his disappearance. He sounded happy. The death was handled by the local constabulary who refused to discuss it with the Rhodesian security personnel.

68 In his book, The Battle for Mozambique, Stephen Emerson explains that these men were from ZANLA's Toronga Training Camp in southern Sofala province which Engelbrecht describes attacking. They escaped in the aftermath and came to surrender.

69 Ken Fowler.

70 Mhanda.

71 Ian Smith

BIBLIOGRAPHY

A Pride of Eagles. Beryl Salt. Covos Day, 2001.

A Right To Be Proud. A.P. Di Perna. Books of Rhodesia, 1978.

Anatomy of a Rebel. Peter Joyce. Graham Publishing, 1974.

The Battle for Mozambique. Stephen Emerson. Thirty Degrees South Publishers, 2013.

Dingo Firestorm. Ian Pringle. Zebra Press, 2012.

Dzino; Memories of a Freedom Fighter. Wilfred Mhanda. Weaver Press, 2011.

Echoes of an African War. Chas Lotter. Covos Day, 1999.

The Elite. Barbara Cole. Three Knights, 1984.

Going to the Wars. Max Hastings. Pan Books, 2000.

The Great Betrayal. Ian Smith. Blake Publishing, 1997.

None But Ourselves. Julie Frederikse. Zimbabwe Publishing House, 1982.

P.K. Van Der Byl. Hannes Wessels. Thirty Degrees South, 2010.

The Rhodesian War; A Military History. Paul Moorcroft and Peter McLaughlin. Jonathan Ball Publishers, 2008.

The Saints. Alexandre Binda. Thirty Degrees South, 2007.

Selous Scouts; Top Secret War. Lt. Col. Ron Reid-Daly as told to Peter Stiff. Galago, 1982.

Serving Secretly. Ken Flower. John Murray Publishers, 1987.

Soldiers in Zimbabwe's Liberation War. Ngwabi Bhebe and Terence Ranger. University of Zimbabwe Publications, 1995.

Special Air Service; The Men Speak. Jonathan Pittaway. Dandy Agencies Publishing, 2009.

Under the Skin. David Caute. Penguin Books, 1983.

The Valiant Years. Beryl Salt. Galaxie Press, 1978. 277